RACE AND MEDIA

Race and Media

Critical Approaches

Edited by
Lori Kido Lopez

NEW YORK UNIVERSITY PRESS

New York

NEW YORK UNIVERSITY PRESS
New York
www.nyupress.org

References to Internet websites (URLs) were accurate at the time of writing. Neither the author nor New York University Press is responsible for URLs that may have expired or changed since the manuscript was prepared.

Library of Congress Cataloging-in-Publication Data
Names: Lopez, Lori Kido, editor.
Title: Race and media : critical approaches / edited by Lori Kido Lopez.
Description: New York : New York University Press, [2020] |
Includes bibliographical references and index.
Identifiers: LCCN 2020016957 (print) | LCCN 2020016958 (ebook) |
ISBN 9781479895779 (hardback) | ISBN 9781479889310 (paperback) |
ISBN 9781479881376 (ebook) | ISBN 9781479823222 (ebook)
Subjects: LCSH: Mass media and minorities. | Mass media and race relations.
Classification: LCC P94.5.M55 R3155 2020 (print) | LCC P94.5.M55 (ebook) |
DDC 302.2308—dc23
LC record available at https://lccn.loc.gov/2020016957
LC ebook record available at https://lccn.loc.gov/2020016958

New York University Press books are printed on acid-free paper, and their binding materials are chosen for strength and durability. We strive to use environmentally responsible suppliers and materials to the greatest extent possible in publishing our books.

Manufactured in the United States of America

10 9 8 7 6 5 4 3 2 1

Also available as an ebook

CONTENTS

NOTES ON TERMINOLOGY

The terms used to describe racial and ethnic minorities are dynamic and highly contested, reflecting the complexity of self-determination and the fluid boundaries that surround all identities. The authors in this collection were allowed to choose their own terms, and as a result, there are a wide range of choices represented in the chapters that follow. Below is a brief discussion of some of the terms that are used, but all decisions about racial terminologies are controversial and subject to individual interpretation. Only a few of the authors specifically describe the reasoning for their choice of terminology in their chapters, but all make choices that reflect what is respectful and ethical within the specific communities they describe.

Asian American • Asian/American • Asian-American

The term "Asian American" was coined during the Yellow Power movement in the late 1960s as a deliberate move away from the term "Oriental," which had come to be recognized as pejorative. While journalists regularly use the hyphenated term "Asian-American" to describe Asians of American descent, activists have argued that the hyphen is problematic and should not be used because it connotes a division between the two halves of one's identity, rather than a united whole. Some scholars have followed in the steps of David Palumbo-Liu (1999), who argued that using the slash ("Asian/American") designates an "and/or" relationship between Asian and American where the two halves are equal while also indicating the instability and mutability of this formation. Additional terms such as "Pacific Islander" and "Desi American" have been added to this category as it was acknowledged that the term "Asian American" had become a stand-in for primarily East Asians, resulting in terms like "Asian Pacific Islander American" and "Asian Pacific Islander Desi American," among others. The term "South Asian American" is also sometimes used to describe only those with heritage from the region of the South Asian subcontinent. There are many additional permutations of these terms and the acronyms used to describe them, each calling attention to various specific populations in an attempt to be more inclusive and call attention to minority populations who are often ignored.

Arab American • Middle Eastern • Muslim • Middle Eastern or North African

The terms used to describe Americans from Arabic-speaking countries in the Middle East and North Africa (such as Lebanon, Egypt, Syria, Iraq, Morocco, Palestine, and Jordan, which have the largest populations in the United States) have been unstable since the first immigrants arrived in the 1880s. While Arab Americans are sometimes defined as those with heritage from countries within the Arab League, this is a political category that shifts and does not necessarily reflect actual cultural or ethnic connections within the Arab world. The U.S. census has historically classified Americans from these regions within the category of "White" (with the ability to designate more specific ancestry categories in the American Community Survey), and there are ongoing debates about whether there should be a category designated as "Arab American" or "Middle Eastern or North African (MENA)" on future versions of the census. While many ethnically Arab Americans are religiously Muslim, and people of both identities experience systematic oppression in the United States in similar and related ways, the two categories should not be conflated. Arab Americans can practice a wide variety of religions and Muslims can be from any racial background.

Black • black • African American

The term "African American" is used to describe those living in the United States who are descendants of African nations, largely as a result of the Atlantic slave trade. The terms "Black" or "black" are used to describe the racial category of peoples all over the world, both in Africa and in the diaspora, with African heritage. While there are geographic specificities to the terms, many use the terms "Black" and "African American" interchangeably to describe people with African heritage in the United States. There is debate about whether the term "black/Black" should be capitalized (along with other terms that build from the same root, such as "anti-Black/anti-black" and "blackness/Blackness"). Those who favor capitalization argue that Black is a racial category that is parallel to Asian or Hispanic, which are capitalized, and consistency would demand that White also be capitalized. The term "Black" with a capital *B* is often used with pride to designate the transition from Africans to Black people in the tradition of W. E. B. Du Bois, and is sometimes used in conjunction with lowercase "white" in order to deliberately center those who have historically been marginalized. Those who favor lowercase argue that black can be used as an adjective, a general racial descriptor, or an abstract concept such as "blackness" or "black audiences." Some authors switch between "black" and "Black" in order to clearly distinguish when they are talking about Black Americans versus the larger racial category.

Indigenous • Native American • First Nations • Indian • American Indian

The term "Indian" is a potentially offensive term, as it is the designation created by European colonizers to the Americas who erroneously believed that they had landed in India. It connotes the history of settlers perpetuating genocide against the original inhabitants of what is now called North America, as well as the ways native cultures have often been commodified, depoliticized, and misunderstood. While there are many individuals who use the term "Indian" to describe themselves, particularly when among their own in-group, it is often seen as offensive for non-Native individuals to use this term. The terms "American Indian," "Native American," "First Nations," or simply "Native" are seen as more respectful, and there are a wide range of conflicting arguments about which is more accurate or appropriate. Many individuals also choose to identify primarily with their specific tribal nation. The terms "indigenous" or "Indigenous" are used to describe peoples who existed prior to colonization, and can be used to describe the Indigenous peoples of the Americas. The lowercase "indigenous" is often viewed as an adjective, while the capitalized "Indigenous" is considered a more respectful way of designating the term as a proper noun. Political recognitions of

Indigenous peoples are connected to a global political movement resulting in the adoption of the UN Declaration on the Rights of Indigenous Peoples in 2007, which aimed to collectively recognize the human rights of global Indigenous peoples.

Latino • Latina/o • Latinx • Chicano • Chicanx • Hispanic

The term "Hispanic" is often used interchangeably with the term "Latino," but there are some specific differences—namely, "Hispanic" is used for people from Spain and the Spanish-speaking countries of the Americas, while "Latino" is used for people from Latin America, or countries with histories of Spanish colonization. The term "Hispanic" also has connotations of being a demographic category created by the U.S. government. In the U.S. context, a number of variants of the term "Latino" have emerged to increase inclusivity and respond to feminist concerns about the gendering of language. "Latina/o" and "Latin@" are used to maintain both the masculine and feminine version of the noun, and avoid allowing the masculine version of the noun to stand in for all people. The term "Latinx" moves beyond the male/female gender binary to indicate inclusivity of all gender identities, including those who are gender nonconforming and transgender. There are debates about whether the term "Latinx" should be widely adopted, as it is not common among Spanish speakers and thus may privilege English syntax and the educated communities from which it emerged. "Chicano" became popularized during the civil rights movement in the 1960s as a term of self-identification and pride for Mexican Americans, and it has a similar history in evolving toward the use of "Chicanx" by some.

mixed race • multiracial

Individuals who have heritage from more than one racial or ethnic category are an extremely diverse and heterogeneous population, and the words used to describe them are similarly varied. The terms "mixed race" (sometimes hyphenated when used as the adjective "mixed-race," or simply "mixed") and "multiracial" are generally seen as neutral and flexible enough to accommodate many different backgrounds. There are many words that are no longer used because of their specific histories.

For instance, given the significance of Black/white racial divisions around citizenship in the United States, the government historically defined certain individuals according to the exact percentage of Black heritage—"mulatto" was used for those who are half Black and half white, "quadroon" for one-quarter Black, and "octoroon" for one-eighth Black. These terms are viewed as pejorative due to their connection to slavery. But there are many other terms that individuals choose to use that help point to their specific backgrounds, or feel more accurate in their personal identifications. The term "mestizo" has Spanish roots and has been used for people with mixed ancestry of white, Latino, Indigenous, or Filipino origin. There have been many terms for Americans with white and Asian heritage, such as "hapa," "Eurasian," and "Amerasian." The term "hapa haole" is Native Hawaiian for half white and has been used by many who are white and Asian American, but has been reclaimed as a word that can be used only by those who are mixed-race Native Hawaiian. Those with Black and Asian heritage have used the terms "Afro-Asian" or "Blasian" to describe themselves. In general, the mixed-race community has a multiplicity of terms associated with it because there are so many different communities who are included (such as using the term "Métis" to describe mixed-race descendants of Indigenous peoples and the settlers who colonized what is now known as Canada) and because individuals sometimes choose to name their own personal racial category (such as Tiger Woods calling himself "Cablinasian" to reference his Caucasian, Black, Indian, and Asian heritage).

White • white • Caucasian • Anglo-Saxon

"White" is the racial category used for people with light skin who primarily descend from European countries. But it is noteworthy for constantly shifting to include and exclude various communities; for instance, on the U.S. census people of Latin American, Middle Eastern, and Central Asian origin can be racially white. Moreover, many immigrant groups in the United States have shifted from being racially othered to being identified as white, such as Irish Americans, Jewish Americans, and Italian Americans. As a racial color scheme, white people are distinguished from "black," "brown," "yellow," and "red" races (with the terms "yellow" and "red" being pejorative). The term "Caucasian" is originally part of a nineteenth-century taxonomy that classified those from the Caucasus mountain range as superior and "Mongolian" and "Negro" as inferior human races. It later became a more generic descriptor for white people in the United States, and its contemporary usage does not necessarily connote this racist history. The term "Anglo-Saxon" originally described people from Great Britain, and is sometimes used to describe English-speaking people or is shortened to "Anglo" to describe white people in the United States. But the term "white" has become most common, and has been widely taken up by academics such as in the naming of "whiteness studies" and "critical whiteness studies," as well as in concepts like "white privilege." Similar to the debates surrounding the capitalization of "black/Black" and "indigenous/Indigenous," there is disagreement about whether "white/White" should be capitalized. Some argue that "White" should be capitalized to mark the term as similar to other racial categories, as is recommended by the APA guidelines. Others feel that "white" should be lowercase, as is recommended by the MLA, Chicago, and Associated Press style guides, or because capitalization connotes superiority.

Introduction

LORI KIDO LOPEZ

Discussions of race dominate the media landscape in every possible form, ranging from news coverage of Black activist movements and political battles over immigration, to actors and celebrities discussing the significance of race in movies and on television, to the spread of thousands of race-related social media posts. Our understanding of what race is, how race works in U.S. society, and what it means to belong to a specifically racialized body are all informed by media and technologies. As such, engagements with media can lead to a confirmation of racist ideologies and the structures that sustain racism, or can open up possibilities for resistance, struggle, and rethinking.

It has become a truism to affirm that these questions and the analytical skills required for answering them are more important now than ever before. Indeed, it is difficult to think about systems of power and their impact on racial ideologies in the twenty-first century without mentioning Donald Trump and the fact that his election in 2016 was largely premised on the promotion of racism, xenophobia, and state-sponsored violence against people of color. His administration has called attention to the rampant racism that has long undergirded political discourse and policy in the United States. We now regularly witness political leaders (including President Trump himself) openly invoking racial hatred as a justification for policy decisions, and have seen the concurrent rise and increased visibility of hate groups and the domestic terrorism of white nationalists, neo-Nazis, neo-Confederates, and the Ku Klux Klan.

Yet for scholars of race and racism, this form of leadership and its threats are nothing new. Racial discourse is always shifting, but our understanding of social inequalities and the systems of oppression that sustain them remains the same. Against this backdrop, it is safe to say that any fantasies and myths of postraciality have sputtered into failure.

The concept of postraciality or postracism refers to the enthusiasm that followed the election of the first African American president, Barack Obama, and the assumption that this accomplishment heralded an era of racial progress. Catherine Squires (2014) affirms that media outlets played a significant role in defining and debating the concept of "postrace," and points to the dangers of wrongly connecting postracism to anti-racism. These emergent rhetorics around race are also evidenced in what Eduardo Bonilla-Silva (2003) calls colorblind racism, a framework that indirectly contributes to the maintenance of social inequalities by masking racial realities. These postracial discourses and beliefs can be understood as one part of the catalyst for the racist backlash that has followed, and the preponderance of both overt and covert racial projects that work in tandem to maintain the status quo. It is now unarguable that the maintenance of a racial hierarchy premised on white supremacy remains at the core of contemporary U.S. society, and unfortunately the preponderance of explicit racial hatred often overshadows the structural inequalities that have never disappeared.

While manifestations of racism at the highest levels of power and explicit manifestations of racial hatred provide one site for considering the communication of racialized discourse, scholarship in this book aims to show that there is far more work to be done in unpacking their mediation. Each of the chapters points to the multitude of other ways we can understand the relationship between race and the media. This includes the way racial ideologies are propagated through fictional narratives and imaginary textual creations, ranging from television sitcoms and art films to video games and web series. It also asks how race is inflected in the construction of communication technologies, through their infrastructures and interfaces and algorithms. Scholars in this collection consider the active roles that people of color have played in authoring their own vehicles for communication, developing, producing, and starring in their own media. Beyond the specific texts that are created, it is also important to consider the role that audiences and consumers play in responding to media texts, as well as in creating racialized communities through media networks and digital platforms. Together these different investigations continue to reveal how hegemonic ideologies and racism are propagated, while also reminding us of the resilience and innovation that people of color have always shown in their acts of resistance and self-determination.

The scholarship included here primarily focuses on race and ethnicity in the context of the United States, acknowledging that the specific sociopolitical histories of a region significantly impact its racial dynamics. While the broader questions posed and the conceptual frameworks utilized may be useful and applicable in other regions, it would be naïve to attempt to fully address the vast diversity and complexity of global racial dynamics and media systems from all over the world in this single collection. Rather, it is the case that in addressing the particularities of racialization in North American and U.S. media industries, some of this scholarship must necessarily extend into transnational relations and diasporic frameworks. The global movement of peoples and ideas has a significant impact on people of color in the United States that cannot be overlooked. This book addresses these realities in chapters that are rooted in the racial dynamics of the United States and help us to explore its specific heterogeneity and complexity.

Expanding Studies of Race and Media

Many generations of cultural studies and media studies scholars have worked to develop the study of race and ethnicity and produce the theories that support research in this area today. This includes canonical works by scholars such as Stuart Hall, bell hooks, and Herman Gray, who called attention to racialized systems of power and the ways racial ideologies are propagated through media structures and representations. Given how disruptive their work was to institutionalized scholarly paradigms around race, I use the term "canonical" advisedly, but it is an indication of how influential these texts are that they can now carry that moniker.

Stuart Hall (1997a) described the social structures of Blackness in relation to marginalization, theorizing the significance of representation and discourse in giving meaning to those experiences. He called attention to the complexities and contradictions that were contained within racial identities, as well as within the ideologies that media communicate about race that make struggle necessary but difficult. bell hooks (1992) turns to the experiences of Black female spectators who have the agency and power to subvert the ways they are represented by means of a critical gaze that looks back and struggles against domination. Her work emphasizes the fact that our specific bodies and experiences in this world are shaped by race, but also other identities such as gender and sexuality. She is critical of the way mainstream media offer up representations of difference for the purposes of commodification and the pleasures of consumption, and sees media production by Black women as an important vehicle for creating radical Black female subjectivities that recognize and challenge these assumptions. Herman Gray (1995, 2005) also recognizes the shifting political discourse around representation, helping us to make sense of the proliferation of African American imagery in popular culture and the role of Black cultural forms as a site for cultural struggle. In adapting his theories of Black representations to address the rise of new media ecologies and other technological advancements that shift our media landscape, he forwards an emphasis on Black structures of feeling and the circulation of affect as an alternative to our endless preoccupation with representation. The scholarship that followed has consistently built from these foundations, acknowledging the significance of these core theories and the way their understandings of the world remain as relevant as ever.

As with all fields of study, research on race and media has tended to cluster in certain areas that have gained more visibility, while others remain at the margins. This book is designed to accompany and strengthen previous works on race and media, affirming the continued importance of using classic analytical frameworks, theories, and methodologies to make sense of the changing media landscape. But this collection also emphasizes scholarship that points to new directions and ways in which the field is continuing to expand and change shape. These transformations can be understood as taking place across methodologies, platforms/mediums, and the communities of people being studied.

In terms of methodology, textual analysis has traditionally been the most common way of approaching race and media. Early scholars performed close readings of media texts to understand the meaning of racial representations by deciphering both the broad patterns they have fallen into and the specific nuances of individual plots, dialogue, scenes, or characterizations. For instance, Charles Ramírez Berg (2002) has contributed many insights on how to identify stereotypes and counter-stereotypes in Latino media and images of Latinidad. In this vein, Racquel Gates (2018) centers representational analysis in her theorization of negativity in Black popular culture, complicating the simple binary of positive/negative that has long hampered our analysis of racial imagery.

This book includes a chapter by Mary Beltrán that instructs readers in how to perform a nuanced image analysis that includes consideration of broader sociocultural contexts, narrative complexities, and media genre. But in addition to visual analysis, Dolores Inés Casillas, Jennifer Lynn Stoever, and Sarah Florini emphasize the analysis of sound, focusing on accents and vocal qualities as well as the rise of audio media such as podcasts. Authors in this book also deploy methodologies from production studies and media industry studies that consider what is happening behind the scenes to create media texts and distribute them to audiences, and digital methodologies such as platform and interface analysis that help us to understand technological architectures and infrastructures. When collecting data about the experiences of people who are involved in producing or interpreting media texts, methods such as interviews and ethnographies of participant observation provide insights. Indeed, the broad repertoire of media studies methodologies can all be used to approach this subject, and this book attempts to explore some of the insights that they can produce.

Scholarship on race and media has also largely centered on the medium of film and television. This makes sense because of the popularity of these formats, the extent of their cultural impact, and the large number of workers who are employed in the creation of Hollywood movies and network television. Moreover, film studies was one of the first forms of media studies to become institutionalized through university departments and academic journals, so its scholarly influence looms large across the field. Much of the scholarship on Native Americans and media in particular has focused on cinema, including excellent books by Elise Marubbio (2006), Michelle Raheja (2010), Michael Hilger (2016), Johanna Hearne (2012), and Jacquelyn Kilpatrick (1999). Yet the chapters in this book spread expansively across the media landscape, including a wide variety of mediums and platforms in their purview. This includes mainstream film and television produced by Hollywood studios and broadcast television, as well as digital forms of television such as web series and independent films that are made and distributed outside the studio system. Jacqueline Land and Kishonna L. Gray examine the interactive medium of video games, and part III of this book, titled

"Digitizing Race," contains analyses of a wide range of digital platforms, including YouTube, Twitter, podcasting networks, and blogs.

Finally, we can consider who has traditionally been included in the communities being studied by scholars of race and media. Race is often understood as a "Black and white" phenomenon both within academic studies and U.S. culture more broadly, which has resulted in the development of much important scholarship on African American and Black communities. African Americans comprise the largest population of people of color in the United States and have a history of creating many culturally specific forms of expression that have had a profound impact on American culture. As a result, there is a deep body of scholarship analyzing the rise of forms such as Black cinema, Black sitcoms, hip hop and other Black forms of music and performance, as well as more recent explorations of digital networks such as Black Twitter. This collection continues in this tradition while also centering studies of Latinx, Asian American, Arab American, and Indigenous communities. Beyond these specific ethnic and racial communities, scholars like Ralina L. Joseph, Meshell Sturgis, and Mari Castañeda examine mixed-race communities. This focus on hybridity and the fluidity of identity is also highlighted in the work of Lia Wolock and Susan Noh, who consider diasporic and cosmopolitan frameworks that extend beyond the United States to consider transnational communities across the globe.

How to Use This Book

This description demonstrates some of the different ways the chapters of this book seek to diversify and expand the way we study race and media, but another way of understanding the relationship between different chapters is through the thematics that distinguish the four parts: "Representing Race," "Producing and Performing Race," "Digitizing Race," and "Consuming and Resisting Race." This structure is designed to point readers toward loose connections between the chapters as the book progresses, but of course it is also the case that individual chapters will connect across these thematics, and there are no concrete boundaries dividing the parts. Each chapter heading includes a number of key concepts and terms that are central to each chapter so that readers can more easily locate and organize lessons around the book's contents.

Part I, "Representing Race," focuses on the question of what we learn about race from media industries that are dominated by whiteness and have long histories of excluding people of color. It opens with a chapter by Lori Kido Lopez on the hegemony of mainstream media that shows how racism is persistently sustained in spite of small improvements. This transitions into an archival examination by Mary Beltrán on television Westerns and how we can understand their representations of Latinos. Together these chapters provide foundational understandings of how racism operates within media and instructions on how to perform textual analysis and image analysis in order to uncover hegemonic and counterhegemonic meanings. Meshell Sturgis and Ralina L. Joseph then use textual analysis on the discourses that surround genetic testing and its significance as a technology of race. They particularly examine the role that mixed-race individuals have played in narratives of racial ancestry and genome sciences. Dolores Inés Casillas and Jennifer Lynn Stoever expand these methods of textual analysis to include considerations of sound and audio media, showing us the importance of listening to voices, soundscapes, accents, and audible records as a way of understanding race. The last chapter of this part is an investigation by Jason Kido Lopez of the role that Black athletes have played in bringing anti-racism into sports. He reveals the dynamics of the power struggles within powerful media corporations like ESPN and the professional sports leagues that are so entwined in their productions, arguing that their dependence on the celebrity figures of professional athletes both limits and facilitates the voicing of political concerns. In highlighting the star texts of Black athletes, he reminds us that there are powerful people of color who can leverage their celebrity for various forms of anti-racism, but that there are equally powerful forces of containment that may limit their efficacy.

Part II, "Producing and Performing Race," moves from understanding the power and dominance of mainstream media industries to investigating the multiple ways people of color have asserted their voices through media authorship and production. It begins with Peter X Feng's discussion of the ABC sitcom *Fresh Off the Boat*, which connects parts I and II by outlining the behind-the-scenes struggles and negotiations that shaped this Asian American text on network television. Feng explores the "burden of representation" as a framework for understanding the pressures that are always heaped onto the few texts that do manage to break through into the mainstream. Jacqueline Land asks a similar set of questions about the rise of Indigenous video games and the struggles that Indigenous game developers have faced. She illuminates the way video game industries maintain a power structure that systematically delegitimizes and ostracizes Indigenous games and their developers. This is followed by Mari Castañeda's chapter on the representation of Afro-Latinidades within U.S. Latinx media, including Spanish-language television, news programs, documentaries, music, and blogs. She models the way that scholars can deploy Latino/a Critical Communication Theory in analyzing media texts, and points to the different ways anti-Blackness is reinforced within Latinx media.

As we can see through Castañeda's overview of Latino/a Critical Communication Theory, it has also been important for scholars of race and media to develop their own frameworks and ways to interrogate communicative practices on their own terms. While the looming presence of mainstream media industries and the enduring tentacles of white supremacy are always a structuring force that cannot be ignored, assessing their impact is not our only goal. Jun Okada's research on the relationship of Asian American film festivals to Asian American independent media helps us to understand how alternative media have developed, been supported, and changed over time. She centers her inquiry on the question of how Asian American film and video were made possible, and what their evolution can teach us about their potential for the future. Amy Villarejo closes out part II with a chapter on Black trans expression and its movement across different media—including live performances, photography, film, and digital media. Using the concept of remediation, she considers the way that processes of media transformation can help us to better understand trans experiences and politics.

Many scholars throughout this collection help to expand the emerging (but already expansive) field of scholarship on race and digital media, including a focus on many different digital texts. Part III, "Digitizing Race," specifically highlights the concept of digital and online networks as a theoretical framework that does not fit neatly into the traditional media approaches of text, production, and reception. Chapters in part III demonstrate how the specific affordances of digital media have allowed for the creation of networks that many different communities have utilized. This includes Aymar Jean Christian's development of an online network for distributing indie web series made by those with intersectional marginalized identities. Sarah Florini examines the ways Black podcasters have created sonic networks that rely upon the technological affordances of audio media and digital media, as well as the cultural specificities of Black sociality. The concept of enclaving is also central to the research of Raven Maragh-Lloyd, who argues that Black Twitter provides both a space for retreat from the mainstream and the opportunity for education and resistance. Sulafa Zidani and Lia Wolock close out part III with their analyses of how Arab American and South Asian American communities have created diasporic networks that expand beyond the United States, building communities through humor, cultural affiliation, and the need for solidarity.

The book's final part, "Consuming and Resisting Race," considers the wide range of audiences, listeners, viewers, users, consumers, players, and participants who engage with media. While media scholars often put forward their own interpretations and ideological analyses of media texts and platforms, it is also important to consider the experiences of real people who are making sense of racialized messages and sometimes asserting their political power to change them. Meredith D. Clark opens this part with research that connects to the previous chapters on digital media, as she explores the way journalistic practices have been challenged and resisted through conversations on Black Twitter. Jillian Báez explicates the different kinds of scholarship that have focused on Latinx audiences, and the way they have forwarded an understanding of Latinx communities as a variegated mosaic of identities. The final three chapters continue to explore the active and intentional role that communities of color have played in fighting for social justice through, within, and in response to media. Miranda J. Brady investigates histories of media activism in the Red Power movement, including the use of documentary film and press briefings to call attention to Indigenous activism in the United States. In Kishonna L. Gray's research on Black video gamers, she finds that live-streaming platforms like Twitch and YouTube have allowed Black participants to challenge the prevalence of racism and misogyny within digital gaming cultures. Finally, Susan Noh looks at the controversies surrounding the Japanese organizing guru Marie Kondo, arguing that fans who come to her defense rely on cosmopolitan logics that ultimately affirm Orientalist ideologies.

We hope that after finishing this book, readers will have enriched their understanding of the relationship between race and media in a number of different ways: connecting historical representations of racial minorities to newer developments in contemporary media, identifying evidence of how racism is systematically upheld through media, and evaluating the strategies and tactics people of color employ to struggle and resist domination through media. Most importantly, we hope that this collection inspires future scholars to continue this conversation by authoring research questions and projects of their own that will continue these vital lines of inquiry into studies of race and media.

PART I

Representing Race

1

Racism and Mainstream Media

LORI KIDO LOPEZ

racism | systemic oppression | mainstream media industries

Media produced by mainstream U.S. media industries must be under-stood as racist. This is not to say that the individual people who work in Hollywood or produce television shows or provide news analysis are immoral, or that they actively wish harm upon people of color. It also does not mean that every single media text contributes to harmful outcomes for people of color. But if we consider the concept of rac-ism as a complex and interlocking system of oppression rather than merely individual or interpersonal, it becomes clear that the powerful structures that work together to create and support the most popular media are indeed inarguably racist. Together they serve to margin-alize, criminalize, hypersexualize, and otherwise disempower people of color, all in service of upholding white supremacy. This then is affirmed in media that are produced in the United States and exported all over the world.

An understanding of mainstream media as fundamentally racist might seem to fly in the face of much progress that has been made with regard to the representation and participation of minorities in today's media landscape. Indeed, it is important to acknowledge and celebrate the successes and accomplishments of people of color, and there have been many exciting strides forward in the twenty-first cen-tury. This includes the popularity of movies like *Black Panther, Get Out*, and *Crazy Rich Asians*, all of which smashed box office records despite the fact that they centered people of color in historically white genres (superhero, horror, and romantic comedy, respectively). There have also been a number of television series with casts that predomi-nantly feature people of color such as *Empire, Fresh Off the Boat, black-ish*, and *Jane the Virgin*, while the astoundingly successful Black showrunner Shonda Rhimes helms a diverse body of popular television programming.

We have also seen widespread conversations about the need to change norms in Hollywood and disrupt its racist histories. In a rousing speech at the 2018 Academy Awards, white actress Frances McDormand dropped the phrase "inclusion rider" to inspire Hollywood elites to refuse to sign onto future projects without promises for the inclusion of historically underrepresented groups (USC Annenberg 2018), after which, actors like Michael B. Jordan and Brie Larson took up the call. The Academy Awards themselves have been a focus of activism following the popularity of the hashtag #OscarsSoWhite, which called attention to how few people of color were being nominated (Reign 2018). In response, the Academy made efforts to diversify its membership with more women and people of color, and changed its voting structure. In the years that followed, films like Barry Jenkins's *Moonlight* (2016) and Spike Lee's *BlacKkKlansman* (2018) were awardees, while Viola Davis, Mahershala Ali, Regina King, and Rami Malek won acting awards. In 2020 Bong Joon Ho's *Parasite* (2019) broke barriers by taking home more Academy Awards than any other film, and was the first non-English-language film to win Best Picture.

Yet we cannot be distracted by these individual moments of success. Despite the fact that news media fixate on the progress they seem to herald, the reality is that as quickly as a glass ceiling is shattered, it is replaced by a newer version that is designed to prevent further breaches. After each of these temporary respites, the status quo resumes with its normal patterns and familiar behaviors. These individual improvements remain the exception to the rule and serve to mask the powerful structures and institutions that change very little. In order to understand why this is the case, we must more carefully assess the ways racism is deeply embedded within mainstream media and culture industries, and how it came to be that way. This chapter explores the complex relationship between race and media in the United States so that we can more clearly understand the array of mediated forces that uphold white supremacy and encumber progress, as well as what it might take to actually bring about change.

What Is Racism?

Accusations of racism have become some of the most potent and unsettling insults that can be leveled against someone, and the fear of being labeled a "racist" can be paralyzing in its perceived character assassination. Yet the reality is that racism is so pervasive in U.S. society that we are all continually at risk of internalizing racist thinking and perpetrating actions that uphold racism; it is the norm into which we are all born and the status quo that we must perpetually resist. The reality that racism is everywhere, rather than embodied by a handful of hateful individuals, also becomes more clear when we understand what this term actually describes.

A commonsense understanding of racism might be the idea that someone is racist when they believe that the white race is superior to others, and treat non-white people unfairly or poorly because of their race. While there are certainly individuals who embody this kind of hatred and it is not inaccurate to call them racist, this understanding is far too superficial to be of much use. To rectify this, scholars and activists have worked to put forward an understanding of racism as a system—a system of advantage that works to continually uphold white supremacy. Michael Omi and Howard Winant (1986) define a project as racist if it "creates or reproduces structures of domination based on essentialist categories of race" (71). This definition forces us to look beyond individual beliefs and attitudes and root our understanding of racism in the institutions and interlocking systems of domination and power that have long histories of contributing to the oppression of people of color. The specificities change in relation to social and institutional development, but their contribution to maintaining racial hierarchies is stable over time. As Stuart Hall describes, racism is "grounded in the relations of slavery, colonial conquest, economic exploitation and imperialism in which the European races have stood in relation to the 'native peoples' of the colonized and exploited periphery" (Hall 1981, 42). He helps us to see that even when these specific practices have ended, their traces are easily identifiable throughout contemporary ideologies. The inequities and injustices of racism are upheld by dozens of institutions that shape everyday life and the possibilities that are available to people of color.

To understand the way racism is deeply embedded within every aspect of U.S. society, we can look at some specific ways that people of color have faced discrimination in broad arenas such as housing, education, employment, and healthcare. For instance, with regard to housing, there have been laws forcing racial minorities to live in certain neighborhoods by denying them leases or mortgages. The neighborhoods they end up in are the ones with substandard housing, less access to grocery stores, and more environmental pollutants, which lead to health problems. Schools in these neighborhoods get less funding and have fewer resources, which means that it is difficult to attract talented educators, and students are more likely to struggle. Fewer students of color end up prepared for college, or with the finances to afford college, while white students benefit from policies such as legacy preferences for those whose parents attended the same college. Hiring practices and employment policies are also rife with racial injustices, as white workers have an easier time learning about jobs, being recruited for jobs, and being hired. People of color are seen as less qualified, less appropriate for promotions and management positions. There is often unequal access to healthcare because minority neighborhoods have fewer clinics and substandard institutions that serve too many people, which decreases quality of care and creates health disparities. People of color are often uninsured because their jobs don't provide health insurance. In general there are fewer doctors and researchers who are people of color, and a dearth of research on the health of people of color, which means that racial differences in health may be overlooked.

This description obviously only scratches the surface of the myriad ways racism as a complex system is upheld over time through institutions, policies, and practices. Yet hopefully it begins to clarify the importance of understanding racism as a system of oppression, rather than an interpersonal attribute based on individual attitudes or behaviors. This understanding helps us to see why racial identities are not a neutral descriptor of one's ancestry and heritage, but a value-laden array of cultural factors that deeply shape what kind of experiences and treatment are likely for different members of society. Further, it helps us to see that to analyze and understand racism and its impacts, we must look beyond the most obvious markers such as the expression of a racial slur or explicit instances of hate speech and hostility. Racial inequities are upheld through the conscious and unconscious decisions made by those in power; by the recurrent patterns that have been established over time and whose impact spans generations; by the policies, architectures, infrastructures, geographies, and technologies that uphold the decisions of their creators long after those individuals are gone; and by the educational materials and mediated narratives that convey our understanding of the world.

While this description has focused on racism and the treatment of people of color, this understanding of oppression as an interlocking system applies to other disempowered groups as well—including women and gender nonconforming people, LGBTQ+ people, disabled people, certain religious minorities, and others. For each of these identities we can trace a similar history of the way that individuals with those identities have been systematically oppressed. We all possess multiple identities, and theories of intersectionality remind us that individuals can experience multiple forms of oppression that cannot be disentangled (Crenshaw 1990). That is, a Black woman or Muslim lesbian or transgender disabled person each experience oppression differently from one another, and we must be careful not to overlook these other identities.

Media as a System of Oppression

Media clearly play a role in these systems of oppression and contribute to upholding them. In order to understand what this means for people of color, we can analyze many different aspects of media production, reception, and meaning-making. First, we can recognize the cultural power of mainstream media in conveying messages about race. This includes feature films made within Hollywood's studio system, and television shows produced for network, cable, and streaming platforms like Netflix and Hulu. It also includes mainstream news media, radio, video games, magazines, popular music, advertising—all of the forms of mass media that constitute major media industries. While there are significant differences between these different forms of media and the ways they are produced and consumed, they each represent a powerful force in society. They are part of million-dollar (or billion-dollar) industries, and their products are consumed by millions of individuals across the world. Their messages shape our reality and teach us about what it means to be a member of society.

Like all corporations under capitalism, media companies are organized in a hierarchical fashion that accords more influence, decision-making ability, and financial benefit to a small handful of executives and creatives. This includes top-ranking executives at news corporations like the New York Times or news conglomerates like the Tribune Publishing Company and News Corp, tech leaders like those at Google and Amazon, and massively powerful multimedia conglomerates like Comcast, Verizon, AT&T/Time Warner, and Disney/21st Century Fox. In an era where the caps on media ownership were ended through deregulation, we have seen the rise of a handful of media giants that control the vast majority of all media production (Baker 2006). And if we look at the racial identities of the owners, presidents, vice presidents, and general leadership of these corporations, they remain persistently and predominantly white (in addition to privileged identities such as cis male and heterosexual, among others).[1]

At the level of media production, we must also consider the identities of the directors, producers, showrunners, writers, hosts, and news anchors who play significant roles in shaping the direction of content. People of color are largely absent from these roles as well, as reports from the Annenberg Inclusion Initiative have continued to show (Smith et al. 2019; Smith et al. 2018). Maryann Erigha (2019) examines how racial inequalities in Hollywood specifically limit African American directors, whose career trajectories are limited by the unfounded assumption that their films are "unbankable." This reliance on market logics to guide hiring decisions then justifies the upholding of racial stratifications throughout the film industry.

While one's identity cannot be guaranteed to impact content in any specific way, and those with privileged identities can certainly play a role in diversifying content, these historical inequities are nonetheless important to address. The more power an individual has, the wider their influence can spread—including to decisions about who else to hire, what kinds of storylines to include, and the direction of character arcs and portrayals. All mainstream media are produced through the collaboration of many different voices and contributors, but some voices are louder than others. On this note, we can also consider the significance of below-the-line labor, or the vast array of individuals with roles including camera operation, editing, set decoration, lighting, hair and makeup, location scouting, post-production and visual effects, craft services, and much more. These roles have traditionally been devalued as more technical than artistic and the individuals who contribute their labor in these areas are often not considered "authors" (Banks 2009). Traditionally feminized roles like hair, makeup, costume design, and casting are primarily helmed by women, but the rest continue to be predominantly men, and people of color are underrepresented across the board. With movies like *Black Panther* leading the way in celebrating the gender and racial diversity of their entire cast and crew (including below-the-line workers) (T. Gray 2018), we can consider the need for disrupting hiring practices beyond just the most visible or traditionally high-status roles to include every level of employment in media creation.

Then we can consider the actors. There are a number of different problems that shape the experiences of actors of color, beginning with struggles around casting. Nancy Wang Yuen's (2016) research on the racism faced by actors reveals the way they suffer from being excluded, tokenized, and stereotyped. This means that they are rarely given roles in the first place, with the vast majority of all roles going to white actors, who then benefit from the increased exposure, experience, and capital. Yuen describes how this leads to a division between stars (who are predominantly white) and the large number of "working actors" (the category most actors of color find themselves in), who face labor insecurities and discrimination throughout their careers. Casting agents and others who have power over casting often have a certain "look" in mind when they envision a role, and this often defaults to the notion that heroes and romantic leads and stars who will draw audiences all must be white people. Actors of color are rarely even allowed to audition for starring roles, and when they do it is risky for their career, because they will be individually blamed if the resulting product fails to be financially profitable. They are more likely to become typecast and limited to playing the same role over and over, rather than being allowed to expand their artistic repertoire and take chances in their performances. This creates a vicious cycle where it is difficult for actors of color to gain the kind of celebrity status, marketability, and accolades that are desirable and can lead to a sustainable career.

Representational Inequities

The way media are created and what happens behind the scenes then affect the representations we end up seeing on-screen. What kinds of roles are people of color given, and what messages do those roles send to audiences? The most common way to assess the answer to this has been through stereotype analysis. Stereotypes are the patterned ways we sort people into collections of traits. At a basic level they represent the generalizations that we hold about certain groups, such as that people with gray hair are elderly or that people with dirty clothes and many bags are homeless. Our brains are constantly sorting our encounters with society into these groups without our knowledge. We may be able to intellectually reason that there are individuals who break from these molds, but if we do not constantly interrogate our expectations and beliefs about these stereotypes, we will continue to make decisions based on them and unthinkingly reproduce them. This has dire consequences for people of color in particular, because their status as minorities means that most people have had fewer in-person encounters and depend heavily on media representations to build a mental portrait of that group. And unfortunately, the media portrayal of people of color has not been kind.

When we analyze the stereotypical ways people of color have traditionally been depicted, their tropes are so resilient that we can easily identify them. African Americans are dull-witted coons, violent brutes, hypersexual hoochie mamas, welfare queens, and servile mammies; Asian Americans are perpetual foreigners, asexual nerds, weaponized martial arts villains, alluring geisha dolls, and conniving dragon ladies; Latinas are spicy spitfires and docile maids, while Latinos are gun-toting gangsters and macho Latin lovers; Native Americans are sexy princesses and warmongering savages, papoose-wearing squaws and wise elders. Many scholars have documented the nuances of these stereotypes and their harmful variants (Bogle 1973; Collins 2000; Berg 2002; Bird 1999; Ono and Pham 2009). In contrast to the exotic "Other," white characters are intelligent, civilized, and moral; they propel the narrative forward and offer a perceived point of identification for the audience. But more importantly, there are a wide range of possibilities accorded to the multiplicities of white male characters depicted in fictional narratives, and as a result, single undesirable representations cannot challenge the social power and privilege of white people in society. Each denigrating portrayal of people of color, on the other hand, becomes part of the conglomerate upholding the idea that they are inferior and subordinate, deserving of mistreatment and neglect. Patricia Hill Collins (2000) calls these stereotypes "controlling images" because they powerfully manipulate our social values by justifying oppression as natural and normal. As she reasons, if Black women are really aggressive and irresponsible mothers who refuse to work hard, then there is no reason to support them through government assistance and welfare. The stereotype makes injustice seem inevitable, as if it were brought on by those who in reality are suffering from undeserved mistreatment.

While these stereotypes and histories of underrepresentation persist, there have also been shifts in representation that attempt to respond to the negative treatment of people of color. For instance, there have been momentary increases in the number of roles given to minority actors alongside the creation of roles that celebrate and uplift their narratives in the past few decades. Yet scholars have also helped us to make sense of these changes, which are nearly always short-lived and do little to alter the status quo. Evelyn Alsultany (2012) offers the term "simplified complex representations" to address the fact that negative representations are often countered with a positive representation that is meant to offset its harm, as she has seen proliferate in the representation of Muslim Americans post-9/11. An example of this would be that a plotline involving a Black criminal will also include a Black police officer who is tasked with bringing him to justice. This strategy is designed to enhance representational complexity, but Alsultany argues that it actually contributes to postracial discourses that deny the realities of racism and do nothing to alter racial biases against people of color. Part of the continuing problem is due to the fact that even these supposedly "positive" images are still authored by hegemonically white media industries that do not attempt to actually understand the experiences of people of color. Kristen Warner (2017) describes a moment of increased visibility for people of color that is marked by "plastic representations"—artificial, superficial, and flattened rather than culturally specific and multidimensional. Such representations are a by-product of media executives seeking to respond to pressures for progress by adding diverse bodies without actually spending time "developing and appreciating the meaningful cultural and historical differences of those bodies."

We can also assess representations of racialized bodies from a technical perspective, asking how the formal components of media production shape their imagery. The way darker-skinned people appear in movies has suffered as a result of racial bias in the formulation of film stock and the practices of cinematography. Just like Band-Aids, hosiery, concealer, and anything labeled "nude" or "flesh-colored," film emulsions have also been created under the assumption that white or Caucasian skin color is the norm that can stand in for all humans. Photography printers like Kodak and Polaroid calibrated their colors using the image of a light-skinned white woman who was understood to provide a "flesh-tone" (Roth 2009). Moreover, film emulsions were not designed for sensitivity to the ranges of yellow, brown, and red tones that are present in the skin color of many human beings. Gaffers have struggled to adequately light scenes featuring dark-skinned actors, and film schools have been slow to incorporate lessons on improved techniques for doing so. As a result, people with darker skin have often ended up distorted, shadowy, overly lit, or discolored on-screen.

Talking about Media

After media are produced and exist in the world, we must also consider the ways they are distributed, discussed, understood, and valued. Audiences do not encounter texts in a vacuum, but instead are guided toward (and away from) particular forms of media, as well as certain interpretations of those media. We can consider how movies and television programs are reviewed by critics, who get access to content in advance of regular audiences and then determine whether they deem it worthy of thumbs up or down. A report from the USC Annenberg Inclusion Initiative (Choueiti, Smith, and Pieper, 2018) finds that the vast majority of film criticism is written by white males, and that these critics systematically underrate films with women and people of color as leads. Underrepresented female critics are substantially fewer in number and write fewer reviews in total than white male critics. Although media criticism does not totally determine the success of a media product, a critic's decisions about what to review can impact visibility and audience size—two factors that are even more critical to media products made by or about minority communities, which are at high risk for flying under the radar.

The awards and accolades given to media products also contribute to visibility, profitability, and value. This includes the extremely prestigious Oscars bestowed by the Academy of Motion Picture Arts and Sciences, but also the Peabody Awards, the Emmy Awards given for television, the Grammy Awards given for music, as well as prizes awarded from film festivals like the Cannes Film Festival, Sundance Film Festival, South by Southwest Film Conference and Festival, and many more. Indeed, there are hundreds of titles and honors given to media products, all of which contribute to hierarchies of value that shape the discourse surrounding that text and those who played a role in creating it. Careers in media industries are always precarious, as even the most successful producers and performers work on a project-by-project basis and are always on the precipice of unemployment and career stagnation. Producers and performers who win awards (or are accepted to screen at well-attended film festivals) have an easier time advancing and prolonging their careers, and develop the industry clout to support future projects by simply being attached to them. Each awarding body has a different relationship to media products that feature or are primarily made by people of color (for instance, the music industry has done a better job recognizing the outsized influence of Black performers and professionals), but it is generally the case that the more prestigious awards have long histories of celebrating white performers and white creators. When awardees then become part of the body that determines future awardees, this cycle is perpetuated.

These hierarchies of value that shape how we understand the role of people of color in media texts can also be traced to genre. While media genres like comedy, reality television, and sports are home to a wide variety of Black performers, they are degraded and devalued in comparison to "high art" media forms such as dramatic movies and prestige television. Yvonne Tasker (1993) points out how a cultural emphasis on Black physicality contributed to the rise of Black masculine action stars, but they have remained sidekicks and buddies in comparison to the centrality of the white hero. This is then connected to the above observations about both media criticism and awards, as the genres that are more likely to feature people of color are not considered to be "quality." Most critics and awarding bodies overlook texts like those from Tyler Perry's comedic oeuvre and fail to recognize the social contributions of television content like *The Real Housewives of Atlanta*. Racquel Gates (2018) and Kristen Warner (2015) have worked to rewrite our understanding of "ratchet" representations of Blackness, arguing that performances commonly disregarded as "trashy" or excessive actually serve important cultural roles. Not only may they have been misunderstood and unfairly demonized, but these so-called "negative representations" actually impact and shift mainstream popular culture in addition to having profound reverberations throughout long-standing Black cultural traditions.

The racial hierarchies that delimit genre can also play an increased role in obscuring content made by or about people of color due to the increasing power of digital algorithms in our media landscape. Streaming platforms like Netflix and Amazon play an enormous role in delivering content and making suggestions to audiences about what they should consume. While these platforms are often celebrated for their extremely large catalogue of content, they still have very little content produced by and about communities of color. Tim Havens (2017) asks us to look closer at the programming decisions, content availability, and user interfaces of platforms like Netflix in order to understand why African Americans often feel sidelined and misunderstood by them. Black users have complained about Netflix promoting content through images that featured Black actors who actually have very minor roles in the overall story, while Black comedians have noted that Netflix pays them less than their white counterparts (Tiku 2018; Zinoman 2018). Meanwhile, even the most celebrated Asian American documentary filmmakers have struggled to get their content onto Netflix and Amazon Prime and often must resort to educational distributors in lieu of the more popular streaming platforms. Together these factors mean that people of color struggle to find the content they are looking for on these platforms, and mainstream white users are continually guided away from the few offerings that do focus on people of color.

Possibilities for Change

While it should be clear that the persistence of racism throughout mainstream media industries will be difficult to challenge and unsettle, this does not mean that all efforts toward change are fruitless. Michel Foucault (1978) reminds us that where there is power, there is always resistance, and there are many different kinds of resistance that take place from within power structures such as media industries. Rather than viewing oppression as an interminable unified force, he helps us to consider how networks of power relations are complex and unstable— and if we work to better understand how they operate, we can develop better strategies for opposition. Isabel Molina-Guzmán (2016) points to what she calls the "Hollywood paradox," where on-screen diversity has increased, but institutional structures such as labor practices and employment remain the same. While she acknowledges the racial power dynamics in Hollywood that make it slow to change, she also finds hope in the fact that the turn to digital platforms is already causing ruptures in business as usual for media producers. Other groups have also adapted their strategies in response to changing industrial norms. Asian American media activists originally focused on traditional activist strategies like meetings with network executives, which rarely garnered results, but they have begun to see more positive results from hosting digital conversations on Twitter that reveal vast networks of support for Asian American content (Lopez 2016a).

If we recognize the persistence and embeddedness of racism throughout media, we can also be attuned to the ways resistance and counterhegemonic efforts are incorporated and defanged—for example, through postracial discourses that work to obviate these realities around racial inequalities. Sarah Banet-Weiser, Roopali Mukherjee, and Herman Gray (2019) identify postrace as "*the* racial project of our time" in the way that it serves to "manage, adjudicate, and redistribute advantages, handicaps, vulnerabilities, and risks based on racial difference" (5–6). Indeed, many of these activist efforts will result in the kinds of individual, exceptional cases of improvement that are quickly absorbed in order to allow for the redistribution of advantages to those already in power. Yet the persistence of efforts at every level is the only way we can ever hope to see lasting change—including challenging the way that media are produced and who participates in media industries, critiquing the representations that we see, and calling upon everyone—from everyday audience members to media critics to digital strategists to awards selection committees—to join in the demand for change.

This chapter has revealed the many different ways we can understand mainstream media as racist, but it also establishes this fundamental understanding as the basis for moving conversations about race and media forward in the twenty-first century. While it is important to continue to be attuned to the ways racism persists, the resiliency of these norms reminds us to expand our understanding of the relationship between race and media to the complex ways people of color are engaging with media representations in ways that move beyond the simple dichotomy of harmful or progressive, racist or anti-racist. If we accept that racism is always the starting point from which mainstream media emerge, we can then direct our inquiries toward the abundance of media studies theories and concepts that would be enlivened by a consideration of media's specific relationship to racial formations and racialized communities. This is the exciting direction in which other chapters of this book take our understanding of race and media, and future scholars in the field will continue to enliven and enrich these conversations with the development of new approaches in the years to come.

2

Image Analysis and Televisual Latinos

MARY BELTRÁN

image analysis | representation | semiotics | television Westerns

A useful method to illuminate how particular ethnic and racial groups are represented in film and television is the study of individual characters and their contexts through image analysis. Particularly when combined with other research approaches, image analysis can illuminate a great deal about a media text's racial politics, as well as its implied ideological messages about ethnic and racial groups and race relations. In this chapter I share some of my research on the representation of Latino protagonists in 1950s children's television Westerns in the United States, particularly *The Cisco Kid* (1950–1956) and the animated series *The Quick Draw McGraw Show* (1959–1961). In doing so, I illustrate how such research is conducted and the kinds of information that can be gleaned from this method.

Image analysis has roots in both the humanities and the social sciences. Humanities-based scholars like Ferdinand de Saussure (1959) and Roland Barthes (1964, 1972) studied how language and media narratives make meaning. In early studies of semiology and semiotics, they revealed how language and signs make meaning. Later, scholars such as Edward Said (1978), Stuart Hall (1997a), and Ella Shohat and Robert Stam (1994) built on this work in their studies of how citizens of Eastern countries and people of color have historically been depicted in constrained ways that have perpetuated their marginalization. And in the social sciences, early studies of the representation of particular ethnic and racial groups, genders, people of particular sexual orientations, and other marginalized groups often have been based on image analysis, with the earliest studies focusing in particular on whether characters were stereotypes.

Stereotypes are images of a social group that homogenize that group, often by assuming that members possess denigrating traits. This term has disciplinary roots in philosophy, psychology, and sociology. As cognitive psychologists note, we make sense of the world by categorizing objects and people into types, and with the addition of xenophobia—the fear or dislike of people we deem different from our own group—this can result in denigrating stereotypes (Berg 2002). Sociologists similarly point out that dominant groups use stereotyping as one way to justify social stratification. When these ideas become integrated into media narratives, stereotypes can take the form of stock characters that come to falsely stand in for a group. Yet the analysis of mediated stereotypes does not enable in-depth analysis of the overall ideological thrust of a media narrative or an understanding of whose stories and perspectives are being privileged. On its own, stereotype analysis can glean some useful information, but it is also important for media scholars to combine with other critical approaches (Beltrán 2018).

Image analysis begins by using the principles of semiotics, or the study of "signs," as a way of understanding how a particular social group is represented in a film, television episode, or other media text. In this case the "sign" under study would typically be a mediated character or characters. Such an analysis first involves an in-depth survey of a character and its most manifest, external qualities. This part of the image is known in semiotics as "the signifier," or its denotative meaning. Analyzing this would include noting all of the visual and audio aesthetic elements of the image after a thorough stylistic examination. The analysis can then shift to discerning the meanings, ideologies, and myths associated with these external traits. In semiotics, this part of the image is described as "the signified," or the image's connotative meaning. For example, for a character that always speaks in broken English, some connotations might include that the character is not very bright, or is perhaps lazy, foolish, or all three of these things. Connotative meanings are not simply attached to a particular image, however, but are culturally constituted in relation to the particular era and place in which an image circulates. For this reason, it may be important to learn more about the time period from which an image originates in order to gain a full understanding of the potential meanings attached to it. One way to do this can be to seek out and study journalists' reviews of the film or television episode in question at the time of its release.

To more fully understand the characters, we may also find it infor-
mative to conduct a narrative analysis that discerns the function of the
character within the narrative. A series of questions can be asked to
glean a greater understanding of the character and how that character
relates to other characters: Whose story is being told? Which characters are fully developed? For instance, do we learn about their home life
and personal motivations? And what is the relationship and balance of
power between the characters? In addition to studying characters individually, seeking responses to these questions can illuminate the significance of racial representation in the narrative as a whole.

It should be acknowledged that mainstream Hollywood storytelling
traditions tend to encourage constructing characters as broadly as possible, using shortcuts to efficiently relate a story. Classical Hollywood
storytelling also encourages the creation of fully developed protagonists
but less-developed side characters and villains, making it rare to find
fully developed characters of color in contemporary films and television.
Given these expectations and the privileging of whiteness throughout
film history, it is important to develop tools for critical analysis that can
go beyond merely condemning a character for possessing stereotypical
attributes that have long been recognized as the expected norm.

To illustrate the way image analysis can show how media genres
shape ideologies about Latinos, I examine the Latino main characters
in two children's Western series that aired on television in the 1950s and
early 1960s. For my case studies, I chose to focus on two popular but
radically different series, the live-action Western drama *The Cisco Kid*
(1950–1956) and the animated Western spoof *The Quick Draw McGraw
Show* (1959–1961). While these series at first may appear almost identical, image analysis and narrative analysis with attention to genre and
historical and social context clarify that they are in fact antithetical at
times with respect to their portrayals of Mexican Americans and their
implied meanings regarding white superiority.

Latinos and Children's Television Westerns of the 1950s

Latina and Latino depictions in 1950s TV Westerns suffered from a number of problems. They routinely included one-dimensional, unflattering
characterizations of Mexican Americans and other Latinos, as had been

established in frontier fiction and in Western films, and were rarely a point of pride for Latina/o audience members. Mexican American characters in Western narratives were typically portrayed as reprehensible criminals or simpleminded servants who spoke broken English. Latinas, if they appeared, were often hapless peasants or flirtatious barmaids. In other words, Latina/os as a whole were typically construed within the genre as ineffective victims and servants.

In contrast, the children's Western *The Cisco Kid* was unique in that it featured a fair-skinned Latino gunman who helped others and charmed women, echoing representations of Hollywood's white Western cowboys, or what Charles Ramirez Berg (2002) identified as Latin Lovers. The Disney Productions adventure series *Zorro* (1957–1959) similarly featured a fair-skinned Spanish vigilante as its hero. *The Cisco Kid* also was one of the first scripted series to become a smash success with American viewers. Produced and broadcast by Ziv Television, the series arguably helped to popularize the new medium. Curiously, in *Cisco Kid* and *Zorro*, a heroic Latino main character is paired with a less admirable Latino sidekick (or in the case of *Zorro*, nemesis). What encouraged the long-term appeal of this pairing? To answer this question, I examine *The Cisco Kid* and its relationship to common American notions of Latinos at the time.

As mentioned previously, the study of how a particular group is represented in a media text needs to begin with an understanding of the social context during which the text was produced and exhibited to the public. For this reason, I begin with the United States in the 1950s. As documented in the scholarly surveys of historians such as Rudolfo Acuña (2014), Vicki L. Ruiz (2008), and Eric Ávila (2006), this was a decade of economic and cultural challenges faced by Mexican Americans. Despite the fact that many Mexican American men had fought bravely for the United States during World War II, Mexican Americans still experienced political disenfranchisement, labor discrimination, redlining, and many other inequities in this decade. They and other Latina/os also had little voice or visibility within the national popular culture. For instance, as scholars such as S. Robert Lichter and Daniel Amundson and this author found in surveys of Latina and Latino television histories, they were almost nonexistent on 1950s English-language television in popular genres of the time, such

Figure 2.1. This promotional photo for the series *The Cisco Kid*
(1950–1956) features Leo Carrillo as Pancho, the somewhat
dim-witted sidekick of the Cisco Kid (*left*), and Duncan Renaldo
as the more heroic Cisco Kid. Moviestore Collection Ltd / Alamy
Stock Photo.

as variety shows, anthology dramas, or family comedies, aside from
the smash hit *I Love Lucy* (1951–1957).

It was in this period that *The Cisco Kid* made its way to television,
alongside other Western-themed children's shows such as *Hopalong Cas-
sidy* (1948–1952) and *The Lone Ranger* (1949–1957). Meant to appeal to
children but watched by many adults, these adventure dramas now can
seem almost interchangeable. Their "good" characters typically never
falter, their villains are purely evil, and each episode contains a problem

or conflict that the heroes resolve within the half hour. *The Cisco Kid* was unique among these series, however, for making the hero Mexican American. It also established the pattern of pairing a Spanish-Mexican gentleman vigilante character with a sidekick who was shorter, mestizo (of both Indigenous and European ancestry, with tan skin and Indigenous facial features), and who provided comic relief. At least twenty-eight Cisco Kid films and a radio series were produced between 1914 and 1994.

In-Depth Character Analysis of "Boomerang"

The television series pilot for *The Cisco Kid*, titled "Boomerang," aired on September 5, 1950. It begins in the middle of the action, without a great deal of exposition about the Cisco Kid and Pancho, undoubtedly counting on young viewers (and their parents and grandparents) to be already familiar with them from the earlier films and radio series. In the narrative, bandits have impersonated Cisco and Pancho to commit a series of bank robberies. Initially jailed when they are mistaken for the imposters, the duo has to break out of jail and trick the bandits to prove their innocence to the local sheriff. The episode also includes all the trademark story elements expected of *The Cisco Kid*. The physical and personality differences between Cisco and Pancho (which, not coincidentally, reinforce Latino stereotypes) are played up for laughs, as I describe below. There are adventurous clashes with villains, and also quieter moments when the duo ride their horses, Diablo and Loco, across "Western" terrain. Finally, as in most episodes, Cisco gets to kiss a pretty young woman on the cheek after the two have vanquished their foes. Their good deed done, Cisco and Pancho tease each other as they ride off at the end to another adventure.

To begin a more in-depth analysis of the characters, we can examine the racial dynamics of the actors playing them. While a variety of non-Latino actors voiced Cisco and Pancho for Frederick Ziv's earlier radio series, the television series cast the actors who had most recently played the roles in films, Duncan Renaldo and Leo Carrillo. Renaldo was of Romanian descent, which arguably "whitens" the character of Cisco even while he is implied in the narrative to be of Latin (Mexican American or Spanish) descent. Mexican American fans at times thought of Renaldo and his predecessors as Mexican, however, given the character they were playing (Candelaria 1988, 123). Carrillo, in turn, was Spanish American, from a family that had lived in California for generations. Yet he was often thought to be Mexican American. The confusion over ethnic labels attached to the actors in these years was a reflection of the lack of common knowledge about Mexican American and Spanish history and identity in this period, as I discuss further below.

With respect to the external contrasts between Cisco and Pancho, audiences are schooled in a number of ways. The first contrast can be found in the different body types of the two actors and thus the characters—Cisco is lithe, Pancho is portly, Cisco has fair skin, while Carrillo as Pancho is made up to appear more tan. Carefully chosen costumes also help to establish their distinctions. Cisco wears the heavily embroidered shirt and tight-cut pants of a Mexican *charro* in a dramatic white-on-black. This outfit was worn by individuals of Spanish heritage and class privilege in Old Mexico who engaged in *charrería*, a gentleman's tradition of horsemanship that the Spanish brought to Mexico in the sixteenth century. Even though he spends much of his time on a horse, his outfit is never rumpled, dirty, or dusty. Pancho, in contrast, is dressed in an outfit expected of a cowboy or *vaquero* (a lower-class livestock or horse wrangler), in drab browns. Cisco's outfit reinforces that he is not associated with the racialized labor and economic histories of Mexican Americans in the Southwest, while Pancho's links him to these histories.

The two characters' command of English, their accents, and their dialogue also have clear connotations with respect to race and class. Cisco speaks like a well-educated and well-to-do gentleman, with just a hint of a Spanish accent, while Pancho constantly butchers English, has a broad Spanish accent, and speaks in malapropisms. For instance, he's known particularly for fearfully saying to Cisco, "Let's went!" These traits had already been well established in the *Cisco Kid* films and in radio. As Shilpa Davé (2013) argues, dialogue and accents deployed in television and other media meaningfully underscore characters' privilege and power, with these dynamics "intertwined with social relations and part of larger cultural formations" (2–3). In other words, we are subtly taught to make race and class associations based on individuals' accents and word choices; we come to apply these to our social relations and our consumption of media.

Examination of the two characters' typical actions and attitudes reveals meaningful differences as well. Pancho generally is presented as less intelligent than Cisco, and as following Cisco's lead most of the time. Moreover, at times he is portrayed with clear weaknesses that Cisco does not possess. He has to be pushed by Cisco to not give in to his impulses for petty thievery, as in the pilot when he has to be warned by Cisco to keep his eyes—not his fingers—on money in the sheriff's safe. He also is often timid while Cisco is brave, as we see in his line, "Let's went before we find ourselves dancing at the end of a rope. Without music!" While Cisco is forever romancing young women—even long enough to occasionally steal a kiss—Pancho often appears to be running away from women. Pancho's gunmanship and cool do help him seem competent, but these moments are rare at best.

Narrative analysis aids in further understanding these constructions. The series as a whole is Cisco's story—as confirmed in the series title. Cisco functions as the hero, with Pancho's support and comic relief. Their friendship also often takes center stage, however, and the two characters treat each other with utmost respect. Another narrative choice is that the two main characters very seldom speak Spanish or express a connection to Mexican American or Spanish American communities or culture. Narrative analysis also encourages examination of other, less-developed characters. For example, analysis of the entire run of *Cisco Kid* reveals that its villains are usually white. This is somewhat mitigated, however, by many well-developed and "positive" white male and female characters also featured in the episodes. In contrast, there are very few Mexican American characters to provide a balance to the Mexican villains who appear in a few episodes. The young women presented in various episodes as love interests for Cisco (if a kiss on the cheek qualifies) are all white as well.

In all, these characterizations and narrative choices ultimately position Cisco as ambiguously white American or Spanish American, and Pancho as Mexican American. This in turn encourages ambivalent attitudes toward Mexican Americans, given that Pancho's behavior generally implies that Mexican American assimilation might not be possible. The series further positions white American culture (as embodied by

Cisco) as undoubtedly superior in values and integrity to Mexican and Mexican American culture (as embodied by Pancho). At the same time, the series and its merchandising did stretch the archetype of the American hero, even if only slightly, to include male adventurers of Latino descent.

To understand the enduring appeal and impact of these characterizations, we should also consider the historical context of the southwestern United States and what Carey McWilliams (2016) coined the "fantasy heritage" of California. The term refers to a popular, mostly fabricated vision of California history that emphasizes and romanticizes its Spanish colonial era. McWilliams points to the many festivals honoring Spanish heritage in towns throughout California in the late 1940s. As he elaborates, the appeal of fantasy heritage is its submergence of uncomfortable facts regarding the history of race relations for Mexican and Indigenous Americans in the state. For instance, while Spanish Americans, whose ancestors had subjugated Mexicans and Indigenous people during the mission era, began to be included in California civic life after the turn of the twentieth century, Mexican Americans were still typically shut out. The enduring contrasts established between the Cisco Kid and Pancho (as well as other similar pairings, such as Zorro and Sergeant Garcia) in radio and television episodes make more sense if one thinks about how they echoed and reinforced ideas of fantasy heritage, which also tended to erase Mexican American history. *The Cisco Kid*'s pairing of "good" and "bad" Latinos can be understood in this light as enacting a pedagogical process that teaches viewers that Mexican Americans of darker skin tone, Indigenous features, shorter height, and accented or less than perfect English are "Mexican" (and *not* American), and that Mexicans are less intelligent and unable or unwilling to assimilate to American life.

Beyond Image Analysis

Yet a strict focus on image analysis and the construction of characters can be limiting, as it leaves out many significant elements of a media text and can result in misinterpretation. Ella Shohat and Robert Stam (1994) recommend focusing on the perspectives and ideologies that are expressed in a text to get beyond its surface. This can be helpful for recognizing multiple and contradictory discourses that may coexist in a media narrative. For example, it is useful to note that seemingly "positive" characters can actually serve conservative ideologies. Moreover, satirical or seemingly "negative" characters can actually serve to sharply criticize racial hierarchies or otherwise challenge the status quo. In this regard, it's important to begin to look to what Shohat and Stam called the "mediations" of a film or television episode to also explore the significance of its narrative structure, genre conventions, and cinematic style. This includes asking, What sorts of messages are embedded about social and class hierarchies and the status quo in this country? How is that message expressed—is it obvious or implied? The intent is to come to understand voices and discourses (points of view and related ideologies) expressed within a media text.

A quick exploration of *The Quick Draw McGraw Show* provides an excellent illustration of how looking beyond stereotypes is necessary to come to a nuanced understanding of a satirical media text. The animated series of short (ten- to fifteen-minute) episodes is in many ways a parody of the Cisco-Pancho pairing, although it was not acknowledged as such at the time. It featured the comic misadventures of an inept, anthropomorphic horse gunslinger named Quick Draw McGraw and his burro sidekick, Baba Looey. Baba Looey, while costumed in manner reminiscent of Pancho in *The Cisco Kid*, is a smart and wily character, especially in comparison to the hapless Quick Draw.

A cursory image analysis might initially presume that the character constructions and related ideological takeaways are identical to those of *The Cisco Kid*. Baba Looey is a sidekick with less stature and status than Quick Draw, much like Pancho. A short burro, he is clearly meant to evoke a short Mexican American man. In addition, he speaks in an exaggerated Mexican accent and broken English (he calls Quick Draw "Quicksdraw," for instance). When overcome with emotion, he occasionally speaks in a parody of Spanish gibberish—a string of Spanish-sounding non-words laced with a few nonsensical words, like "burrito." Baba Looey's characterization is so clichéd as to be rendered absurd, which highlights how satire at times can change the meaning of a stereotype. And his similarities to Pancho stop there.

Both Quick Draw McGraw and Baba Looey were voiced by Daws Butler, with distinctive accents that reinforced their characterizations as a goofy white cowboy and his English-butchering but *smart* Mexican American companion. Examining the details of the animation in the two characters' construction also confirms that Baba Looey is confident, jaunty, and above all clever, while Quick Draw is earnest, egotistical, and dumb. The episode narratives confirm this as well. While Baba Looey is often discounted by villains who judge him merely by his size or accent, he always gets the upper hand. In "Bad Guy Disguise," for instance, he has to pretend to be a baby but uses this guise to shoot the bad guy in the face, time and again. (It's a violent show, with the fantasy conceit that characters are never permanently hurt.) In "Masking for Trouble," the villain Sundown Sam says to Baba—they're the same size—"Maybe you'd like a nice punch in the nose!" Baba simply responds, "No. But you have one!" This is followed by a loud boing as his hoof bops the guy's nose.

Baba Looey also constantly foresees and warns Quick Draw of potential danger or embarrassment. He's always right, even if Quick Draw seldom heeds his advice; a common refrain from Quick Draw is, "I'll do the thin'in' around here . . . and do-o-on't you forget it!" One of the running gags is that Quick Draw constantly blunders because he won't listen to Baba Looey. In some episodes Baba is cunning, tricking villains and Quick Draw alike. In "Slick City Slicker," Baba Looey dresses up like a hotel bellhop in order to help Quick Draw arrest the Raindrop Kid, a criminal hiding out at the hotel. In this role, he's easily able to trick the Raindrop Kid—and Quick Draw—into thinking that they're stuck to the ceiling by nailing the furniture to the actual ceiling. Thus while the series spoofs the conscribed roles of *The Cisco Kid*, it simultaneously upends those expectations.

The Quick Draw McGraw Show and other Hanna-Barbera series of this time period were known for creating funny and facetious characters that were appealing because of their irreverence and skewering of American culture. They illustrate how satire can at times critique stereotypes, resulting in radically different ideological meanings. In this case, the dialogue and narratives demonstrate that Baba Looey does not fit the Latino buffoon stereotype, even while his costuming would seem to reinforce it. As Jason Mittell (2003) notes, Hanna-Barbera series like *The Quick Draw McGraw Show* worked in a dual register, "aiming the visuals and the 'wacky' sound effects at the 'moppets,' and the dialogue at adults" (43). Adults who saw through the thinly veiled discourses of white superiority and Mexican American stigmatization in children's Westerns such as *The Cisco Kid* could enjoy their satirization in *The Quick Draw McGraw Show*. In all, the show's satire offered a clever parody and convincing critique of the Mexican American erasures that undergird the earlier children's Westerns, even while the visual appearance of Baba Looey appears to reinforce that mythology.

While six decades have passed since these television episodes first aired and we are less likely to see obviously racist, sexist, or otherwise xenophobic images or media narratives in more recent decades, social inequities and the stigmatization of some groups still are manifest in a variety of ways in films, television, and other entertainment media. For this reason, image analysis can be a useful method for media scholars exploring the racial politics of representation to have in their arsenal. This is especially important in our contemporary environment, in which complex media texts can appear to signal that racial discrimination and oppression no longer exist.

3

Visualizing Mixed Race and Genetics

MESHELL STURGIS AND RALINA L. JOSEPH

mixed race | race and genetics | advertising

What does it mean to "look mixed"? This problematic question should elicit incredulity and head scratching, given the vast diversity of mixed-race people. But because race is hegemonically understood through the visual, what might emerge is a picture of someone with curly hair, light brown skin, freckles, and light-colored eyes—that is, someone who "looks mixed" by way of a Black and White background.[1] Within the institutions of both science and media, race rarely remains rooted in culture, place, and kinship, but is instead biologically mapped onto the body as phenotypic "looks," physical traits, and now even genes. Paleontologist Stephen Jay Gould (1996) disproves the racist research of scientists like Samuel George Morton who purported that brain size was related to racial differences and levels of intelligence. Similarly, Black studies scholar Alexander Weheliye (2014) describes race as being constructed by a set of sociopolitical assemblages (50), while communication scholar LeiLani Nishime explains how our process of identifying race visually is a learned behavior. Nishime writes that while "there may be quantifiable differences between the people we place in separate racial groups . . . the decision to prioritize the tiny physical differences that separate people along predetermined racial lines is culturally dictated" (Nishime 2014, xiii).[2] In other words, while scientific indulgences about race are not a biological necessity, they are a social fact (Joseph 2018, 8; Jackson and Garner 1998, 51).

A reliance on the social operation of race also meant that there was no way to definitively ascertain who was mixed-race other than by traditional forms of genealogy, self-identification, and assessment of appearance.[3] Yet following the completion of the Human Genome Project in 2003, advanced genomic sciences have allowed for the translation and tracing of an individual's DNA using specific genetic markers and variants. Web-based companies such as 23andMe, AfricanAncestry, and MyHeritage have introduced direct-to-consumer genetic tests that can specify someone's ancestry using regional and country-sourced reference populations. The results are then provided as one's ethnic makeup, which can easily slip into understandings of one's racial identity (Jackson and Garner 1998, 52).[4] These companies attempt to answer questions of genealogical gaps and mixed heritages by offering origin stories that are entirely removed from the way a person looks. Simply spit into a tube, seal it in an envelope addressed to the company, and wait six to eight weeks for the results to be digitally released. This streamlined process now costs roughly $75 to $250 and promises more ancestral accuracy than any other genealogical method.

Companies like 23andMe are shaping global conversations around race and ethnicity, driving how consumers conceptualize what it means to be ethnically mixed, and relatedly, influencing how one "looks mixed." In a blog post entitled "A New Survey on Attitudes about Race and Genetics," the company explains, "What people think about when they think about race usually focuses on skin color, which, although heavily influenced by genetics, is controlled by a tiny fraction of our genome" (2018d). Even though about a third of the Americans surveyed believe that there is a connection between DNA and racial difference, 23andMe proposes that the outcome of direct-to-consumer genetic testing is "the opposite, reminding people of how mixed we all are" (2018d). Yet there are two different "mixes" being addressed here. While the science looks at *how* people are ethnically mixed, the media of 23andMe develop a repertoire of *what it "looks" like* to be mixed, and subsequently, what it means to be racially mixed based on those looks.

But being "mixed" is far from a self-evident proposition. Depending on sociopolitical context, location, and time, the way people identify with and read race and ethnicity is structured differently. For example, a mixed-race person's complexion may change drastically depending on season, climate, or hairstyle, all of which can fluctuate day to day. These malleable factors can greatly impact how a stranger might read their race, proffering dramatically different reads depending on time, place, and the strangers' experiential references (Sims 2016). Critical mixed-race studies scholars such as Nikki Khanna have also demonstrated that mixed-race subjects themselves will choose their racialized identities in accordance with "reflected appraisals," or the way they are identified as one singular racial identity or another (Khanna 2004, 2010, 2011). Race, like beauty, is in the eye of the beholder (Saperstein 2013). While there is no uniform "look" for those who are mixed-race, representations in the media repeatedly guide audiences toward singular stereotypes such as the tragic and new millennium mulatta and the exceptional multiracial tropes that Ralina L. Joseph (2013) identifies as particular to representations of mixed race. Patricia Hill Collins (2000) reminds us that these stereotypes then become "controlling images," justifying the systematic mistreatment of minoritized communities.

23andMe contributes to a hegemonic establishment of a mixed-race look. With a vast advertising campaign that includes commercials, sweepstakes, and in-depth testimonials by satisfied customers, 23andMe frequently uses images of Black multiethnic and mixed-race women to promote its services. This chapter asks how multiraciality is visually and narratively deployed by 23andMe and what its mixed-race imagery conveys about the cultural significance of genome sciences. This includes an analysis of how consumers respond to their genetic results by confirming or denying the "validity" of the results in relation to their self-identification, but also the myriad ways customers can subtly reject 23andMe's dominant racial scripting. We argue that the company participates in fixing the meaning of a racially ambiguous look that narratively frames mixed-race Blackness as an ailment in need of an antidote—as if racial mixture can cure or neutralize the ostensible harms of Blackness. Ultimately we critique the company's optimism about a global, race-less, postracial society,[5] as well as its problematic implicit idea that science will provide an antidote to racialization.

Half or Whole: Measuring Multiracial Blackness

The census has long served as a site for debating how we recognize and identify the ever-growing population of mixed-race individuals who cannot just "check one box." The "mark one or more" (MOOM) ideology was first and most vociferously articulated by multiracial activists in the mid-1990s (Williams 2006). Multiracial activists, whom Williams describes as largely White women married to Black men, accepted MOOM as a concession after their preferred choice of "multiracial" as a stand-alone and self-explanatory category was rejected. Post-2000 census racial science dictates that being both Black and mixed necessitates delineating that mixture beyond boxes, and the availability of home genome kits means that this can be done to the level of numerical percentages.

This quantitative question is an interesting return to an earlier moment of pre-multiracial recognition that is articulated in the refusal to answer the ever-present question posed to multiracial individuals: "What are you?"[6] (Root 1996, 2001; Winters and DeBose 2003). Teresa Williams-Leon and Cynthia L. Nakashima (2001) resist this question in their book *The Sum of Our Parts: Mixed-Heritage Asian Americans*, while Sika Dagbovie-Mullins (2013) responds that the "sum" of the Black-mixed experience is an attainment of "a black-sentient consciousness" (3). Identity is a negotiation process of both self-import and relational reception. The modern-day "What are you?" question is now measured with both qualitative and quantitative methods. In a society that places cultural value on race-dominated notions of identity, the biological and physiognomic are paramount.

Critical mixed race scholars have traced this process of racializing Blackness as it intersects with multiraciality. Ralina L. Joseph (2013), who designates her subjects as "mixed-race African Americans," uncovers the cultural popularity of anti-Black racism and the notion that transcending Blackness was desirable in mainstream popular culture in the decade before Obama was elected. Quantifying Blackness suits this notion, as it can confirm one's racial purity or unfortunate distance from the horizon. Yet, as Habiba Ibrahim describes and Joseph agrees, multiracialism and Blackness are temporally "defined by the same horizon" (Joseph 2013, 5; Ibrahim 2012, vii). In other words, the quantitative distance from the horizon is meaningless if the horizon itself epitomizes the color line. Michele Elam's use of "mixed folk" in *The Souls of Mixed Folk* makes a "gentle dig" at the "overreaching ambitions and hyperbolic rhetoric of some in the mixed-race movement who advertise mixed-race people as new millennial beings with special souls that warrant their own manifestos" (Elam 2011, xvi). These scholars' terminologies move from what Jayne Ifekwunigwe (2004) calls the "Age of Celebration," when scholars of multiracialism sought to simply stake a claim for themselves, to the "Age of Critique," when scholars sought to consider the role of power vis-à-vis multiracials (8). In a parallel fashion, we seek to bypass the celebration of mixed-race imagery from 23andMe and directly critique the genomic sciences and their capital influence on the relationship between cultural identity and race.

As mixed-race authors, we regularly confront the same "What are you?" question that has become materialized in the form of DNA tests. Indeed, these scientific instruments appear to be yet another opening of the "vein to genealogy that might logically explain [our] oddly racialized looks" (Joseph 2013, xiv). Along with an increase in people who identify as mixed, the discourse of DNA restates what many critical race scholars and historians have already known: the myth of monoraciality runs in tandem with the myth that multiraciality is new. With Blackness as race and race as inferior to culture, then to possess a cultural identity one must negotiate the necessity of transcending Blackness for social and physical survival. Joseph traces the narrativistic transformation of the sick and barren tragic mulatta stereotype into the new millennium multiracial who is a sad "race girl" followed by the unicorn exceptional multiracial. Throughout this historic arc of representations, Black hybridity is portrayed as "unattainable, and perhaps undesirable" (2013, 169). The multiracial Black women in our analysis are similarly plagued by a narrative that "disdains" their Blackness as ailment while "dialectically desiring" their mixedness as a cure to the problem of race, and therefore Blackness (2013, 4).

Is Visualizing "Mixed" an Ailment or Antidote?

Founded in 2006 by Anne Wojcicki, Linda Avey, and Paul Cusenza, 23andMe is a company that analyzes the twenty-three chromosomes that make up a person's unique DNA. The service translates genetic data into a composite of one's ethnic makeup, medical predispositions, ancestral genealogy, and individual genetic traits (such as the number of hair whorls a person has, or whether their ear lobes are attached or detached). With all the data hosted online, consumers can access detailed descriptions of their DNA, connect with relatives, and map their ancestral history. Just as consumers are afforded the autonomy to use their data however they please, the company also retains access to this data so it can increase the accuracy of its reference populations. Additionally, consumers can opt into sharing their data with the company for research purposes like developing therapies and drug solutions. 23andMe's results can vary widely from those of other genetic companies such as those mentioned earlier, as each company sources its results from a unique database of regional and country-based reference populations. This means that the outcomes of 23andMe's marketing are directly tied to the products of the company's science. Interestingly, the company blames institutional racism for fostering suspicion of science within Black communities, as seen in a blog post titled "Diversity Matters in Research," which briefly mentions a history of scientific mistreatment, citing the Tuskegee Syphilis Project as an example (2019b). However, 23andMe does little to actually demonstrate how diversifying its science, or building the accuracy of its tests based on acquiring underrepresented and historically disadvantaged groups, will instead be used toward equitable ends.[7]

The company's YouTube channel features dozens of uploaded videos, including product overviews, featured stories of participants' experiences, educational interviews, promotions, and customer-made videos that reveal their results. These videos can be understood as advertisements that promote the validity and utility of 23andMe's genetic tests. Throughout them, Black women are repeatedly cast as the face of 23andMe: Halleta Alemu hosts "The DNA Download," a quirky newslike weekly clip that shares facts about DNA; Cari Champion hosted the 2018 live broadcast event for DNA Day of Celebration;[8] and Vanessa Freeman, an anchor for Cheddar News, has hosted several segments on genetics sponsored by 23andMe. As the faces of the company, such representations of multiracial Blackness reveal 23andMe's simultaneous desire and disdain for mixed race.

The problem is not limited to what the results say, but also in how the company depicts people using those results. For instance, Cari Champion's inquiry into the 10.4 percent of her DNA that is European was not just a question of what the results were, but the story behind those results. A similar double meaning resounds in the "What are you?" question. As a negotiated answer, there are multiple truths—not simply one quantifiable answer, no matter how rooted it is in biology. Many of the testimonial videos work to build out a story in relation to the test results. People of color are commonly represented as redressing issues of race, identity, and family. In contrast, representations of monoracial White people, or those whose parents are ostensibly White, are seen as inherently beyond race. Many of their video stories begin with a White person describing who they are by sharing details of their life and familial background. The narrative builds up to the DNA results that reveal some predisposed illness suddenly discovered in the consumer's genetics.[9] In these videos, race is not the primary inquiry, as it was in Champion's. White people are not seen as "having a race" in the way that Black multiracial people are. Although the results for everyone undoubtedly challenge the concept of monoraciality, race and ethnicity are not treated as a biological quandary for White consumers. Instead, videos of monoracial White people delve into emotional details such as uncovering a biological mutation or deficiency that impacts their health.[10] 23andMe is repeatedly cast as the hero that saves the fragile White identity by buffering against sometimes unpreventable and otherwise unpredictable biological threats. While 23andMe may be offering resolution for those with unsettled pasts or unknown futures, it fails to critique the highly problematic past of race and science altogether. For the Black or otherwise racialized subject, this has had dire consequences, as the science of the past and present has had a hand in the understanding of race and racism.[11]

In the videos that reveal a customer's mixed ethnicity, they demonstrate what it means to be mixed and what mixed "looks" like as defined by the composite percentages of various ethnicities/nationalities/heritages/races that are revealed.[12] The 23andMe representations of mixed-race subjects that we focus on in this chapter visualize a particular version of what it means to be "mixed-with-Black." Moreover, the mixed experience is depicted as one that fails to be complete without a return to the so-called traditional or "pure" racial categories; in other words, mixed race is illegible without its monoracial signifiers. Rather than focusing on the entire 23andMe mediascape, we narrow our focus to two representations of Black multiracial women. After viewing most of 23andMe's marketing videos, we selected two stories that encapsulate a representative formation of how 23andMe understands mixed-race Blackness and utilizes representations of Black multiraciality in its marketing campaigns.

The ads present two mixed-race women named Angelina and Nicole as incomplete until they discover the traditional monoracial groups to which they belong, using the company's DNA analysis. Angelina's ad frames her as initially content with life as a Black woman. But she is increasingly bothered by not knowing the race of her absent father and turns to 23andMe for resolution. Nicole, on the other hand, does not achieve what the ad visualizes as wholeness or "100%" until she has traveled all of the world, feeling what it means to be "East Asian," "Middle Eastern," "West African," and "Scandinavian." In this way, a Black and mixed-race subjectivity is presented as ailment in need of remedy; the "What are you?" question is presented as incomplete without the ability to articulate the culturally delineated discrete segments that make up the whole person.

In what the media depicts as a global process of becoming mixed, the science of 23andMe posits that we are all already multiethnic although only a selection of us are "seen" as such. Within the company's mediascape, this default toward all results revealing some level of multiethnic background, positions representations of White people as unaffected by issues of race, although they encounter other ailments. But for Black people, 23andMe's news of a multiracial background supposedly clears a path toward racial transcendence. These revolving discourses of mixed race seem to offer an antidote for any and all, heralding us into a future with no biological mystery. Yet the mediascape largely circumvents our true social ailment: racism as a hegemonic power structure supported by the epistemological regime of science. As Barbara Jeanne Fields and Karen E. Fields indicate in *Racecraft* (2012), "The news is not good when scientists studying the human genome . . . hark back to the old notion [of race] . . . to a system of classifying people that is steeped in folk thought" (5). The significance of 23andMe's representational discourse of mixed subjects is that the science risks bolstering postracial rhetoric while at the same time essentializing beauty standards in favor of the demographically ascending multiracial subjectivity.

Angelina's Story

Angelina's video opens to shots of a busy city landscape bursting with urban Blackness: murals of Black icons, hair braiding shops, fruit vendors, and lots of Black and Brown people traversing city streets (23andMe 2017a). The camera catches a strikingly pretty, curly-haired, caramel-complexioned, twenty-something young woman striding

Figure 3.1. Depicted in a kente cloth–inspired hat, Angelina is held in her grandmother's embrace. 23andMe, *Breaking Down Stereotype Barriers: Angelina's 23andMe Story*, YouTube video, June 19, 2017.

down the street while gripping her coffee. We hear a woman's voiceover explain that the place we see is Bed-Stuy in Brooklyn, New York, which she describes as a place where "being Black, our Blackness is rooted in the culture." Blackness, she tells us, is in the historical naming of the neighborhood, with streets named after Marcus Garvey, Malcolm X, and Martin Luther King Jr.

This description of Bed-Stuy as a Black-identified space completely neglects any mention of its recent gentrification, where median home value, household income, and those with advanced degrees have spiked (Szekely 2018). The young woman, Angelina, goes on to narrate: "That history wasn't just in my neighborhood, it was in my house. It was the opportunity for me to really be grounded as a Black woman." As Angelina says these words, we see family pictures with a rainbow of relatives alongside a variety of Afrocentric objects including blankets, toys, Kwanzaa candles, books, and dolls. Through the image of Angelina held in her grandmother's embrace while wearing a kente cloth–inspired hat, we understand that this is a household that unequivocally celebrates Blackness (figure 3.1). The Blackness of place and history is not just outside in her neighborhood; it's inside Angelina's home and family.

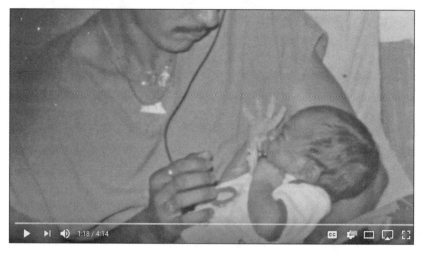

Figure 3.2. In this photo of Angelina and her father, a partial view of his face renders him racially ambiguous. 23andMe, *Breaking Down Stereotype Barriers: Angelina's 23andMe Story*, YouTube video, June 19, 2017.

However, in the second part of the video, Angelina explains that despite her own claiming of Blackness, "out in the world" she failed to register as Black. In her own words, "People would tell me I was crazy for calling myself Black." She describes how difficult it was when teachers would ask "if I was Native American or Puerto Rican or something else." The video falls silent for a beat, before Angelina's narration doubles down on her feelings of disconnection as she explains, "My father was absent from my life. . . . I don't know my father's race and ethnicity." To visually illustrate this disconnection, the camera shows a picture of a man holding a baby. The shot is framed so the viewer can see only a slice of the tip of the man's nose and mouth, his serious face gazing down at a crying infant Angelina (figure 3.2). From the quick image, her father's skin color is difficult to ascertain and the aging photograph doesn't provide access to the "truth" Angelina and the viewer are seeking. Angelina continues her story, saying that her mother would not give her the answers she was looking for about her father.

Part 3 of the video, the resolution, provides the solution to Angelina's mixed-race affliction: DNA testing through 23andMe. Angelina narrates that with the answers provided to her through DNA testing, she begins to feel comfortable in her skin. As she says, "I began to piece together the puzzle of understanding who my father was . . . [and] that felt exciting." In the crescendo of the video, Angelina remarks, "We are so much more alike than we are different. These barriers separating ourselves don't really need to exist and it enhances conversations if we aren't looking at each other through the lens of what stereotype and what box I put you in." This blandly multicultural statement stands in stark contrast to the pro-Black ones in the first third of the video that establish Angelina's personal and community history, shifting to focus on the product for sale.

Yet the visuals themselves do not confirm such bland multiculturalism, as we see that Angelina has become a motivational speaker for young women of color (figure 3.3). She states, "As I speak to young women I want them to feel encouraged to also be who they are and not let the world tell them to be something other than what they are. I feel very much at peace with my identity and who I am as a woman. I feel complete." As Angelina concludes her narration, the camera follows her running through the streets to Central Park, taking in a multicultural array of people on the street, not just Black and Brown ones as in the opening images. The closing shot of her is a triumphant one of her

Figure 3.3. In the resolution to Angelina's story, she is seen confidently speaking to young women of color. 23andMe, *Breaking Down Stereotype Barriers: Angelina's 23andMe Story*, YouTube video, June 19, 2017.

Figure 3.4. Angelina ends the video in a triumphant pose as she faces the world. 23andMe, *Breaking Down Stereotype Barriers: Angelina's 23andMe Story*, YouTube video, June 19, 2017.

overlooking a pond in a power pose with her arms firmly planted on her hips (figure 3.4).

There are a number of ways we can read Angelina's story. One understanding is that it moves from her identity as Black to a troubling mixed-race confusion (where 23andMe is presented as antidote) to her postracial stance (as 23andMe has healed her from Black to mixed to now complete). In this formulation Blackness functions as a stand-in for "race," and thus mixedness becomes the postracial antidote to the illness of Blackness. But this narrative is more complicated than moving up and out of Blackness through 23andMe. Interestingly, it is not being Black but being mixed-race that represents the illness in this metaphor. In fact, Angelina's initial description of Blackness does not even relegate it to the biological (as race) but instead concludes that it is something cultural— rooted in place, people, and processes of communication. As Angelina mentors a group of young women of color, including Black girls who look like the ones from her narration of her family and neighborhood, Blackness returns her to wholeness, not 23andMe. While the commercial's voiceover narration uses bland multicultural rhetoric to suggest that 23andMe is what makes her complete, the images and setting in fact depict Angelina as complete by the work she performs in her Black community. Her sense of wholeness comes from being engaged with her Black community and her family, resisting the conclusion that wholeness comes from knowing some truth about her mysterious genetic background.

Nicole's Story

While Angelina's story is available only through 23andMe's YouTube channel, the second story we explore was additionally broadcast as a commercial on national television. In early August 2018, 23andMe closed its Golden23 Sweepstakes, where twenty-three winners were selected for a travel extravaganza. The official reward included six days of travel (up to $20,000 for themselves and one guest) to any location that appeared on their genetic test, complete with spending money and hosted cultural activities. The one-minute video ad for the sweepstakes featured model and creator of Black Girl Beautiful (blackgirlbeautiful.com) Nikia Phoenix. Her video was first uploaded as *100% Nicole* (23andMe 2018a), but after several iterations was later titled *We Are All Connected: Celebrate Your DNA* (23andMe 2018f).[13] The video's description reads: "There are parts of all of us / Yet to be discovered / And through our DNA / We are all connected / Celebrate your DNA."[14]

The video *100% Nicole* begins with the image of a woman (Nicole) riding over a bridge on a motorbike. The song "Getting to Know You," from the movie *The King and I* (1951), is sung by Gertrude Lawrence in the background while the text "Follow your DNA around the world" fades in and out, left of center. The woman's braids are mostly concealed by the helmet she wears, but her prominent freckles, light honey skin, and gold-hoop nose ring are revealed as the camera centers her face. She peers through her dark round specs at lush mountains in the distance and is then shown wearing a bandana on her head; she smiles and nods to Asian agricultural workers as she asks for directions. In a following scene, Nicole heads into the ocean with a woman, both settling onto their surfboards as water splashes, laughing with each other as the sun sets in the background. Here, her braids are fully revealed as cornrows. In a third scene she laughs and dances her way into the night, toasting drinks with a crowd of people enjoying festivities at an Asian night

Figure 3.5. Nicole's race is visually communicated with pie charts depicting portions of her DNA results. 23andMe, *100% Nicole*, YouTube video, June 12, 2018.

market. Nicole holds her arm out to capture a selfie in the moment and just as she does this, an orange pie chart figure appears around her head, like a halo, along with the words "29% East Asian" (figure 3.5).

Dressed in a helmet and eyewear once again, the clip continues as she catches air in a dune buggy heading over a large mound of desert sand. After Nicole and her company race through the dusty terrain, she lies on a table for a soapy massage from a woman whose face is not shown. The text says "12% Middle Eastern" as another pie chart halo forms around her. She rinses off in an orange bathing suit, floating on her back in water, and then takes a short bus ride to catch a game of street soccer with several Black boys and men. Nicole is shown holding a local West African man's hand, as the two of them swing their hips down the dirt road when a larger pink pie chart halo appears around her with the words "46% West African." As she departs, the words "We are all connected" underline Nicole's broad smile (figure 3.6).

Following the West African scene, she emerges out of a dark lake with snow-covered jagged mountains as the backdrop. Before she can shiver and wipe the water from her eyes, she materializes in a sauna, wrapped in a towel. She leans forward and as she exhales, "3% Scandinavian" appears with the pie chart halo around her. As Lawrence sings in the background, "Haven't you noticed, suddenly I'm bright and breezy, because of all the . . ." Nicole appears in the same shot as figure 3.6, but instead of the tagline "We are all connected," a fully colored and slightly animated pie chart halo appears around her with the words "100% Nicole." The scene concludes with a man's voiceover explaining the details of the Golden23 Sweepstakes.

The video positions Nicole as exploring the deepest part of herself alongside a transnational exploration of different cultures and "Others." The advertisement exploits place and looks in order to sell the idea of genetics, and blurs the lines between reality and fiction in doing so. For example, Nicole's real name is Nikia. Nikia wrote on her Instagram page that the data presented in the video do not reflect her actual DNA results; at the time of the video, she had not yet received her 23andMe genetic report (Phoenix 2017). Not only is the name Nicole an anglicized alternative to Nikia, but the DNA results are fabricated. The helmets, eyewear, and the camera's long shot from behind initially cloak her racialized identity, allowing the monoracial viewer to identify the protagonist as any woman. As the ad progresses, Nicole is revealed to be a very particularly mixed woman. Here again, we see the simultaneous desire for mixed race (and postrace) alongside disdain for Blackness (and race) (Newman 2019, 108).

Figure 3.6. Nicole smiles alongside a statement of global communities as connected through multiraciality. 23andMe, *100% Nicole*, YouTube video, June 12, 2018.

The video *100% Nicole* demonstrates a desire for everyone to be multiracial, or at least multigenerationally multiethnic, with the hope of ameliorating race. Such a statement privileges mixed race in order to distance Blackness, a move we understand as ultimately postracial, or one that diminishes the significance of race. In this way, Nicole's actual DNA results become less important, while her mixed-race "look" continues to signify particular meanings in relation to the data. To portray Nicole as 100 percent authentic, the ad neutralizes her image by disguising elements of her mixed-race physicality such as dark freckles and curly hair. Yet the displacement of the text "100% Nicole" with the newer version of "We are all connected" builds 23andMe's postracial agenda, where race ultimately doesn't matter as we are all evolutionarily connected to Africa through ancestry. The ad uses its mixed-race subject to exemplify the process by which one becomes whole through genetic data.

Conclusion

These media samples do two distinct things when it comes to our initial question of what it means to "look mixed." First, they allow immediate access to the complexity of what makes someone mixed as manifested by both scientific biology and culture. Nicole travels around the world as she pieces together the percentages of her identity and experiences the cultures of the groups with whom she now identifies. In Angelina's case, her mixedness is signified by people's curiosity about her, and her own curiosity about her past and biological parents, while simultaneously claiming a Black identity rooted in her local community and local culture. Blackness as rooted in culture is offered second but remains intact despite the prioritization of biology.

Our analysis suggests that representations of mixed-race Blackness provide a way of knowing that comes about by way of looking. Angelina expresses the inability of others to know her racial makeup by her looks, and yet, in the clip we explore, we come to know her mixed identity by seeing where she comes from and with whom she is in community. The video *100% Nicole* promotes looking at others in order to know oneself, and at the same time, obscures the look of mixed race. The only thing knowable for certain, according to 23andMe, is the claim that "we are all connected," by knowing our DNA. The beauty of knowing ourselves through our DNA, 23andMe tells us, is that we are delivered into a future where race, ostensibly, doesn't have to matter at all.

It is no coincidence that "Nicole," with her freckled-face, light-brown-skinned, mixed-race poster girl aesthetic, has been chosen as the face of 23andMe's two-year-long advertisement campaign. Racial mixing is not a new phenomenon, but something that has been occurring for as long as groups were divided across lines of region, race, religion, and nation. Simply saying "We are all mixed" negates this reality, and ultimately allows the people who have appropriated and colonized practices of "vetting" and blood quantum to continue such transgressions. The science of 23andMe problematically focuses on the ways we are all descendants of Africa, even when our histories, languages, and physical appearances do not so easily demarcate such a diaspora. We cannot elide the structures that have been built to fortify such a racial divide, and we cannot flippantly overstep these boundaries for the sake of a fantastical "prodigal daughter" on the horizon who returns to Africa. This attempt to measure identity is one-sided, negating the reality that "identity is relational" and emerges from a negotiated process of communication (Jackson and Garner 1998, 46). It is impossible for 23andMe to provide data that answer the "What are you?" question even as the science can document one's entire genome. What 23andme considers as whole, or 100 percent, is only but half, or a sum of many parts.

These representations and the multiple meanings they present suggest that direct-to-consumer genetic testing sites such as 23andMe do not pose an actual threat to our "racial order of things," as Roopali Mukherjee (2006) describes, even as they shake the concept of monoracial identities. Their turn to the "mixed look" only reveals the impossibility of a postracial subject position by converging the fragments of racial identity into one scientifically knowable truth. Mixed race is heralded as the vanguard of our future, offering a clean slate for racial tensions by somehow dissolving or exploding the notion of monoracial identity as it troubles notions of authenticity and purity. However, what these sites and genetic consumer practices and media are in fact doing is reinscribing what Weheliye (2014) calls our current racializing assemblage by affirming Blackness as something rooted in biology (or outside human construction) as seen in race. In other words, even though race seems to be located on and in the body, as in these examples of mixed-race sub-jects, race is always assembled in a way that suggests that it is ordained outside human agency, even though it is something entirely constructed by humans; Blackness is cultural. And in these two cases, it is being reconstructed by the mediascape of 23andMe and its genomic science practices and campaigns.

Just as mixed-race people are not new, the genomic science of 23andMe is also not new. The representations in 23andMe videos sug-gest instead a revolving racial discourse. The media of 23andMe are a source of power that work to reinscribe traditional notions of race while re-prescribing how to look mixed. Mixed race is not an ailment, and 23andMe is not an antidote. Instead, perhaps the reality of race, mixed race, and home genomic kits is as frustrating as race itself: mixed-race subjects are afflicted with a host of unknowable truths and 23andMe merely complicates the possibility of ever really knowing what the "look" of mixed race really means.

4

Listening to Racial Injustice

DOLORES INÉS CASILLAS AND JENNIFER LYNN STOEVER

sonic color line | vocal bodies | televised trials

Are you listening?
—Rachel Jeantel, witness in George Zimmerman case

While research on race and media has long focused on visual representations and visible markers of race, scholars from fields such as American studies, ethnic studies, rhetoric, film, history, English, anthropology, and media studies have been producing exciting new scholarship on *listening* as a method of analysis.[1] This chapter builds from these works in order to make the case for shifting attention from the visuality of race to the aural, sonic dimension of representation. Doing so helps to disrupt the privileging of sight as the only path to knowledge by acknowledging the epistemological work of listening. This shift is particularly valuable in an era when attention to vocal and audible features have increasingly become stand-ins for racial cues or as a means of signaling race. Moreover, this work can help to counter the many flawed and problematic public claims made by media pundits and politicians about the United States being a "colorblind" society, or the popular misconception that as a nation we "see no color" because racism no longer exists. As Eduardo Bonilla-Silva (2003) and others contend, colorblind ideologies actually sustain social inequalities based on race in areas such as housing discrimination, police brutality, all-White courtroom juries, health disparities, voter disenfranchisement, and unequal access to media. We encourage scholars to direct their theoretical, methodological, and political attention toward the relationship between sight and sound and how the insistence on *not* seeing race is tied tightly to our ongoing, disregarded penchant to listen to race.

Our way of directing more attention toward sonic facets of race and complicating visual understandings of race centers on two key concepts—*vocal bodies* and the *sonic color line*. Dolores Inés Casillas, Juan Sebastian Ferrada, and Sara Hinojos (2018) explain that audible representations of *vocal bodies* translate the voice into textured indications of race through factors such as cadence, pitch, and volume coupled with word choice, slang, and regional accents. This emphasis on a voice's texture or audible details moves beyond gauging how long a character or person of color on television speaks in a given role to include analysis of how voices are staged or heard as accented, slow- or fast-cadenced, low- or high-pitched, and so forth.[2] In essence, the vocal body prompts listeners to associate sound with racialized understandings about "different"-sounding voices. This analysis can then be deepened through consideration of the *sonic color line*, which Jennifer Lynn Stoever (2010, 2016) defines as the historical processes through which sound has been racialized, and the creation of hierarchies between the sounds of different racial groups. While the concept of vocal bodies directs our attention to how people sound "unusual" or non-White, the sonic color line points to the social stakes involved in sounding "different" or non-White. The sonic color line explains how ideologies of race help us make sense of what we are listening to and also how troubling, racialized assumptions are internalized through listening. For instance, when a group of African American women in Napa, California, were forced to exit a train tour due to their loud laughter (O'Neal 2015) or when school teachers in Arizona were removed from their teaching posts for having "heavy" accents (Leeman 2012), White listeners evoked and reinforced the sonic color line. In incidents such as these, we see how vocal bodies—as identified through the sonic color line's shaping of racialized perceptions of volume and accented styles of speech—can end up promoting a form of social respectability defined by dominant White norms of language, voice, and sound.

To demonstrate the efficacy of vocal bodies and the sonic color line as theoretical approaches to analyzing mediated expressions and assumptions about race, we examine the highly mediated murder trial of George Zimmerman, self-appointed neighborhood watchman, accused of murdering teenager Trayvon Martin in Sanford, Florida. Media coverage from 2012 and 2013 generated national debates about the racialized, violent experiences inherent to being Black in the United States. The news coverage focused on Blackness within a visual frame, yet numerous sonic vocal cues were key to constructing Blackness as an aural concept. We argue that by *listening* to the live televised court proceedings and post-trial musings on news shows broadcast on major television networks and court-entertainment networks, we can clearly see that racialized assumptions about the speech of witnesses and the victim impacted the jury's not-guilty verdict.

Listening to Trials

On February 26, 2012, seventeen-year-old Trayvon Martin was walking home from the corner store carrying a bag of Skittles and a can of Arizona Iced Tea. While he carried on a playful teen text-and-talk session with his friend Rachel Jeantel, vigilante George Zimmerman started following the high schooler by car and then on foot. After Martin started to run away, Zimmerman engaged him in a physical altercation and shot him. Jeantel, an eighteen-year-old high school senior, became an earwitness to his death.[3] Zimmerman was charged with second-degree murder for profiling and shooting Martin, to which Zimmerman pleaded not guilty by claiming self-defense and was acquitted.

The heavy media coverage of the crime and Zimmerman's trial fit into many common media tropes. National news coverage of Trayvon Martin routinely mentioned his tall height, his muscular build, and the dark hoodie he wore—racial signifiers that positioned the youth as a dangerous Black man. Doing so helped craft a legal rationale that Zimmerman had a legitimate fear of the seventeen-year-old child, as was heard during trial coverage that was broadcast to over 10 million cable viewers.[4] Such framings align with the consistent racial bias on television, where African Americans are disproportionately seen as deviant criminals (Dixon and Linz 2000) who are disproportionately shown in handcuffs and mug shots (Entman and Rojecki 2000). Reality television focusing on crime also positions people of color as the ones to be chased and caught, as seen on shows like *COPS*, *The Border Patrol*, and *The First 48*; the latter show was actually referenced during the Zimmerman trial. As the *Guardian* reports, a "distinct feature of the show is that almost all of the suspects in it are Black" (Green 2013).

Televised trials such as Zimmerman's must be understood as media "megaspectacles" that capture the nation's attention via live feeds, interruptions to regularly scheduled programming, discussion on talk shows, and the "self-promoting hype of media culture itself" (Kellner 2002, 93). Ralina L. Joseph notes that the Zimmerman trial became a megaspectacle only after Black Twitter users and #BlackLivesMatter activists "shamed the popular media into covering the tragedy" (Joseph 2018, 96). Nonetheless, like the O. J. Simpson murder trial in 1995, the Zimmerman trial blurred the already fuzzy border between information and entertainment. It became a megaspectacle that dramatized cultural conflicts regarding race, gender, class, and sexuality (Kellner 2002), impacting spectators' daily lives as well as the construction and consumption of other kinds of media texts. For instance, the television series *Law and Order: Special Victims Unit* aired an episode inspired by the Zimmerman case in 2013, and Jay-Z produced a docu-series for Paramount called *Rest in Power: The Trayvon Martin Story* in 2018 that reenacted the trial.[5] The nation's captivation with the case as it unfolded and these later televised portrayals speak to the national emotive response to his murder.

Yet the ways the Zimmerman trial sparked conversations about racial tensions, inequities, and profiling practices can be understood only through an analysis of sound. As legal scholar James Parker (2015) argues, we need a widely expanded notion of *acoustic jurisprudence*, or "an orientation towards law and the practice of judgment attuned to questions of sound and listening"—especially in a media landscape in which high-profile trials can become global media sensations (40). Moreover, Stoever (2016) reminds us that race in the United States clearly has an "audible contour" (3). She provides compelling examples of the violent stakes involved when communities of color do not adhere to dominant listening and speaking practices, revealing the racial privilege embedded in who is forced to understand whom. Indeed, state-sanctioned violence—either through slavery or institutionalized racism—has often occurred based on learned assumptions of what it means to *sound* Black to dominant ears. In this next section, we use understandings of vocal bodies and the sonic color line to closely analyze the role of earwitness Rachel Jeantel in the Zimmerman trial.

"That's How I Speak": Rachel Jeantel Testifies

Much of Zimmerman's trial hinged on the end of Martin's phone call with Jeantel—two minutes that resulted in five and a half hours of testimony in open court. Jeantel's manner of speaking would come under verbal assault from just about every authority in the courtroom: the judge, the court reporter, the lead defense attorney, Don West, and even Bernie De La Rionda, the state's attorney who called her to testify. These four people repeatedly criticized the way Jeantel spoke and interrupted her while testifying to tell her, in various ways, that her language was inarticulate and not "proper" enough for the courtroom. Her vocal body was framed by these individuals for the jury—comprised of five White women, all but one middle-aged or retired, and one woman of color— but was broadcast to millions of television viewers and radio listeners who also sat in judgment.

Jeantel's speech is best characterized as African American Vernacular English (AAVE), as influenced by her neighborhood and her family's Haitian background (Rickford and King 2016, 957). She refuses to codeswitch or styleshift (Alim and Smitherman 2012), two frequent practices where people of color are forced to change their voice's register and word choice in order to sound less threatening or more palatable to White people. Linguist Jon McWhorter describes Jeantel's language bluntly: "Her English is perfect. It's just that it's Black [AAVE] English" (McWhorter 2013). Beyond her use of AAVE grammar, syntax, and vocabulary, her self-expressed vocal body includes a low-volume voice and soft-edged, flowing words without pauses. While none of these qualities or characteristics have any bearing on Jeantel's capacity to serve as a reliable earwitness, her speech and voice nonetheless become contested sites for evaluating her contributions to Martin's case. Through an analysis of competing vocal bodies throughout her testimony, we can see the way the sonic color line serves to discredit Jeantel, position Martin as a dangerous aggressor, and ultimately acquit Zimmerman.

Zimmerman's defense attorney Don West played a key role in ascribing meaning to Jeantel's vocal performance. In questioning Jeantel in front of the jury, West exaggerated the difference between her speech and Standard English by repeating Black vernacular phrases from her testimony in dramatic fashion. In his infamous repetition of the phrase "creepy ass cracker"—a phrase Jeantel testifies Martin used to describe Zimmerman as he followed Martin in his car—West depicts Jeantel and Martin as aggressive in their estimation of Zimmerman. He also slows down the pace of her testimony to the point of unintelligibility, spending over thirty minutes of the court's time parsing out the phrase "I coulda heard Trayvon," which Jeantel insisted was a mishearing of "I could hear it was Trayvon" by the court reporter. West insisted on playing the recording of Jeantel's deposition multiple times for the jury, first because he claimed that his own White male vocal body could not perform her words. In this instance, West maintained that Jeantel's speech could not be rendered via his (White) Standard English speech and tone. Instead, he remarked, "I have to play it . . . ," trailing off for a second, then returning with "The transcript isn't accurate enough because of the way it was said." As he played the recording multiple times, West visibly pantomimed confusion and disbelief to the jury, performing the reactions of a "reasonable person" assessing Jeantel's vocal body. Even after the repeated playbacks, West still stumbles and trips over Jeantel's words to indicate that it is she who wields an unruly vocal body, rather than him. He performs for the jury—and for a large television and Internet audience—how his "reasonable" listening practice connects Black vernacular English to a lack of intelligence, a failure to listen properly, and therefore an inability to bear reliable witness in court.

Even though prosecutor Bernie De La Rionda was the counsel who called Jeantel to the stand, he too performed damaging aural condescension in many ways. He began by identifying Jeantel's ethnicity with a racist joke, referencing the sonic color line's stereotypes of diasporic Blackness as loud: "I know you grew up in a Haitian family, so please speak up so everyone can hear you." Later, he verbally coached Jeantel during her testimony, ostensibly in response to the judge's comments and seeking to help the jury to understand Jeantel. However, by doing so, he confirms her vocal performance as deviant and supports those who work to discredit her. He tells her, "You have a very soft voice. . . . [The jury's] having a hard time hearing you." Ironically, De La Rionda insinuates that Jeantel will be legible to the White-dominant jury as a witness only if she speaks in a tone, volume, and rhythm—a vocal body—already identified by the sonic color line as sonically "Black." He marks her voice with excess, deviance, and unreasonableness that he needs to minimize with caveats and framing phrases. "Let me make sure that the jury understands that," he said to Jeantel after finishing an answer. Eventually he stopped waiting for her to finish sentences and began breaking into Jeantel's answers. "Let me interrupt you a second" became De La Rionda's polite refrain, damaging her credibility by portraying Jeantel's speech as always already needing his interruption and interpretation. In other words, De la Rionda's performance attempted to motivate the jury to understand and be compelled by Jeantel as a witness by offering himself as a medium, aurally representing his speech *and* his listening practice as a reasonable translation of Jeantel's testimony. Television viewers are accustomed to seeing and listening to White professionals—doctors, lawyers, civil rights activists—speak on behalf of communities of color. In his attempt to help Jeantel by coaching her speech, De La Rionda communicates to viewers through what Christie Zwahlen (2015) has called an intrusive and presupposing "power-laden filter of 'neediness.'" Zwahlen argues that, when Jeantel's voice was positioned by and against White professionals, many home viewers understood her voice as sounding "a great longing for help"—for better education, speech coaching, mentorship, even for fashion advice!—rather than as offering up crucial information in a criminal proceeding.

This treatment reveals the reality that Jeantel always already carried the burden of understandability with her into the courtroom. No expectation existed for anyone else in the courtroom to exert any additional effort to understand her speech. As John R. Rickford and Sharese King remind us, translators for "deep AAVE and other vernacular speakers" have yet to be instituted in U.S. courts, even as an option (Rickford and King 2016, 981). If the court reporter failed to understand her—and her numerous demands for Jeantel to repeat herself suggested that she frequently did—it was up to Jeantel to styleshift and/or translate her own testimony to accommodate the court reporter's ear. Tellingly, not once did the judge call the court reporter's listening ability or linguistic competence into question (or her own, for that matter), no matter how many times she asks Jeantel to "one more time please give that answer again," or the court reporter states, "I can't hear the witness." Eventually, the judge begins talking *over* Jeantel's answers to indicate her lack of understanding, as well as her power to stop Jeantel's testimony at will. Such literal fits and starts performed the illegibility of Jeantel's testimony for the jury, enabling the lawyers to chop, reorder, mistranslate, and parse her testimony so extensively that, at times, they prevented the jury from hearing Jeantel finish a sentence.

The frequent emphasis on her speech being excessive—too soft, too low, too fast—communicated that her language, and by extension Jeantel herself, should be heard as unruly, uncooperative, and "out of place" in the witness stand. Court officials repeatedly marked Jeantel's speech as inappropriate for the formal setting of a courthouse and amplified the dominance of White modes of formality and communication in this setting. Courtrooms are hailed as noble, democratic, truthful, "colorblind" spaces responsible for carrying out justice. Yet an examination of Jeantel's experience on the witness stand suggests that "truthful" testimony has a recognizable accent, tone, and volume, a particular vocal body encoded in the abstract U.S. legal standard of the "reasonable person." Unfortunately for Jeantel, Martin, and the American justice system as a whole, the vocal body amplified within courtroom settings resounds with audible Whiteness, masculinity, and middle-class signifiers of "propriety," even for those on the witness stand.

These judgments on Black women's speech by White listeners have long served as a racializing tactic in American culture, both to depict Black women as angry and/or unreasonable, and to attempt to silence them as they protest this very treatment. While "Americans adore sassy Black women, . . . those caricatures of finger-waving, eye-rolling Black women," feminist theorist Brittney Cooper argues, "the truth is that Angry Black Women are looked upon as entities to be contained" (Cooper 2018, 1, 3). Such stereotyping and suppression are precisely how the sonic color line operates in the United States as a shifting analytic rendering certain sounds—and the bodies that produce and consume them—as Other. The sonic color line indelibly links Othered corporeal bodies to stereotyped vocal bodies, marking both as noisy, different, out of place, dangerous, ignored, improper, or what Cornel West describes as "incomprehensible and unintelligible" under White supremacist epistemologies in the courtroom and beyond (West 1982, 28).

This analysis reveals the way the sonic color line marks Jeantel's manner of speaking and performance of her vocal body as non-White—and therefore less reliable, less truthful, and even less human—to

White-dominant listening ears. Jeantel's testimony reveals that the "reasonable person" standard extends beyond even the jury's often problematic imaginings of a defendant's actions. Everyone in the courtroom imposes the social discipline of the sonic color line, ensuring that reasonable doubt can be heard only by people whom the jury hears and understands as "reasonable." One's testimony will be deemed truthful insofar as it is delivered in a standardized English, properly colored with the increasingly muted tones of civility.

Hearing Sonic Ratchetness

Throughout her testimony, Rachel Jeantel challenged audiences both within and outside the courtroom to recognize the racialized limitations of the "hearing" that people of color receive in courtrooms as structured by the sonic color line. Jeantel deployed what Regina Bradley (2013) has termed *sonic ratchetness*, or a "means of navigating sliding representations of respectability" within American culture. Bradley argues that Jeantel expresses agency over her testimony by calling attention to the sound of her speech, while simultaneously amplifying the attempts by the White officers of the court to suppress it. Her frequent and brilliantly subversive use of the word "sir" in her wary responses to Zimmerman's attorney Don West, for example—low, monotone, and exaggeratedly polite—powerfully exerted her continued presence in the White space of the courtroom and warily sounded out the racialized edge of her treatment in court for those who were able to listen.[6] At a key moment, Jeantel clarified for West, "That's how I speak. You cannot hear me that well." In doing so, she called attention to the burden the U.S. justice system places on witnesses to styleshift in order to make themselves legible and audible.

The racialized power dynamics of the courtroom construct a "reasonable person" as identifiable by a particular normalized accent, grammar, diction, and syntax, and a concomitant "reasonable" listening practice disciplined to identify this idealized vocal body and punish, dismiss, and/or misunderstand those who do not conform to it. Witnesses risk being silenced by lawyers, reprimanded by judges, misinterpreted by court reporters, and tuned out by jurors if they refuse to aurally conform to the sonic color line. Refusing to styleshift has high stakes, both in individual cases and for our culture as a whole. Most immediately, Zimmerman was acquitted. Jeantel later told CNN correspondent David Mattingly that she felt "a little bit" responsible for the jury's decision; in retrospect, she said she would have "act[ed] different" because the jurors "judge how *they* talk, how *they* look, and how *they* dress." Since the trial, a Miami-based group of Black professionals calling themselves The Village have offered Jeantel counseling, tutoring, and voice coaching (Thompson and Parker 2014). Ironically, while the defendant Zimmerman was freed, it was prosecution witness Jeantel who was shamed and coerced into a form of rehabilitation.

The broadcast of Jeantel's refusal to speak via a vocal body other than her own invited us to listen to the ways the U.S. justice system mutes, distorts, and denies its witnesses a real hearing, forcing some to structure their experiences through linguistic performances that potentially deem key parts of themselves and their testimony inaccessible precisely when it is most needed. Hopefully, the echoes of Jeantel's testimony will resonate in the afterlife of the Internet until we actually listen to her demands for attentiveness.

5

Branding Athlete Activism

JASON KIDO LOPEZ

sports media | celebrities | activism | branding

When Cleveland Cavaliers star LeBron James and other NBA players donned shirts emblazoned with the phrase "I Can't Breathe" during a warmup in 2014, basketball fans and media pundits asked what role athletes should be playing in broader political activism. These conversations ignited into a full-blown culture war in 2016, when quarterback Colin Kaepernick started kneeling during the playing of the national anthem and other football players followed suit. These political expressions by Black athletes from the National Football League (NFL) and the National Basketball Association (NBA) were part of a long history of athlete activism in sports, and so too was the predictable controversy that followed. Athletes who have critiqued White supremacy and racism have historically been censured based partially on the assumption that professional sports leagues produce spaces free from politics, and the broader hegemonic discomfort around Black citizens and activists demanding social justice. The ensuing debate about the right of Black athletes to express themselves spread throughout media. These moments of athlete activism and their hypervisibility provide opportunities to interrogate the way sports media cultures and specific values of professional sports leagues shape the possibilities for Black athletes to participate in anti-racism expressions.

One of the factors that allow athletes to speak out about issues that are important to them is the fact that both the NBA and the NFL significantly rely upon their players to create and maintain their branding. At the most superficial level, there would be no game without people playing it. But even the most cursory glance at the substantial media presence of the NBA and the NFL reveals an extensive dependence on the players that goes beyond their roles as quarterbacks or power forwards. The players are the stars of narratives that play out both inside and outside the confines of the game. These stories include past and future competitive performance, but can also incorporate team chemistry, compatibility with the coach and/or team owner, health, workout routines, contracts and agents, business arrangements, families and romantic relationships, hobbies, fashion, and so on. The resulting league-friendly picture is one that emphasizes the qualities of liveness and realness—fans get to see the athletes as they really are, and watch them in narratives that unfold live both inside and outside the athletic arena,

The fact that liveness and realness are essential in the branding of the NFL and the NBA then leads to complex negotiations and struggles over athlete behaviors. Athlete expressions that are consistent with the leagues' usual messages and ideologies about race are encouraged and magnified, while contradictory behaviors are punished and marginalized. Given that activism against racism is traditionally deemed too radical or too political for the leagues, many forms of player activism are censured or silenced. Yet league strategies designed to shape athlete behavior and expression are limited by the desire to protect a sense of liveness and realness for their fans. Since athlete activism can be understood as a real part of the lives of the players and it frequently occurs in the midst of live mediated events, it then becomes folded into the leagues' product.

This chapter explores these conflicts within the NFL and the NBA that simultaneously curtail and enable athlete activism through a contradictory set of brand values. After examining how the NFL and the NBA brand themselves and engage in attempts to silence and marginalize athlete activism, I analyze their dependence on constructions of liveness and realness through an array of multimedia products—including game broadcasts, commentary television shows, websites, and social media. I argue that they collectively manufacture the notion that athletes partake in real narratives that play out live and, in doing so, they consistently afford activist athletes the opportunity to reshape the branding of the NFL and the NBA to include messaging focused on anti-racism.

The Brands of the NFL and the NBA and Political Expression

As with all large companies, the NFL and the NBA are constantly shaping the values of their brands. This involves work toward coordinating the engagement of viewers and fans, as well as producers, sponsors, and employees (C. Johnson 2012). As dynamic, interactive objects, companies must juggle all of these parties' relationships to the company and to each other in order to try to create a unified set of attitudes, feelings, and values around their brand (Lury 2004). Amidst these efforts toward building a particular set of shared expectations around the NFL and the NBA, one significant component of both brands is the idea that their products are apolitical. Specifically, both leagues forward the notion that they are free from a particular sort of politics: those that explicitly critique institutionalized racism and White supremacy.

This is connected to a more general tendency to view the sporting realm as an apolitical space. The commonly held notion that sports are broadly free from politics is connected to the fact that sports are taken to be pure meritocracies where the most talented players get to play and the best teams win. Questions about worth and ability are revealed objectively through competition, and any considerations outside of skill—including considerations of politics and race—are thus irrelevant and have no place in sports. Indeed, the regular representation of success by athletes of color reinforces the idea that sports are free from race-based discrimination (Griffin 2012; de B'béri and Hogarth 2009; Guerrero 2011), and this picture of sport is imagined to parallel a picture of American society (Grainger, Newman, and Andrews 2006). If people in sports and the wider U.S. culture earn what they deserve according to merit, then people who have less deserve to have less. Of course, this ignores institutionalized reasons why resources and opportunities are unevenly and unfairly distributed (Grainger, Newman, and Andrews 2006). Sports cultures "reject the infusion of racial politics into sports" (Smith 2009, 224) because it contradicts both the myth of sports as a meritocracy and the myth of sports as an apolitical space. The conception of meritocracy is so deeply ingrained in sporting cultures that it seems apolitical, and expressions about racism seem out of place and overtly political.

When NFL and NBA athletes raise the issue of racism, both the issue and the player are held to be distractions that must be censured because they fall outside the norm of apolitical meritocracy. When Eric Garner was choked to death by the police in 2014, his death and last words, "I can't breathe," were caught on camera and widely distributed. In response, many NBA players like LeBron James wore black shirts emblazoned with Garner's dying words during pregame warmups. Though some celebrated James's actions, many critiqued them (Coombs and Cassilo 2017). For example, after an interview in which James and Kevin Durant discussed race and critiqued President Trump, Fox News personality Lauran Ingraham proclaimed on her show that they should "shut up and dribble" (Sullivan 2018). The implication is clear—athletes, even off the court, should not be speaking about politics or race.

Perhaps an even more powerful expression of the censure of athlete expression is quarterback Colin Kaepernick's expulsion from the NFL. After sitting and then kneeling during the national anthem to protest racial injustice and police brutality in the 2016–2017 season, Kaepernick was not rostered by any NFL teams in the following two seasons and as of this writing in 2019 is still a free agent. To some, it seemed like Kaepernick was being blackballed by the NFL due to his activism. Kaepernick filed a lawsuit claiming as much (Lauletta 2017), which was then settled out of court (Draper and Belson 2019). James's censure and Kaepernick's unemployment demonstrate the pervasiveness of the ideology that the NBA and the NFL are apolitical meritocracies.

Sports Leagues and Race

The idea that athletes are silenced or marginalized for speaking up about race or racism must be understood within the broader context of the NBA's and the NFL's relationship to race. Unlike the common tendencies in U.S. media to symbolically annihilate people of color and to establish Whiteness as the norm, the labor force of both leagues includes mostly men of color, and Black men in particular. Indeed, the racial makeup of their players means that both leagues consistently represent those who have been historically marginalized and silenced in mainstream media. As a result, ideologies about race are not peripheral, but instead are fundamental to the branding of both leagues.

Yet the relationship between these professional sports leagues and their largely Black labor forces have been marked by ambivalence. Boulou Ebanda De B'béri and Peter Hogarth (2009) designate this ambivalence as a "paradoxical hate-love articulation" (100) due to what David J. Leonard (2006) identifies as an "embracement and demonization of Black male bodies and cultural practices" (160). The source of this ambivalence is the fact that the largely White-owned leagues commodify the largely Black labor force for White, middle-class consumers (De B'béri & Hogarth 2009; Leonard 2006). To do so, they must construct a picture of Blackness that attracts its desired audience—a process of branding that includes the crafting of labor policies alongside the creation of media campaigns.

One of the ways the NBA and the NFL have benefited from their largely Black labor forces is from the massive popularity of hip hop and other forms of Black popular culture (Rhoden 2006). Black athlete expression can be co-opted by the leagues and sold as a picture of authentic and cool Blackness that is designed to appeal to their desired White, middle-class audience (Andrews, Mower, and Silk 2011). Yet this usage of Black popular culture can also serve to repel their desired audience, as portrayals of Black masculinity in the context of hip hop culture have also inspired moral panics about its connection to street culture, criminality, and violence (Grainger, Newman, and Andrews 2006; Leonard 2006). Such fears about professional athletes then become detrimental to the brands of the NFL and the NBA, necessitating the careful management of Black players. This control has been enacted through a number of policies that surveil and punish NFL and NBA athletes who step outside the league-friendly portrayal of Blackness. Both leagues have rules about age, pay, behavior, appearance, and speech that are designed to constrain representations of Blackness while profiting from their commodification (P. Cunningham 2009). For instance, basketball players are required to wear business casual outfits during pregame activities, while football players are prohibited from touchdown celebrations deemed offensive, like twerking. Both leagues reserve the right to punish violent behavior during and outside the game. These policies take a particular construction of Blackness, and attempt simultaneously to magnify the aspects deemed profitable and to minimize those deemed threatening—for example, that young Black men tend to be uncivilized or violent.

Beyond these labor policies, the NBA and the NFL also produce media campaigns in order to establish their players as model citizens and to fight against problematic narratives. For example, the NFL reacted to the perception that domestic violence was an issue for the league by starting a campaign that highlighted its players as fathers and husbands (Oriard 2003, 175–78). Social responsibility initiatives such as NBA Cares (NBA 2019a) and Let's Listen Together (NFL 2019) display players engaging in mentoring and charity work, as well as speaking with law enforcement personnel. As a way of addressing the specific activism of players like Kaepernick and James who targeted police brutality as a problem, the leagues have started their own brand-friendly campaigns that send a unifying counter-message: problems are caused when the police and those who are policed don't listen to each other. Both the NFL's Let's Listen Together and the NBA Voices (NBA 2019b) campaigns include media images showing players sitting on public panels with community members and police, and riding along with police patrols. Even the names of the campaigns themselves imply that the problem is not with the unjust policing of people of color, but with lack of communication between the police and those policed. Therefore, the responsibility for the violence done to Black bodies by the police falls both on the perpetrators of the violence and its victims.

These campaigns play a significant role in attempting to render athlete activism palatable and ineffective. This is an example of a general pattern between sports and athlete activism. As Douglas Hartmann (2003) argues, such activism tends to be "effectively trivialized, diluted, or even erased altogether, rendering our memories of their gestures either shamelessly sentimental and meaningless on the one hand, or subject to political manipulation, reckless commercialization, and all manner of wanton co-optation on the other" (9–10). In these particular cases, the two leagues claim and rework the original activism of their athletes into messages that are more conducive to their interests. As we saw above, activism against racism cuts against the leagues' brands, and both leagues tend to silence and rewrite Black player expression that does so. The removal of Kaepernick from the

NFL and the Let's Listen Together campaign work simultaneously to censor Black athlete activism and recast it.

The Live and Real Expression of Activist Athletes

We can see that there are significant barriers for athlete expression about race and racism, including policies and punishments that attempt to discourage activism and media campaigns that redirect anti-racist activism toward other issues. Yet given that professional sports leagues remain dependent on athlete celebrity and expression, there is a tension between the need to allow athletes to appear to be real people enacting live narratives and the demand to constrain and rewrite those narratives. While this tension can simply result in the contradictory treatment of professional athletes, it also must be understood as opening up the possibility for athletes to play an active role in reshaping the otherwise conservative and supposedly apolitical brands of the NFL and the NBA. This becomes visible through the conventions of sports broadcasts and in the online platforms such as social media.

First and foremost, the NFL and the NBA are purveyors of a game and therefore need to attach their product to liveness and realness. Because games are competitions with undetermined results, the winners cannot be known for certain until after the games have been played. The competition plays out in an unscripted and unrehearsed fashion, and therefore the events during the game are purported to be real. Although games may certainly be watched after the fact, these real events are understood to have initially been broadcast live. Along with the games themselves come a host of other features such as pregame and postgame discussion, expert analysis, and announcer commentary, all centered on a live and real competition. For this reason, live sports commentary seems to be more real than other media texts (Billings 2008, 17–18).

In this context, when players use the events around the games to spread activist messages, that activism is naturally incorporated into these mediated narratives. For example, both James's and Kaepernick's statements about police brutality happened in pregame moments, and therefore were covered as though they were any other important live and real pregame occurrence. This was amplified in the postgame coverage of these actions. For James, there was speculation about the nature and the timing of the activism (e.g., Strauss and Scott 2014), and Kaepernick's coverage focused heavily on the question of whether he was a distraction to the team (e.g., McManamon 2017). Many sportswriters pontificated on the larger cultural disagreements about both the actions and their meanings (Adande 2014; Jones 2017). Discussions of these athletes, their actions, and their meanings dominated the media coverage of the NBA and the NFL at these points in time.

This amplification of athlete activism also happens online through the official websites, Twitter accounts, and Instagram accounts of the NBA and the NFL. These digital platforms parallel the values of their television coverage, generally benefiting from the production of news and analysis of live and real occurrences. Therefore, just as with the televised commentary, player activism must be addressed. One major response is the online presence of the Let's Listen Together and NBA Voices campaigns discussed above. Additionally, Twitter and Instagram afford the opportunity for fans and activists to discuss athlete activism using the leagues' account names and hashtags. The widespread discussion of the activism of athletes like James and Kaepernick ends up directly linked to the leagues. Fans discuss pregame activism through and around the leagues' online social media presence just as they do with in-game player performance, thereby imbuing the brand with discussions about police brutality and racism.

In addition, Twitter and Instagram accounts afford the ability to link to individual player accounts, which adds to the feeling of realness. Athletes use their personal social media accounts to give the impression that their real personalities are on display, and offer an interactive space between athlete and fan (Price, Farrington, and Hall 2013). Audiences get to know the players beyond their performances, consuming live updates about their everyday lives and recent developments. Social media also enable athletes to brand themselves and express their personally held political opinions (Schmittel and Sanderson 2015). Despite the fact that the official accounts of the NBA and the NFL will not feature posts that contradict their values and that they can punish players for certain kinds of expressions, they do frequently link to these individual accounts because they want fans to get to know the players. Given these values, all forms of player expression end up being amplified through social media—including expressions of activism.

The qualities of liveness and realness are part of what distinguishes sports media from other media genres, and here we can see some of the political consequences of those qualities with regard to athlete activism. Beyond a simple power struggle over labor and athlete expression, this conflict has effectively allowed athletes to shape the meaning of their own professional sports leagues, requiring that their activism become part of the branding of the NFL and the NBA. When players like James and Kaepernick speak out against racism and White supremacy, their activist messages end up getting intertwined with the branding of their professional sports leagues. As long as the leagues depend on the players to build live and real narratives, athletes will continually have the ability to rewrite their brands in this way.

Conclusion: Rewriting the Brand

As dynamic objects that are built through the interaction of many parties, the brands of the NFL and the NBA are shaped by more than just the interests of their owners. The brands are built through policy and media campaigns that serve the largely White owners' attempt to attract a largely White audience, but they are also dependent on live and real athlete expression. As core components of the leagues' brands, they will perpetually offer athletes the ability to speak out against racism and White supremacy and, therefore, imbue the brands themselves with messages contrary to their usual conservative and apolitical values. Despite the leagues' usual interests, the players can make the NBA and the NFL brands that fight race-based injustices.

A star athlete like LeBron James has this ability due partially to his fame, but even those who are not superstars are part of the leagues' live and real brands. Popular athletes might have more of a platform and might face less resistance from the leagues, but all players can make use of the nature of the brand to express themselves about topics that are important to them. Of course, as with Kaepernick, censure and marginalization loom for these players, but by their nature the leagues offer opportunity for activist uses. The cost might be high, and we should not criticize players who do not want to pay it, but allowing for liveness and realness also allows for live and real activism against institutionalized racism.

For those who choose to do so, there is significant power in acting not against sport, but through it. As Hartmann (2003) points out, there is power in challenging "an institutional-symbolic system that had made great claims about being a positive, progressive force for African Americans to explicitly recognize and represent face, to finally—and formally—live up to its claims" (22). Athletes like James and Kaepernick operate within the NBA and the NFL and hold them to their own ideologies. If the leagues are meritocracies and oppose discrimination, then activist athletes demand a consistent and comprehensive commitment to these values.

That censure, marginalization, and rewriting of the activist messages always loom demonstrates that part of the dynamism of the brand is conflict between players and management. Philip Lamarr Cunningham (2009) explores how, despite the efforts by the NBA and the NFL to marginalize and appropriate hip hop and street culture, the players can still use these cultures to defy the league. A similar power struggle occurs over athlete activism, and in both cases athletes can use the leagues' dependence on live and real narratives to rewrite brand values. However, the case of activism shows how leagues that are usually hesitant to engage with race-based activism end up amplifying these messages. Contemporary athletes within this system not only rewrite the leagues' brands, but also have their messages spread widely through the brands themselves. Despite hegemonic forces working against them, the leagues' dependence on live and real narratives represents a persistent route for courageous activist athletes to raise and critique institutionalized racism and White supremacy.

PART II

Producing and Performing Race

6

The Burden of Representation in Asian American Television

PETER X FENG

sitcoms | authorship | burden of representation

When we speak, we want to be heard; the less often we speak, the more important it is that we be understood. In mainstream film and television, minority communities are represented infrequently, so minority audiences pay special attention when they are depicted. It is also the case that minority artists are frequently misunderstood by outsiders who may lack a frame of reference to interpret a cinematic text—as well as by insiders who may be frustrated that one of their own has not conveyed the salient details that illuminate the life of the community. It is a terrible irony that those of us who infrequently see ourselves represented on the screen often attack artists from our own communities. This phenomenon is known as the "burden of representation."

The burden of representation is borne by any media text (or work of fiction) that is perceived to speak for a marginalized and "underrepresented" group. Because media depictions centering on minority groups are rare, the community starts to expect individual texts to take on the task of redressing systematic patterns of misrepresentation. This means that minority filmmakers are held responsible for countering mainstream media's negative or stereotypical depictions of the group, with audiences from that community desiring characters whose experiences mirror their own as a way of alleviating oppression. Minority audiences may also be concerned that members of their group may internalize negative representations if they are not countered by divergent viewpoints. This burden is not faced by movies that depict dominant groups because there is a plethora of such representations—for example, straight cisgendered white males may be depicted as villains but they are also depicted as heroes, as loving fathers, as competitive siblings, and so on. By contrast, the relative scarcity of representations produced by minority filmmakers means that they cannot possibly meet the expectations that they redress prevailing representational schemas; the minority audience may hold filmmakers from the community to an impossibly high standard.

The burden of representation (or simply, "the burden") is a direct result of underrepresentation. While I use the terms "minority" and "marginalized" somewhat interchangeably in this chapter, it is important to recognize that the relative lack of Asian American visibility in the mainstream media is not just a function of the size of the Asian American population. Rather, Asian American media production is incommensurate with the size of the Asian American population because mainstream media have actively pushed Asian American representation to the margins. Of course, media gatekeepers may not be deliberately excluding Asian American stories, but the habitual attention paid to the dominant culture is tantamount to deliberate exclusion—which is to say that marginalization is the result of deliberately *centering* certain kinds of storytelling.

An attendant result of this act of centering is that minority audiences have been taught to identify with mainstream viewpoints. To consume a film centering on a straight white male protagonist is in a very real sense to learn how to empathize with a straight white male perspective, and prolonged consumption of such narratives leads to the normalization of those perspectives. This may result in the internalization of racist and sexist attitudes. For instance, it may be that a Native American youth brought up on film and television Westerns in the 1950s simply looks past the dehumanized depictions of "American Indians" in those narratives—but to the extent that those representations are fundamental to the Western, consumption of a Western narrative compels the spectator to adopt (perhaps without conscious awareness) the view that "Indians" are subhuman savages instinctively bent on the destruction of white settlers. It follows that the best-case scenario for Native American filmgoers would be cognitive dissonance (as they struggle to reconcile the cinematic depictions with their own sense of a rich cultural heritage), while the worst-case scenario would be the gradual development of self-directed loathing.

The absence of diverse representations in mainstream filmmaking may have an even more damaging effect on majority audiences, who have seldom been asked to identify with minority perspectives. This is a concrete instance of privilege—the ability to consume popular culture without needing to learn how to empathize with the protagonist's perspective. In my classrooms, I have often had the occasion to ask my students whether they think women understand men better than men understand women; my female students almost without exception agree with that statement, even if they can't articulate why they feel that way. In my view, to the extent that James Brown was correct and "this is a man's world," women have to learn how men operate in order to survive—but the reverse is not true. If Sigmund Freud was never able to figure out "what does a woman want," that is because he never had to learn how to empathize with women. I may be overstating the impact of mainstream media (as a film scholar, I am biased), but I sincerely believe that growing up in a world that is saturated with stories centering straight white male experience produces a generation of men who (at best) are not practiced at empathizing with marginalized communities and who (at worst) are completely mystified by them—how else could they ask, "What do they want?" When Hollywood executives resist casting female and minority actors as leads in big-budget movies, citing concern that audiences will not accept them, I do not disagree: Hollywood has not made a concerted effort to teach mainstream audiences how to identify with minority protagonists. Marginalized audiences may be able to identify with stories centering on straight while male heroes—we have had to be able to consume movies in this (white) man's world—but mainstream spectators have not been forced to learn how to empathize and identify with diverse viewpoints.

In this context, it is understandable that Asian American audiences, accustomed to being ignored or insulted by mainstream media, would turn to Asian American filmmakers and television producers (henceforth, I'll use the term "makers" to refer to film, TV, and media producers generally) to see Asian American experiences depicted on-screen. While audiences often state that they enjoy movies and television as a form of escapism, that does not mean that audiences always want to see representations that are completely removed from their own quotidian existences; audiences also look to the mass media for affirmation, and to signal that the wider culture is aware of the experience of minority subcultures. It may be that Asian American audiences wish to see and consume representations of Asian American life, perhaps out of an awareness that stereotypical depictions may affect our own sense of self-worth (for example, a mother may want her son to see a depiction of a confident Asian American man instead of the representations of sexual perverts in films like *Breakfast at Tiffany's* and *Sixteen Candles*). It may be that Asian Americans want to consume more media depicting Asian Americans. But it may also be that Asian Americans desire to see themselves more fully represented in mainstream media so they know that the dominant culture is exposed to Asian Americans—that non-Asian Americans can see both the distinctiveness of Asian American life and also the experiences that we share with other Americans and indeed with all humanity. In short, Asian American audiences may want more access to mainstream media so that we know that everyone else can learn about and empathize with our humanity.

Origins of the Burden

The phrase "burden of representation" is often attributed to James Baldwin, but the phrase initially referred to political representation rather than artistic representation. G. W. Prothero (1888) and Robert Rait (1915), both historians of nineteenth-century English politics, used the phrase, perhaps euphemistically, to refer to the significance of representation with regard to taxation. Another commentator on the nineteenth century, Karl Marx, famously discussed the emergence of a subaltern class into political discourse with a phrase that has been oft-repeated in English translation as "They cannot represent themselves; they must be represented" (1978, 608). As Gayatri Spivak (1999) has pointed out, Marx uses the German word *vertreten* in this passage, not *darstellen*, which means "to re-present" in the sense of an artistic representation (256–60). This tension between the artistic and political senses of "representation" points to the way media depictions of Asian Americans can affect the ways the political interests of Asian Americans are "spoken for." Ella Shohat and Robert Stam (1994) point out that "representation" also has religious connotations, in that "the Judeo-Islamic censure of 'graven images' and the preference for abstract representations such as the arabesque cast theological suspicion on directly figurative representation" (182). They point out that all three forms of representation—political, artistic, and religious—share the notion "that something is 'standing for' something else, or that some person or group is speaking on behalf of some other persons or groups" (183).

In the late 1970s through the 1980s, the art historian John Tagg (1988) uses the phrase in a different context: he traces the use of the photograph as evidence, arguing that the deployment of specific representational practices and the circulation of photographs in specific institutions serve to produce ideologies. Photography was linked to the nineteenth-century institutions and practices that, as described by Michel Foucault, produced a new social order shaped by discipline and surveillance. Tagg's use of the phrase is thus distinct from the term's usage within the study of popular culture, in the sense that he is discussing photography's link to technologies of domination while we are interested in minority makers and audiences and expectations that they redress dominant representations. That said, Tagg's exploration of the way photographic conventions lead us to identify certain kinds of images as truthful representations of human relationships is of course directly relevant to our understanding of the way cinematic representation works.

In the context of race and media, the most forceful articulation of the "burden of representation" comes from Kobena Mercer (1994), who situates the burden in the context of "a restricted economy of minority representation" in Great Britain in the 1980s (21). He is especially interested in the ways institutions that attempt to redress the hegemony of dominant representations by promoting minority makers can exacerbate the burden. For instance, minority filmmaking is often supported through public funding "on the implicit expectation that they 'represent' and 'speak for' the community from which they come" (92) and thereby perpetuates the view that "every minority subject is, essentially, the same" (214). By defining the burden of representation as an economy, Mercer reveals that minority makers' accountability and obligation to their communities are false constructs, since a maker does not have the agency to make artistic choices, constrained as s/he is by the horizon of expectations that accompanies institutional access (240).

Mercer's point is important, but almost always forgotten, perhaps for the same reason that it is so difficult to sustain a large-scale analysis of systems in everyday conversation. It is much easier to talk about oppressors and victims than it is to examine networks of power; easier to believe that we succeed or fail based on our merits than to examine privilege; easier to attribute sentiments and assign blame to individuals than to acknowledge the systems that constrain what individuals can say and do in the first place. To blame a maker for misrepresenting the community is easier than recognizing the material conditions that shape the way that audiovisual texts are produced, distributed, and consumed.

The Burden of *All-American Girl*

I now turn to the reception of two family sitcoms from network television: *All-American Girl* in the 1990s and *Fresh Off the Boat* in the 2010s. *All-American Girl* features Korean American Margaret Cho and is based on her own autobiographical stand-up comedy. It lasted for only one season and was criticized widely in the Asian American community. Cho has been embraced in the years since the show aired, in part because she was able to articulate her own frustration with the way the production largely rejected her creative input. In contrast, many Asian Americans immediately embraced *Fresh Off the Boat*, which also centers on an Asian American child who rejects the "model minority stereotype" and struggles with parental expectations. *Fresh Off the Boat* is based on a memoir by Taiwanese American chef and restauranteur Eddie Huang. Like Cho, Huang was involved in shaping the direction of the first season, but publicly broke with the show's producers (the show continued without his involvement).

Both of these sitcoms draw on autobiographical material, but their similarities end there. *All-American Girl* is a multi-camera show that aired during President Bill Clinton's second year in office: an era of four national networks, when streaming video was nonexistent. By contrast, *Fresh Off the Boat* is a single-camera show from the post-network era that debuted during Barack Obama's second term as president as part of a diverse lineup of new ABC sitcoms (*black-ish* and *Cristela* had debuted earlier in the same season). Unlike Cho, Huang had a Twitter account and a blog and the willingness to air his differences with the showrunners while *Fresh Off the Boat* was still in production. While *All-American Girl* offers a classic case study of the burden of representation,

Fresh Off the Boat illuminates something stranger still: a writer who uses his own access to the media to distance himself from a successful show that he feels does not accurately represent the truth of his experience as a Taiwanese American. What can we learn from contrasting these two sitcoms, one that was crushed by the weight of the burden and the other that succeeded despite its own author disavowing its authenticity?

To begin, we can note that there were inconsistencies with how the authorship of these television shows was understood. Cho bore the burden because an on-screen credit for *All-American Girl* declared that the show was "based on the stand-up of Margaret Cho," but this fact exists in uneasy tension with another on-screen credit: "created by Gary Jacobs." My point is not that Gary Jacobs should have borne the brunt of criticism directed at the show, but that a television show has stakeholders rather than simply "authors." In this case, the stakeholders included a network (ABC), multiple production companies (Sandollar Television, Heartfelt Productions, and Touchstone Television), a showrunner (Gary Jacobs), and a star (Margaret Cho) who shared the same given name as a character (Margaret Kim).

All-American Girl tells the story of Margaret Kim, a young Korean American woman, and her family: her brothers, Stuart and Eric; her parents, Katherine and Benny; and her grandmother, Yung-hee. Stuart is a doctor and Margaret's parents own a bookstore in San Francisco, while Margaret works in a department store with two white friends. Most of the plots center on conflicts between the "assimilated" Margaret and "tiger mother" Katherine. The program's predominantly white writing staff was dominated by veteran television writers, so it is not surprising that many episodes recycle familiar plots. Compared to contemporaneous family sitcoms such as *The Cosby Show*, *Roseanne*, and *Grace under Fire*, *All-American Girl*'s plots are well-worn.

When *All-American Girl* premiered in the fall of 1994, I was a graduate student in the University of Iowa communication studies department and taught a class on Asian American independent media. I frequently participated in online forums (Usenet newsgroups) on popular television and Asian American issues, and belonged to a listserv of Asian American graduate students largely based in the Midwest. We were a group of young scholars who held each other to high critical standards, and when *All-American Girl* debuted we held out some hope that it would become a cultural touchstone in the way that *A Different World* was for my African American friends in media studies. But I think we all knew that *All-American Girl* was unlikely to satisfy us. Even though we understood that the show could not possibly fulfill our hopes for bringing young Asian Americans into the television mainstream, and even though we knew all about the burden and how unfair it would be to expect this show to get everything right, we could not hide our disappointment from each other—a disappointment all the more painful for being entirely anticipated. We eviscerated the show. We were grad students, after all: we were trained to tear texts apart.

A quarter century later, most of the specific criticisms we shared have faded from my memory—but I remember one particular conversation vividly. During the Kim family's dinner, mother Katherine entered the kitchen and lifted the lid off the rice cooker, scooping up a portion of rice and pouring it out. The rice fell in a cascade. One of my Korean American colleagues was incensed: "Korean rice is sticky! It clumps together!" We all recognized that the show's set dressers and prop department were certainly not Asian, and while they knew that the Kims' kitchen would have a rice cooker, they thought that the rice that emerged would resemble a pilaf. I seem to recall that I haltingly offered a defense: "Maybe the rice sat under the hot lights for so long that it dried out?" My friend was not having it, and I conceded the point. Even though we had many bigger issues with the show—the tired generation gap tropes, the gendered contrast between overachiever Stuart and rebellious Margaret, the casting of Chinese American and Japanese American actors as Korean Americans—this completely inauthentic rice is what saddened and infuriated us the most. Or, more precisely, it was because we had bigger issues with the show that we channeled our disappointment into this detail; had the show gotten the big things right, I think we would have rolled our eyes and let this little thing go. But because the show felt so keenly inauthentic, we seized on this one detail and made it encapsulate our critique: "They couldn't even get the rice right." Maybe the show was reaching the non-Asian audience and communicating that we were just like everyone else—Asian Americans could star in lame sitcoms, too—but we who most wanted the show to succeed were the least inclined to cut it any slack. It was certainly unreasonable of us to expect that this one show would redress years of retrograde depictions of Asian Americans on network television, but it was inevitable that we would hold *All-American Girl* to a high standard—it was the nature of the burden.

Margaret Cho went on to talk about her sitcom experience in her 1999 comedy tour called *I'm the One That I Want*, which was also released as a film and a book. Both the show and the memoir discuss the producers' attempts to shape her performance to be "more Asian" and their insistence that she lose weight to play the role, and Cho is by turns funny and poignant in relating these stories (her weight-loss regimen resulted in her hospitalization). Speaking years later, in a 2014 interview with *KoreAm*, she noted that concerns about her weight were not voiced before camera tests. She speculated that the technicians and producers had no experience in photographing Asian faces. Cho also expressed support for *Fresh Off the Boat* and noted that she was able to share her experience with Eddie Huang; as the pioneer, she had no one to turn to for guidance (Woo 2014).

All-American Girl ran for nineteen episodes but was not renewed for a second season. It would be understandable if Margaret Cho took the "failure" of "her show" personally, but to her credit she quickly came to understand the nature of the burden, and much of her comedy since has highlighted the absurdity of the burden. In a bizarre twist, when Tilda Swinton was criticized for taking the role of "the Ancient One" in Marvel's *Doctor Strange*, she contacted Cho to discuss the matter, initially asking for help in understanding "the lay of the land" (Gettell 2016). Cho was thus put in the position of educating a Scottish actor about the economy of racial representation in a Hollywood film. Perhaps Swinton reached out to Cho because she was aware of *All-American Girl* and hoped that Cho would express sympathy for a performer targeted for criticism, but it may also be that Swinton was only aware of Cho's hard-won standing in the entertainment industry and approached her hoping that she would help to defuse the situation. The ultimate irony is that Swinton was asking Cho to speak for the Asian American community one more time.

The unfortunate story of *All-American Girl* reveals many of the typical consequences of the burden of representation. Because the Asian American community was starved for images of Asians on television, it held the sitcom to an impossibly high standard. Discussion of the show did not focus on whether it was funny or on the pressure put on Cho as a pioneering performer, but rather on the perception that the show did not advance an authentically Asian American perspective. Asian American audiences criticized the show for reproducing misperceptions about our community (immigrant parents focus on their children's professional success and not on their individuality) and for failing to showcase the distinctiveness of Korean American culture (with its preference for sticky rice). Even when audiences are aware that the economy of representation will inevitably produce an impossible burden, we still express our disappointment when a show falls short of our expectations. On the other hand, it could be said that *All-American Girl* precipitated a discussion about television representation, and that the resulting "controversy" gave a marginalized community the opportunity to be heard by the dominant culture. A cultural dynamic like this may also be an inevitable consequence of the burden: an underrepresented community, frustrated at its marginalization, seizes upon a television sitcom to call attention to the mainstream media's failure to produce diverse material.

The Burden of *Fresh Off the Boat*

Fresh Off the Boat is inspired by Eddie Huang's memoir of the same name, focusing on the Huang family's experiences after leaving a Taiwanese American enclave near Washington, DC. They end up in the predominantly white suburb of Orlando, Florida, in the 1990s (which means that the show's setting is contemporaneous with *All-American Girl*). Eddie's interest in hip hop sets him apart from his younger brothers, who, as high-achieving students more fluent in Mandarin than he, seem to better fit the model minority stereotype. Most episodes in the first season incorporated multiple storylines, typically giving equal screentime to the parents and to Eddie; younger brothers Evan and Emery gained screentime over the following seasons. The overarching storylines of the first season—father Louis's efforts to establish his ranch-themed family restaurant, mother Jessica's personality clashes with suburban neighbors, Eddie's outsider status at school, and conflict between Jessica's efforts to maintain a Taiwanese identity and Eddie's interest in contemporary African American culture—are familiar "culture clash" tropes but are developed with a certain degree of nuance that can be attributed in large part to the writers' efforts to build around Huang's distinctive authorial voice. If at times the show takes a more assimilationist tone than Huang's at times militant memoir, that is in part managed by setting the show in the recent past, which encourages nostalgia and flatters twenty-first-century viewers by enabling them to assign the show's depictions of intolerance to a less-enlightened time: this effect was arguably reinforced by the first season's use of voice-over narration, which framed childhood conflicts as retrospectively seen by the adult Eddie.

Eddie Huang was only thirty-one when he published his first memoir, but his outsized personality, tenacious intelligence, and continual reinvention place him firmly in the tradition of American autobiography. After graduating from Yeshiva University's Cardozo School of Law, Huang worked as a corporate lawyer, ran a streetwear company, dealt drugs, performed stand-up comedy, opened a sandwich shop and a restaurant, appeared on the Cooking Channel and on Bravo's *Top Chef*, created a nonfiction series for Viceland, and blogged. *Fresh Off the Boat: A Memoir* was published in 2013 and attracted the attention of 20th Century Fox Television, who attached Persian American Nahnatchka Khan as the showrunner and secured a commitment for a "put pilot" with ABC (a pilot episode that the network agrees to air as a stand-alone special or a series). ABC introduced the series as a midseason replacement in February 2015.

In January 2015, before the show aired, Huang published an article in *New York* magazine airing some of his differences with the show's creative team. The article opens with an anecdote about the show's eighth episode, "Phillip Goldstein." At the end of the show, when young Eddie forges a connection with an African American student, the script called for Huang's narration to cap off the episode by observing, "Check this out: an Asian kid and a Black kid bonding over music by white Jewish rappers. America is great!" Huang describes how he fought about this line with the executive producer, asking, "Did you read the book? If you can find any crumb of complete thought in the book that remotely infers 'America is great,' I'll read the line." The producer replies that the show is "never going to be the book" and proposes a compromise: "America's not half-bad!" Huang responds by suggesting that if the idea is to compromise, he could allude to a compromise enacted in the U.S. Constitution:

"America ain't three fifths bad" (Huang 2015). The actual line that eventually ran in the episode isn't as pointedly critical of our nation's racial legacy, although it comes much closer to replicating the memoir's narratorial voice: "Check this out: an Asian kid and a Black kid bonding over music by white Jewish rappers. America is crazy!"

Huang's objection, that the sitcom script does not reflect the "complete thought" of his memoir, suggests that the issue is the way Huang's autobiographical text is being distorted—Huang does not invoke the burden but instead the desire to have this show reflect his own perspective. After ongoing friction with the show's producers, Huang (2015) describes finally watching the pilot episode on his laptop:

> I had crossed a threshold and become the audience. I wasn't the auteur, the writer, the actor, or the source material. I was the viewer, and I finally understood it. This show isn't about me, nor is it about Asian America. The network won't take that gamble right now. . . . People watching these channels have never seen us, and the network's approach to pacifying them is to say we're all the same. Sell them pasteurized network television with East Asian faces until they wake up intolerant of their own lactose.

Huang acknowledges that the show does not present his perspective, suggesting that he isn't even the "source material." Instead, he acknowledges the discursive terrain of network television and suggests that space can be made for authentic Taiwanese American representation only by beginning with an essentially familiar sitcom family that is only superficially Asian.

Huang's conflicted attitude toward the sitcom adaptation of his memoir caused him to continually wrestle with his feelings about the show and his participation in it. In an interview with the *Hollywood Reporter* published on the day of the show's premiere, Huang revealed that he had pushed for the show to incorporate an arc drawing on his memoir's account of the impact of domestic violence on his childhood (Goldberg 2015). He took to Twitter on April 7, 2015, and stated that while he stood by the pilot, subsequent episodes had strayed too far from his experience: "I understand that this is a comedy but the great comics speak from pain" (Bacle 2015). Sometime thereafter Huang broke definitively with the show (although he continues to be listed as a producer) and starting with the second season, the show has continued without his voice-over narration.

Huang's disavowal of the sitcom inspired by his memoir is a very specific instance of the burden. He has repeatedly acknowledged that a network sitcom is a particular mode of storytelling that is incompatible with the themes he tried to express in his book, but it took him several years to make peace with the fact that the character named Eddie Huang bears very little relationship to his own life as the "real" Eddie Huang. I would suggest that Huang's conflict is analogous to how I felt toward *All-American Girl*'s inauthentic rice: I understand that TV is not reality but a stylized representation, and yet I also know that this stylization affects the way reality is perceived—specifically, it shapes the discursive terrain and thereby affects the way that I am perceived by others as well as by myself. In a very real way, TV creates a representational terrain that we have to negotiate in real life.

The burden of representation results from an imbalance in the discursive terrain: it is the inevitable outcome when a minority community has few opportunities to speak. Just as we pay special attention to taciturn people when they break their silence, we tend to scrutinize texts produced by minority makers. The defense that "it's just a movie"—a somewhat paradoxical plea where an artist asks not to be taken too seriously—is in effect not available to minority artists. People who speak volubly may be discounted if they speak so much that no one knows what they really stand for. Minority makers wish to be taken seriously. They also know that you cannot please everybody. Unfortunately, the burden of representation often means that you cannot please *anybody*.

7

Indigenous Video Games

JACQUELINE LAND

Indigenous media | indie video games | sovereignty

The rise of Indigenous video game development has ushered in a new wave of Indigenous self-representation. Indigenous game developers in the United States, Canada, Australia, New Zealand, and Finland are working to challenge racist stereotypes about Indigenous people that have long been perpetuated in mainstream games (Sharam 2011) as well as to explore the possibilities of game design and gameplay rooted in Indigenous worldviews. The equipment and skills needed to produce digital games have become more accessible, giving way to an ever-expanding independent gaming scene that has created opportunities for Indigenous creative workers. Far from representing a singular conception of Indigeneity, Indigenous games reflect the distinctiveness of Indigenous communities around the globe even as contemporary Indigenous movements have fostered transnational alliances (Wilson and Stewart 2008). While encompassing a huge range of aesthetic, technological, economic, national, and cultural contexts, Indigenous games share a common goal of putting Indigenous people in leading creative roles, opening up space for Indigenous perspectives within digital game culture, and advancing Indigenous self-determination and sovereignty. As Cherokee, Hawaiian, and Samoan scholar and game developer Jason Edward Lewis (2014) has argued, Indigenous people's involvement and agency within new media technologies and gaming in particular can "expand the epistemological assumptions upon which those systems and structures are based" and allow them to "stake out our own territory in a common future" (63).

The promise of Indigenous games has become a popular topic within Indigenous-controlled spaces such as Native Twitter, Native news sites like *Indian Country Today*, and Indigenous events such as the imagine-NATIVE film festival and Indigenous Comic Con. However, outside these spaces, few people know about the surge of Indigenous games being created within and outside commercial media industries from communities around the globe. The invisibility of Indigenous games is perhaps not surprising, given the broader gaming industry's struggle with diversity and inclusivity. A 2018 survey for the International Game Developers Association found that the most desirable game industry worker was "a 32 year old white male with a university degree who lives in North America and who does not have children" (Weststar, O'Meara, and Legault 2018, 8). In its review of gaming hubs around the world, it found that 18 percent of game developers are East/South East Asian, 5 percent are Hispanic or Latino, 3 percent are Pacific Islanders, 2 percent are Arabian or West Asian, 2 percent are Aboriginal or Indigenous, and 1 percent are Black/African American or African (Weststar, O'Meara, and Legault 2018, 11). Further, the lack of diversity within the industry operates in tandem with norms in digital games culture that distinguish between hardcore and casual gamers (Juul 2010; Vanderhoef 2013). As Alison Harvey and Tamara Shepherd (2017) have argued in their examination of women in indie games, the gaming industry targets white cisgender males as the ideal hardcore gamer subject who demonstrates "cultivated player knowledge, dedicated play experience and consistent investment of time, money and energy in digital games" (494). Casual gamers can then be understood as a relegated category that is distinguished from "real" or hardcore gamers. Further, game critics and players often closely scrutinize the creativity, gaming capital, and technical skills of game creators. These discourses work to delegitimize initiatives to increase women and other marginalized peoples' participation in games, devalue their games, and thus justify their continued exclusion.

To demonstrate the need for more nuanced analyses of the boundary policing and gatekeeping mechanisms within digital games culture, this chapter uses a critical media industry studies framework (Havens, Lotz, and Tinic 2009) to examine trends in Indigenous video game production. This approach emphasizes an attentiveness to the broader industrial landscape in which games are being produced, discussed, and played—including the Indigenous game developers working in service of community-based needs and global Indigenous political efforts, as well as the normative valuations within digital games culture that exclude and dismiss Indigenous games. To begin, I interrogate the categories of diverse, multicultural, and "serious" games to suggest that they mark Indigenous games as an unwelcome and illegitimate presence within digital games culture. Building on this, the reception of Indigenous games in popular gaming review sites and blogs is examined to show how the goals of Indigenous game developers are narrowly interpreted and presented within non-Indigenous gaming communities. My analysis reveals how the affective and professionalization discourses surrounding Indigenous game developers perpetuate exclusionary logics.

The Struggle for Indie Games

The transformative potential of independent or "indie" games has remained central to video game studies as a discipline despite overwhelming evidence that mainstream blockbuster games are apparatuses of global empire, misogyny, and racial violence (Dyer-Witheford and de Peuter 2009; Higgin 2008; Byrd 2016). Such work highlights the possibilities of creating games for education, activism, and radical social critique (Lipkin 2013; Ruberg 2018). Many indie game developers seek to challenge not only the content of games, but also the production and distribution logics of global capitalist empire. Thus, indie game development, understood in opposition to the mainstream gaming industry, is seen as a promising site for creativity and innovation. Kishonna L. Gray and David J. Leonard (2018) have described how "the yearning for transformative games" fuels indie game developers to challenge hegemonic values through their games.

> Game makers have sought to tear down the walls of the hegemony of gaming and demand equity in each and every space. They demonstrate the potential of games as teachers of alternative narratives and histories, as challenges to the ideologies of hate, persistent inequalities, and violent injustices. They model the possibility of games giving voice to the experiences, (intersectional) identities, and histories of otherwise marginalized and erased communities. (8)

This optimism and vision for what games can do are mirrored in Indigenous-led discourses around Indigenous games. Anishinaabe,

Métis, and Irish game developer and scholar Elizabeth LaPensée has been a strong proponent of the possibility for Indigenous video games as tools of Indigenous sovereignty and cultural expression (Lewis and LaPensée 2011; LaPensée 2014, 2018; Hearne and LaPensée 2017). Similarly, Deborah L. Madsen (2017) has argued that "Indigenously-determined" game-worlds and mechanics allow users immersive experiences rooted in resistance and community empowerment. Game jams, community-based workshops, and tribally backed e-sports leagues are some of the most triumphed initiatives, particularly those that target youth. These often involve working with elders and leaders in the community to gather traditional stories, often in their tribal languages, and create games based on them. For example, the tribal nonprofit Cook Inlet Tribal Council (CITC), based out of Barrow, Alaska, launched the first Indigenous-owned video game company, Upper One Games, in 2012 as part of a social enterprise business model in hopes of cultivating revenue sources outside federal and state funding to serve the community, and released its first highly anticipated game, *Never Alone*, in 2014. In a press release CITC president Gloria O'Neill stated,

> We want to be innovators in social enterprise. With our move into digital games we have the opportunity not only to tell our story—but to chart our own destiny and forge new career opportunities for our youth in an exciting, leading edge sector of entertainment media. We take our duty to be successful while representing our community extremely seriously. (Upper One Games 2013b)

O'Neill's statement illustrates how Indigenous indie game development is guided by both economic and political goals. They hope to create new jobs, raise money to increase community services and programming, and offer youth training in media production and design. Yet, at the same time, they want to create games that challenge stereotypes, preserve traditional culture and stories, and stake a claim in the contemporary media landscape.

This is important because representations in mainstream video games have long been criticized for maintaining toxic cultures and perpetuating racism and sexism, especially against Native people. For example, in Atari's *Custer's Revenge*, released in 1982, the objective is for players to manipulate the character of General Custer to rape a naked Native American woman who is tied to a post (Weaver 2009, 1556). C. Sharam (2011) has argued that the representation of Native Americans in video games over the past thirty years has either perpetuated symbolic annihilation or reinforced harmful stereotypes. He writes, "Many aspects of these characters, whether they have some sort of basis in history or not, are certainly not relevant to the contemporary Native American" (Sharam 2011, para. 1). The common perception of Native Americans as an antiquated and singular people contributes to a general misunderstanding of their cultures (note: the word "cultures" is pluralized because there are many different groups of First Nations people, and their beliefs and values are not necessarily congruous) and could potentially hinder their ability to synthesize with mainstream society. Employing a software and code studies lens, Choctaw scholar Jodi Byrd (2018) has further explored how the technical features and settings of game design reproduce settler colonial logics in design and gameplay.

Game studies scholars have also investigated how gamers of color experience racism within digital games cultures. Kishonna L. Gray (2012a) has shown how voice chat in Xbox Live and other online games are rampant with linguistic profiling and racist and sexist hate speech that can make such digital spaces extremely hostile for women and people of color. Lisa Nakamura (2017) has also strongly critiqued the notion that marginalized peoples are responsible for creating spaces for themselves and earning their spot in gaming culture through their technical mastery and outperforming other players as a form of "procedural meritocracy." Instead, Nakamura shows that the idea that anyone can make and play games is a false promise that ignores the fact that "the 'game' is stacked against many of us, and life is already on the highest difficulty setting for queers, for women, for people of color" (247). Furthermore, as we will see, discourses that circulate under this neoliberal meritocratic understanding also work to delegitimize initiatives to increase Indigenous folks' participation in games, devalue Indigenous games, and thus justify their continued exclusion.

Territorializing Indie Games

The discourses around indie games serve a gatekeeping function that leads to Indigenous games being received as an unwelcome and illegitimate presence. As with other forms of Indigenous media production, these creators and their works are subject to constant containment and backlash (Cornellier 2016; Crey 2016). The perception of Indigenous games as a threat to the settler nation-state was especially visible in the discourses around the game *Thunderbird Strike* (2017), a side scrolling game in which the player controls a flying creature from Anishinaabe mythology and shoots lightning at a snake in order to protect the natural world. Elizabeth LaPensée created the game with the intention of telling a story from her community and initially thought that it would be "played by some friends and family members and maybe some community members" (quoted in CBC Radio 2017). However, it became a major news item in October 2017 when Minnesota Republican senator David Osmek created a controversy around the game, calling it "an eco-terrorist version of *Angry Birds*" (Minnesota State Republican Caucus 2017). In a subsequent statement, Osmek belittled the design of the game, saying that it looked like it was "programmed on a Commodore 64, circa 1985," argued that the grant she received should be repaid, and called her credentials as a professor into question (Dubé 2017). Toby Mack, president of the Energy Equipment and Infrastructure Alliance, also expressed concern that the game would promote violence against oil industry workers. The story was picked up by major news sources, including Fox News. LaPenseé reported receiving violent threats, including death threats, in the wake of the controversy (Kraker 2017). The story reveals how Indigenous game developers are vilified, as well as how quickly the developer's credibility and technical skills were called into question as a basis for her exclusion and to delegitimize her work.

Aside from these open displays of hostility against Indigenous game developers, we can also see how Indigenous games more broadly are viewed as technically inferior and their creators not credible as "real" game designers. Indeed, the very initiatives that make decolonial game design and gameplay thinkable, such as grant-funded programs and nonprofit enterprises, can become the basis for their dismissal. The insistence that "anyone can make games" does not mean that everyone who makes games is evaluated equally. Instead, we continue to see that free community-based gaming is differentiated and seen as lesser than commercial games rooted in individualistic creative labor and career models. For example, one common configuration is to see non-Indigenous professional game developers working with Indigenous elders, storytellers, and community members, who are seen as "cultural consultants." This discourse underpins the Sami Game Jam, an annual five-day game development event in which "experienced game developers and people with Sami background come together in Utsjoki, Finland creating games on Sami culture and phenomena" (Sami Game Jam 2018). Though the event has produced a diverse collection of free online games that explore Sami traditional stories and contemporary perspectives, the marketing materials around the event maintain hierarchies between "real" developers and Sami cultural experts, which may affirm outsiders' expectations that Indigenous people are not technologically savvy or that they require assistance to make their own games.

So far, I have sought to illustrate how the design and production processes of Indigenous video games are narrowly interpreted and devalued. These exclusionary logics are also visible in the reception of Indigenous games by both game critics and players, an issue that becomes all the more important as Indigenous developers attempt to participate within indie gaming markets. Upper One Games' *Never Alone* (2014) was delegitimized in several ways. The game reflects the hybridization of Indigenous cultural production and indie gaming conventions, adapting "Kunuuksaayuka," a traditional Iñupiat story about a young man journeying to discover the source of a major blizzard, into a puzzle-based platform game where players guide a young girl, Nuna, and her pet fox through a treacherous Arctic landscape to unlock "cultural insights," or short video segments that teach players about Iñupiaq culture in the past up to today. Alan Gershenfeld, president of E-Line Media, described the game as the first in a long-term initiative to pioneer a new genre of "World Games" (Upper One Games 2013a). Displaying a strong commitment to cultural storytelling and accountability, game designers from E-Line Media spent several months visiting with Iñupiat communities in Barrow, Alaska, and worked closely with over thirty-five Alaska Native elders, storytellers, and community members throughout the development process (E-line Media 2016).

As with the community-based programs, the production and business model behind the game reinforced some hierarchies between game designers and community members who helped inform the story. Upper One Games was born out of a partnership between CITC and E-Line

Media, a company known for its involvement in educational games and the Games for Change movement. The publicity materials often circulated photographs of elders in the community who recounted the story, rather than professional Iñupiaq designers who were involved in the production, which inadvertently contributes to the minimization of Indigenous contributions and labor. Further, critics often praised the intentions, but found the game mechanics lacking. A critic for *Edge* magazine described *Never Alone* as "a fragile container for a tale of such inestimable value, and what ought to be universally welcoming instead must be approached with caution: come expecting revelation on an emotional level, not a mechanical one" ("Never Alone" 2015). Matthew Elliott, reviewer for Games Radar, similarly wrote, "*Never Alone* is bursting with promise and charm, but is savagely let down by technical flaws and maddening design decisions. Not even the cutest fox in gaming can save it" (M. Elliott 2014). Critics weren't the only ones with complaints, as players left reviews on sites like Steam. Some, such as Grumpy-Reviewer, expressed ambivalence about the game, writing, "I love indie games and I give this 4 because I know the people behind this game have their hearts in the right place. The problem is that, unfortunately, the game is bad" (GrumpyReviewer 2014. Another reviewer, Burn, wrote, "At first I complained 'this isn't a game, it's a short documentary', but once I finished the game I joyfully realized 'this isn't a game, it's a short documentary'. There should be more educational games like this on the market!" (Burn 2015). Dawnbug added, "The story is enjoyable enough, the graphics are decent, and the cultural insights are interesting. However, the game really isn't coded well, and the issues with the coding make the story harder to follow" (Dawnbug 2018). These arguments that *Never Alone* was not a real game and was a poorly made game dominated the game's reception, and worked in tandem with established discourses that delegitimize Indigenous game developers.

Conclusion

It has been my aim through this analysis to trace some of the discursive patterns that reinforce the exclusion of Indigenous game developers despite ever-increasing efforts to make space for Indigenous participation within digital games culture. This is not to treat these initiatives as futile, but to show how efforts to make games more inclusive to the needs and desires of Indigenous people will require reckoning and continued struggle against the toxic norms, taste valuations, and industrial structures that have long marginalized minority-produced indie games and minority participation in gaming culture. While we are seeing more and more Indigenous games produced all the time, it is clear that digital games culture remains an inhospitable space for Indigenous producers and players. As scholars of race and media, we must take these disjunctures between Indigenous games and their perception within the broader culture into account, remembering that the decolonization of games must entail meaningful structural changes.

8

Applying Latina/o Critical Communication Theory to Anti-Blackness

MARI CASTAÑEDA

Latina/o Critical Communication Theory | Afro-Latinos |
Spanish-language media

The rise of the Black Lives Matter movement has helped to call attention to long-standing racist attitudes and policing practices, using the tools of digital communication. While we often focus on its impact in the United States, this movement has extended across the Americas in its call to fight anti-Blackness. Within North American Latinx communities, it has specifically provided a rallying point for Afro-Latinx individuals and communities who have long faced discrimination and racism, particularly within media. For instance, we saw a historic change in Latinx media in 2017 when Ilia Calderón was selected to replace María Elena Salinas after thirty-six years of co-anchoring the national news program *Noticiero Univision* on the fifth-largest network in the United States (Univision 2017). Univision's hiring of Calderón was significant because she became the first Afro-Latina journalist to ever co-anchor a national evening news program on U.S. Spanish-language television, and the first person from Chocó, Colombia, to achieve such prominence in North American Latinx media. Chocó is a coastal region in Colombia that is historically and dominantly Black, and an area that the rest of Colombia has generally treated with racist attitudes and stereotypes.

In my own travels throughout Colombia in 2015, many individuals I encountered made racialized and problematic comments about residents of Chocó even though many people from Chocó were now residing in major metropolitan cities such as Medellín, Cali, and Bogotá. From the perspective of residents from Chocó, the presence of Black citizens in major global cities meant that their issues could no longer be ignored and inclusion was necessary for addressing the systemic racism they had endured over the years not only in Colombia, but across the United States and beyond. The last decade had inspired various social movements rooted in the acknowledgment that the lived experiences and contributions of Black communities (*Afro-descendientes*) in Latin America and the Caribbean were valuable and important. Additionally, the emerging movements recognizing Afro-Latinidades were reinforced by the emergence of Black Lives Matter in the United States and the need to call into question the racist attitudes and policing practices across the Americas in state politics and mass media. According to Yesenia Barragan, the growing political strikes by Afro-Colombians in recent years are also the result of communities fighting for more economic and social justice in the face of ongoing systemic exclusion. She quotes Saidiya Hartman, who notes, "Black lives are still imperiled and devalued. . . . This is the afterlife of slavery—skewed life chances, limited access to health and education, premature death, incarceration, and impoverishment" (Barragan 2016).

The fight to recognize the deep impact that Black exclusion has had on the Americas also extends beyond the social and political economy of everyday life. Movements oriented toward Afro-Latinidades have also included demands for mass media and digital communications to be more reflective of current demographics and racialized histories (see Román and Flores 2010). Newscasts, telenovelas, and everything in between are now being reexamined more closely for the ways problematic and questionable racialized narratives are perpetuated, and how Afro-Latinx individuals in particular are not being granted opportunities to showcase their talents and skills as key members of society and prominent voices in the public sphere (Rivero 2014; Torres-Saillant 2008). The considerable growth of Afro-Latinx as sports figures and global entertainers also demonstrated that Blackness was becoming mainstream in Latinx popular culture but continually marginalized in social-political contexts (Burgos 2009).

Consequently, the selection of Ilia Calderón as the new co-anchor at Univision, and as a person who views her own racial identity as a strength and values the multiracial context of her family (her partner identifies as Korean American and they have a daughter), demonstrates that perhaps (slowly) forthcoming changes to the racialized framework that have been historically promoted on Latinx media are underway in ways that deeply matter to the ethno-racial future of Latinx communities across the Americas. In this context, Latinx media are key in reimagining the racialization of Latinx populations in the United States and possibly challenging the limited understanding of race with regard to Latinx communities. As Littlefield notes (2008), "The media serve as a tool that people use to define, measure, and understand American society. For that reason, the media serve as a system of racialization in that they have historically been used to perpetuate the dominant culture's perspective and create a public forum that defines and shapes ideas concerning race and ethnicity." Additionally, these ideas about racial categories are not static or frozen in time, but influenced by historical, economic, and political contexts, which in turn affect the processes of becoming racialized beings and transforming how racial identities are constructed and experienced through social relations. Understanding how this occurs is important because it can powerfully challenge our preconceived and problematic notions of race and racism.

This is an important shift since Spanish-language media have struggled with this issue and have emphasized Whiteness historically, politically, and culturally. Yet as more Latinx communities across the United States as well as Latin America mobilize, organize, and address the lived experiences and media representation of Indigeneity and Afro-Latinidades, we must understand how Latinx media are making limited spaces for these identities as well. This chapter will discuss how Latinx media have historically participated in the racialization of U.S. Latinx and how contemporary social movements and the ongoing challenges to the historically racist treatment of Afro-descendent and Indigenous communities, including the success of Black Lives Matter, have called into question the reproduction of White supremacy as well as activated action against racist tropes in Latinx media. In an effort to conduct this analysis, the chapter will discuss and apply the Latina/o Critical Communication Theory (LatCritComm) as a pathway for better understanding the current shifts occurring in Latinx media as well as assess what the future may hold.

Latina/o Critical Communication Theory

According to Claudia Anguiano and Mari Castañeda (2014), there is much to gain by applying critical race theory and Latino critical theory to studies of communication, especially examinations of anti-Blackness as expressed through pervasive communicative forms. Most of the theoretical applications of critical race theory and Latino critical theory have occurred in studies of law and education, and have generated a rich body of scholarship that demonstrates the ways racism is institutionalized and racialization systematized. Although examinations of race and media representation have proliferated in the last three decades, there is still much to examine given the vast array of communication practices and the growing media landscape, particularly if we utilize a critical race and Latino critical lens. In an effort to bring together Latinx communication studies with the aforementioned theoretical lenses, Anguiano and Castañeda (2014) developed Latina/o Critical Communication Theory through a set of tenets that can be operationalized in order to critically examine communicative sites and practices in the context of Latinx lived experiences.

The five tenets are as following: (1) centralize the Latinx experience; (2) deploy decolonizing methodologies; (3) acknowledge and address racism aimed at Latinx communities; (4) resist colorblind and postracial rhetoric; and (5) promote a social justice dimension. These tenets are based on the major findings promoted by critical race theorists and Latina/o critical studies theorists, and aim to provide a framework through which communicative investigations centered on a critique of racialization processes related to Latinx can take place. This is not to say that other theoretical frameworks focusing on race, communications, and Latinx are insufficient. On the contrary, LatCritComm Theory is an attempt to add another layer to the flourishing and ongoing scholarly conversations that are deepening our understanding of Latinx subjectivities more specifically and communication realities more broadly.

According to Anguiano and Castañeda (2014), LatCritComm Theory takes a holistic and social justice approach to analyses of communication and cultural experiences of Latinx communities by centering the long history of struggle and resistance by communities of color. For instance, the theory values methodologies that emphasize non-Western modes of knowledge production and recognizes that methods such as counternarratives and autoethnography tell a different (racialization) story that can potentially disrupt historical and contemporary mainstream narratives. Furthermore, LatCritComm Theory "as an analytical

lens allows us to consider how White supremacy has shaped the contours of the audio-visual communications that Latina/o communities
engage with on a daily basis" (Anguiano and Castañeda 2014, 115–16).
This theoretical foundation thus creates a productive context in which to
investigate the history of racialization that has occurred in U.S. Spanish-
language media and the productive changes underway that are reimagining Latinx media as the voices and experiences of Afro-Latinx, for
instance, become more visible and are given credence in the mainstream
Latinx media landscape.

Centralize the Latinx Experience

The theory begins by centralizing the Latinx experience as an effort to
understand how members of this community of color experience racialization in multiple way through their Spanish-language use, immigration
status, and ethnic cultural practices—and how this is judged, often deri-
sively, by largely White populations. It also aims to move away from
race as a Black/White binary and recognize that Latinx lived experiences
(and media representations) are rooted in transnationalism, postcolo-
niality, colorism, and xenophobia. For instance, as a child growing up
in Los Angeles, I watched Spanish-language television and listened to
Spanish-language radio, and was always struck with how Blackness and
Indigeneity were constantly dismissed and stereotyped. Even at a young
age, this dismissiveness did not make any sense since I was growing
up surrounded by a diverse community of people that included Black
families, Mexicans, Indigenous people, Asians, and Latinx from different parts of Latin America and the Caribbean, including Puerto Rico.
Indeed, race and ethnicity were salient factors in our realities, but our
largely positive interactions as kids seemed opposite from what was
being promoted on mainstream and Latinx media. The near-invisibility
of Black, Asian, and Indigenous people on Latinx media, except as
stereotypical caricatures, reinforced a broader notion that these communities did not exist as part of the Latinx diaspora, when in fact they
constitute millions of people.

I remember how a high school friend who was perceived as only
Japanese shocked people when she shared that she was Peruvian of
Japanese descent. Another friend mentioned that she was actually

Afro-Colombian although everyone assumed she was only African American, and another acquaintance who spoke Spanish noted that her parents were predominantly Quechua speakers because they were from an Indigenous community in Ecuador. These lived experiences demonstrate that U.S. Latinx subjectivities are not largely White or mestizo (i.e., mixed race with Indigenous ancestry) but in fact embody a range of racialized positionalities that are often ignored and made invisible by media. Consequently, popular comprehension of what constitutes Latinx lived experiences remains largely limited.

The emergence of digital technologies can help to chip away at ignorance by providing a platform through which counternarratives of Latinidades are produced and distributed. One blog space that has challenged the prevailing story of race in Latinx communities is *Ain't I Latina?* (aintilatina.com). In it, journalist Janel Martinez centers Blackness as another way to understand what it means to be Latina today. She questions the centrality of "Eurocentric beauty standards" and discusses how the stories of Afro-Latinas are often erased and silenced in Spanish-language and Latinx media. Another Afro-Latinx social media creator who has pointed to the absurdity of televisual invisibility when in reality Blackness is very prominent in Latinx cultural contexts is LeJuan James. His YouTube videos aim to show how Latinx can be understood from a variety of intersectional positionalities (mother, student, Caribbean, professional) and in doing so complicates what is often perceived as normative Latinidad.

Scholars in Latinx studies have also challenged normative ideas about race and identity in Latinx communities, media, and academia itself. In her essay "'Too Black to Be Latina/o': Blackness and Blacks as Foreigners in Latino Studies," Tanya Katerí Hernández (2003) notes that although the privilege of Whiteness in Latinx media and popular culture is not surprising, the constant racialized treatment of Afro-Latinx identities as foreigner and foreign in local and the national Latinx imaginary is distressing, disheartening, and ultimately racist. She argues, "What is most disturbing about this multi-layered dynamic of Latino/as putting forth an image of enlightened racial thinking, by virtue of their racially mixed heritage . . . is the way in which the mindset obstructs any ability to effectively work through the complexity of the socioeconomic racial hierarchy." Ultimately, the historical refusal to acknowledge the impact of White supremacy and undo racial prejudice in Latinx communities has perpetuated the treatment of Blackness and even Asianness as foreign and disconnected from Latinidad and has also reinforced a Latinx imaginary that is raceless. Consequently, singling out Afro-Latinx communities as not belonging by characterizing them as foreign, alien, and suspicious for not matching what is considered the norm is a racialization process that needs to be centered if we are to fully understand and center Latinx experiences.

Since the publication of Hernández's essay, other Latinx studies scholars have also explicated the meaning of race in the context of Latinidad and the factors that have impacted the racialization process for Latinx. Ginetta Candelario (2008) notes that "identity formations are responsive to local conditions and institutions" and cultural and ideological contexts; thus, race for Latinx communities is conditioned by a multiplicity of meanings and social relations. The gendered ethno-racial identities of Latinx are in many cases slippery and/or ambiguous, so any understanding of Latinx media must take this into account. By centralizing the Latinx lived experience, LatCritComm Theory aims to show the disjuncture between what is occurring in communities and what is being represented on Latinx media. The shift at Univision to include an Afro-Latina in the national newscast as a co-anchor, the immediate firing of a talk show entertainer who compared former first lady Michelle Obama to a primate animal, and other efforts by Latinx media to reassess how race is embodied throughout its various content products are demonstrations that the unrelenting work by scholars, progressive media producers, and activists to protest against the negative racialization of Black, Asian, and Indigenous Latinx communities is paying off. The issue that remains is the following: as communication offerings expand and race becomes an issue that is dealt with in more complex ways, it is not clear whether such engagement will translate into productive material realities and the equitable treatment of U.S. Latinx communities within the broader sociopolitical landscape.

Deploy Decolonizing Methodologies

The second tenet of the LatCritComm theoretical framework calls for use of decolonizing methodologies that challenge the notion that research can be produced from an entirely objective orientation, and asks scholars to examine how their histories and social positions inform how they understand the multidimensional experience of Latinx. Applying feminist-inspired methods opens the possibility of creating collaborative knowledge production that is not researcher-centric but participant-focused and cognizant of the lingering effects that colonization has had on Latinx communities. For example, the actual racialized experience of Latinx media workers is an area of research that is sorely lacking in the broader literature in digital media and communication. Castañeda (2014b) notes that a Puerto Rican journalist residing in Massachusetts shared that in her past media work she was constantly made to feel that she was incapable of producing real journalism or media content that would be read or engaged with by non-Latinx audiences. Although she identified as a light-skinned Boricua, she was often made to feel that her Latina positionality diminished her journalistic skills. However, this Latina journalist was recently granted the opportunity to host a regional morning radio show, and through her weekly program, she has made many efforts to deploy a decolonizing method to her work as radio talk show host. She has done this by fostering multiracial collaboration, embodying a feminist approach in her interviews, insisting that community voices and issues are centered in the discussion, and making every effort to point to the multidimensional contours of Latinx history, context, and agency.

Similarly, before Ilia Calderón was asked to co-anchor *Noticiero Univision*, she conducted an interview with a KKK member in North Carolina that was televised as an evening program in August 2017. This interview was not only broadcast as a news special titled *En la boca del lobo* (In the mouth of the wolf), but it also became a viral video that demonstrated the degradation and potential danger Latinx media workers like Calderón often face when they are not perceived to be the "right kinds" of people of color—meaning they are deemed not mestizo but only Black. Her steely performance in the face of a contemptuous interview with the KKK Grand Wizard Chris Barker, where he called her the n-word and a mongrel, ironically pushed further ongoing efforts to decolonize Latinx media spaces and dismantle the racist attitudes of Latinx viewers. It was unfortunate, though, that such an eye-opening interaction placed a heavy emotional burden on Calderón. LatCritComm Theory's emphasis on decolonizing methodologies not only turns research on its head by including the testimonios of Latinx lived experiences, but also provides the context through which Latinx media can be reimagined as a decolonizing force. It's important to note, however, that Calderón regarded the interview as a harrowing experience, which points to the reality that decolonization is not without pain and suffering.

Acknowledge and Address Racism Aimed at Latinx Communities

The third precept aims to elucidate the varied personal and systemic disparities and racism that Latinx communities face consistently and the ways such hurtful treatment is reinforced by persistent xenophobic oppressions that occur at individual and structural levels. Racist micro- and macro-aggressions targeted at Latinx populations are often unrecognized because in mainstream discourse, inequities are perceived as being about citizenship status or language ability, for instance, but not race. By acknowledging and addressing the racism faced by Latinx peoples, we can better investigate how race is experienced in conflicting, detrimental, and intersectional liberatory ways.

For example, Latinx media have traditionally operated as not only information and entertainment resources, but also advocates for those who have been mistreated and misunderstood. The anti-immigrant legislation and policies that have proliferated after the initial pro-immigration movements in the mid-2000s have in many ways transformed Latinx media into spaces that acknowledge and address the racism aimed at Latinx communities. Time and again they have covered stories that show the impact that anti-immigrant and anti-Latinx sentiments have produced on the material realities of Latinx, including their mental health. National news journalist Jorge Ramos of Univision has been especially vocal about the treatment of Latinx in the United States. He has gone head-to-head with the forty-fifth president, and in turn is viewed as someone on Latinx media who is fighting the racism directed at Latinx people at a national level. It is important to note, however, that the commercial nature of most Latinx media has also set limits to the kinds of advocacy that can be produced through the airwaves.

In this sense, digital communication technologies have created a platform through which critical analyses and criticism can take place without necessarily fearing repercussions, especially from advertisers. For instance, the websites Latino Rebels (latinorebels.com) and Remezcla (remezcla.com) have become excellent examples of sites where Latinx writers congregate on a digital media platform to expose and discuss racist policies and encounters that many Latinx communities face on a daily basis. In multiple online articles and audiovisual postings, contributors from Latino Rebels and Remezcla have argued that although Latinx-identified politicians, judges, celebrities, and artists may be recognized at a national level and in many ways accepted as legitimate voices in the public sphere, they themselves (including, for example, Supreme Court Justice Sonia Sotomayor) have also experienced racism.

The documentary film *Latinos beyond Reel* also makes this point especially with regard to Sotomayor, who was characterized multiple times as a maid in news coverage during her congressional confirmation hearings. Given the hate-filled vitriol aimed at Latinx, and most specifically at Mexican and Central American immigrants, acknowledging and addressing racism is increasingly a topic of concern for Latinx media. *PBS Newshour* senior correspondent Ray Suarez notes that "even as Latino trailblazers move into professions where they once were rare or that were even closed to them, they are still disproportionately represented in blue-collar work" and consistently racialized as unwelcomed "aliens" (2013, 225). Multiple scholars agree that fear is the factor that drives so much of the racism directed at Latinx communities: fear of their bicultural, bilingual, and multiracial positionalities and the impact these have on what it means to be "American" (K. Johnson 1996; Sanchez 1997; Galindo and Vigil 2006; Huber et al. 2008).

Resist Colorblind and Postracial Rhetoric

The fourth point of LatCritComm Theory builds on the previous principles by asserting that much of the discussion about race in the United States tends to follow a Black/White binary that erases the complex racial experiences of Latinx, Native American, Middle Eastern, and Asian American communities. Media and political attempts to characterize U.S. Latinx experiences as existing within colorblind and postracial frameworks fails to recognize the material and rhetorical forms of exclusion that Latinx populations face on a daily basis. The assumption that because Latinx/Spanish-language media have a presence in the cultural and media landscape of the United States, all Latinx people are accepted as full members in civil society is untrue and damaging to achieving real educational, economic, and political equity. For instance, multiple mainstream newspapers and online venues published and posted articles this past summer about the global success of the Daddy Yankee, Luis Fonsi, and Justin Bieber musical collaboration on the song "Despacito" as a demonstration that Latinx cultural production, and by association Latinx overall, have somehow "arrived." Such media characterizations impart the notion that Latinx now embody a postracial status and any forms of racial discrimination they face is local and personal, rather than systemic and structural.

In many ways, these efforts to create colorblind narratives about Latinx are attempts to homogenize and mainstream their location within the broader U.S. society. For Latinx celebrities and media outlets, colorblind and postracial discourses allow non-Latinx audiences to consume media products that are ordinarily deemed Latinx-oriented. Yet such broadening and whitewashing of Latinx communications diminish the historical struggles that have shaped Latinx communities. They also diminish the ongoing battles to equitably access education, jobs, and political power. As the impact of Afro-descendent, Indigenous, Black Lives Matter, and immigrant movements become more evident in Latinx programming and content production (especially online), the need to resist colorblind narratives about Latinx becomes more important than ever. As long as Latinx immigrants and many Latinx communities are characterized in racist terms, then postracial characterizations of Latinx must be challenged for how they pit seemingly good "White" Latinx people against the "bad hombres." Latinx media's efforts to highlight the Black, Asian, and Indigenous Latinx experiences as they connect with anti-immigration policies and police practices are some of the ways colorblind and postracial narratives about Latinx are contested (although without a doubt, Whiteness still colors the audiovisual landscape). Speaking Spanish is in fact a primary way to push back against postracial and colorblind rhetoric because it signifies, front and center, how difference, cultural connections, and historical dynamics continue to exist for Latinx; and it is a difference that is appreciated and beloved and cannot be erased even with the passage of English-only policies and practices.

Promote a Social Justice Dimension

The final tenet asks, How does one foster a social justice orientation to the study and praxis of Latinx media and race? In many ways, the approach requires the acknowledgment that gaining media access is a political project that requires an intersectional framework that is anti-racist, anti-capitalist, and always critically feminist. Promoting a social justice dimension means the need to examine how capitalism influences much of the media production in the United States and the ways this confines the discussion of certain issues and lived realities. In addition to examining media with an anti-racist framework, the adoption of a critical feminist approach is also necessary for reimagining what Latinx media can be like if social justice was at the forefront of Latinx communications production. More commercial Spanish-language media are limited in their ability to publicly espouse a social justice dimension in their work, although news reporters have argued that in the current context of the forty-fifth president and his support of White supremacists, they are making a social justice intervention by simply existing (Navarrette 2017; Radtke 2017). They are also promoting social justice by covering and discussing the topics that the mainstream English-language media will not address on their broadcast news programs and websites. Certainly, in some ways they are correct, but what they do is not enough. Therefore, online platforms that have adopted a clearly articulated social justice dimension have been key in pushing the discussion of what needs to be done to change the representation and treatment of Latinx on and off the media landscape. Education also has a big role to play in this regard, both in K-12 and in higher education. Latinx professors are working closely with students and community media organizations to produce media content that offers counternarratives about what it means to be Latinx in and across multiple U.S. communities. Scores of these college graduates often become Latinx media workers who aim to create anti-racist, feminist stories about Latinx communities that acknowledge the challenges, beauty, and changes taking place on the ground locally. Thus, it is not enough to examine Latinx media and race; political action that also embodies a social justice element is needed more than ever.

Moving Forward in Examining Latinx Media and Race

Given the historical and ongoing anti-Latinx, anti-immigrant, and anti-Blackness offenses in the United States, it is crucial to understand the role that U.S. Latinx media are playing to address as well as reinscribe the historical and contemporary problematics of race and racism that Latinx communities are facing. The online brand Remezcla has created viral stories that highlight and celebrate Afro-Latinidad in articles such as "#BlackLatinxHistory Highlights Afro-Latinos Who Changed History" (Simón 2016), but the reality is that a recognition of what Blackness means within Latinx communities is still deeply contested within the community as well as Black communities. During February's Black History Month, Twitter postings have argued back and forth whether Latinx communities recognize their Blackness and whether their Blackness even counts since it is (wrongly) perceived to not have been affected by the racism African American populations have endured in the United States. The idea that Afro-Latinx experiences are not influenced by the racist attacks again Blackness fails to understand that anti-Black audiovisual and discursive narratives do not distinguish between ethnic, national, or linguistic backgrounds. Afro-Latinx and Latinx individuals who are Indigenous-looking with dark brown skin are also subjected to discrimination, animosity, and antipathy toward their contributions to broader economic and social relations. Vilna Bashi (2004) notes that we must actually understand "anti-black racism as a *global* immigration phenomenon" (600). Thus, to do so allows us to better compare, contrast, and complicate the treatment and experiences of Blackness, and race more broadly, within and across Latinidades.

For instance, Latinx media have seen themselves as Latinx-oriented but not necessarily as a racialized entity. Yet their increasing relevance to U.S. electoral politics has forced Latinx media to face the racialization of their sector and the people who are both working in and consuming Latinx media. They are no longer outside discussions and constructions of race but very much operating as proxies for racialization and minoritization of Latinx and non-English-speaking communities. They have become a contradictory vehicle for both expressing and calling out xenophobia as demonstrated by U.S. politics and English-language mainstream media. In some ways, it is also causing Latinx entertainment media to reflect on the ways they have also reproduced oppression in other areas such as gender, class, and sexuality, although there is still much work to do.

As noted earlier, the inclusion of an Afro-Latina news anchor from Colombia on *Noticiero Univision* is viewed as a progressive sign for Latinx media in terms of race. It is being heralded as a turning point in Spanish-language media and a wide range of programming streams including entertainment. Historically, the issue of race on Spanish-language media was addressed only in stereotypical ways, with Black folks often represented as inferior. The Afro-descendiente/descendent movement has been ongoing for the past decade in an effort to address the ways colonialism has impacted the Americas and the Caribbean. The need to address race on Latin American media has made its way to U.S. Latinx media as well, and on the flip side, the social movements rooted in heralding Black Lives Matter in the United States have also impacted Latin American social politics and discussions about racialization in media within a transnational context. However, the issue of White supremacy is still not entirely addressed and certain kinds of racialized exclusions still exist on Latinx media, such as the voices of Indigenous populations.

One of the challenges of talking about racialization in Latinx media is the fact that in many ways, to be seen as Latinx is to be racialized in the United States, given the historical relationship between White political economic power and Latinx populations. Therefore, if a people are racialized by virtue of being Latinx, then Latinx media are already racialized by virtue of being for, about, and by Latinx people. Indeed, Latinx media have always been racialized spaces (Castañeda 2017), and will continue to be so as long as speaking Spanish in U.S. Latinx communities is viewed as foreign. This was evident during the 2016 presidential campaign when Jorge Ramos from Univision tried to be at the campaign stops and was kicked out, when the Republican presidential candidate made fun of him, and more importantly, when Univision and Spanish-language media more generally were delegitimized. Univision was seen as not a legitimate news source because of the Spanish-language use and the fact that it was oriented toward Latinx. Yet Spanish-language and Latinx media do not always see themselves as being already racialized, and as a result, they often reproduce the same narratives and images of White supremacy that can reinforce systems of oppression. Radio, on the other hand, has been a broadcast space in which racism has been addressed and examined, and racialization contested (Casillas 2014). The discussions about ICE and immigration that are taking place on broadcast and digital media are not only ways for information about community issues to be dispersed and discussed, but also reminders of how Latinx are systematically, materially, and symbolically othered in the United States every single day.

Conclusion

The tenets of LatCritComm Theory were applied above with the intention to demonstrate how the framework can potentially help us reimagine how we analyze, understand, and perhaps improve Latinx media by more fully addressing anti-Blackness and the systemic exclusion of Afro-Latinidades. If we examine some of the literature about audience responses and reception, we see that issues regarding race and ethnicity, in addition to sexuality, gender, and class, deeply impact how people see themselves and others. This has real consequences with regard to policies and the acceptance of difference in everyday life. It also impacts the ability to build connections and movements across difference that would allow for Latinx populations to see themselves as part of a larger (racialized) community. Online Latinx media are some of the spaces in which the boundaries and discussions surrounding race and racialization are being engaged with and challenged. Latinx media have historically regarded themselves as advocates for Latinx communities, but the importance of pointing out the ways the communities are being targeted and racialized in negative ways is now at a crisis point given the Republican presidency and Trumpism. Race within Latinx media needs to be examined not only because of the number of people they reach, but also because these media are viewed as a voice and communicative space for Latinx lived experiences.

9

Asian American Independent Media

JUN OKADA

film festivals | media independence

The origins of Asian American independent media are often traced back to the Center for Asian American Media (CAAM) and its name-sake annual film festival, CAAMfest. Its events are held each year in San Francisco and the greater San Francisco Bay Area, and have provided filmmakers exposure and access to local and national audiences since 1980. CAAM's history, size, and name suggest that it is the "center" of Asian American media, and it does serve as a clearinghouse of sorts for Asian American media—especially since it is the only Asian American film festival or media organization boasting a fiscal contract with the federally controlled Public Broadcasting System (Gong 1991). Indeed, CAAM and its film festival have exclusive rights to a state-mandated agreement to fund films that may appear on PBS and its affiliates. And yet, despite the power and centrality CAAM appears to hold, it was actually the result of a decade of grassroots media efforts by a diverse, nationwide collective of independent media activists and filmmakers in the 1970s. It was due to their struggle for recognition and representation that CAAM was eventually established in 1980 as one of the five Minority Consortia financed partly by the state-funded Corporation for Public Broadcasting (CPB) to address racial inequality in television.

In addition, the history of CAAM and CAAMfest reveals that the first years of Asian American independent film and video centered strongly around its connection to government funding through the auspices of PBS and the CPB. Yet as the political climate evolved, more recent examples of Asian American independent filmmaking and film festivals show a decentralization and loosening of this original relationship, which now is defined more by private forms of funding and commercial exhibition that exemplify the neoliberal political style of independent filmmaking—that is, the defunding of public media and the rise of do-it-yourself Internet platforms such as YouTube. As Toby Miller and Richard Maxwell (2011) have stated, neoliberalism in media "exercised power by governing [people] through market imperatives, so that they could be made ratiocinative liberal actors whose inner creativity was unlocked in an endless mutual adaptation to the environment." This seeming "unlocking" of creative and fiscal potential, which had been kept in check by institutions like the CPB, was slowly unleashed within Asian American independent media.

But to start from the beginning, while the history of CAAM tells a tale of somewhat linear progress, this chapter articulates the broader context and comparative history of Asian American film festivals in order to reveal the diversity of impulses that have inspired the creation of independent film communities since the beginning of the Asian American film and video movement in the early 1970s. Although there are currently many Asian American film festivals that span the continental United States, I focus primarily on CAAMfest, Cine Vision, and the San Diego Asian Film Festival to better understand the contrast between the early years of a public media-dominated Asian American media and the decentralized, neoliberal style of filmmaking, exhibition, and distribution that is more common today. I problematize the notion of a "center" of Asian American media by outlining alternative and contemporary models for the dissemination of Asian American independent media content as well as the inevitable decentering of the original model as an effect of the so-called neoliberal DIY model. While the PBS pipeline represented by CAAM was important, there is also a long history of conflict and debate about the values it promoted, specifically, how to counter the notion of state-driven Asian American–identified content. I then show how the pushback against the singular funding streams represented by the CPB, however hard-won, resulted in the development of online content delivery and the expansion of audiences. These changes have profoundly altered the landscape for Asian American independent media.

CAAM: Asian American Public Broadcasting

The Center for Asian American Media began in 1980 as the National Asian American Telecommunications Association (NAATA) in San

Francisco. PBS was established in the 1960s to rectify the "vast waste-land" of commercial television that was endangering American viewers' minds, according to then chairman of the Federal Communications Commission Newt Minnow. According to Minnow, television without checks was not in the public interest. This idea led to the eventual development of Educational Television, which was subsequently transformed to the Public Broadcasting Service (PBS). It was created to serve the "public interest," a mission that Minnow believed was crucially missing from the nascent entertainment medium.

Yet by 1979 PBS was suffering from internal critiques that it was not fully inclusive of the diversity of Americans that it purportedly represented. The financial arm of PBS, the Corporation for Public Broadcasting, commissioned the Task Force on Minorities in Public Broadcasting to complete a study entitled "A Formula for Change." This report concluded that public broadcasting did not authentically represent the racial diversity of the United States. In conjunction with media activists focusing on the lack of representation and opportunity for Asian Americans in TV and film, an agreement was struck with PBS and the CPB to ameliorate this issue of institutional marginalization. Hence, by the early 1980s, CAAM and a cohort of other Minority Consortia—Latino Public Broadcasting, National Black Programming Consortium, Vision Maker Media, and Pacific Islanders in Communications—were established to provide content to a national television audience. These consortia were given the responsibility to reach out into their respective ethnic communities to choose films that would authentically represent these communities, films that would eventually be broadcast to PBS television. CAAM's film festival (at the time called the San Francisco International Asian American Film Festival) would show the first iteration of these nonfiction, experimental, and fiction short subjects, feature documentaries, and occasional narrative fiction feature films. After screening at this festival, select films would then have their broadcast premiere on PBS television, usually during Asian Pacific Heritage Month or other targeted PBS scheduled programming.

Since CAAM's establishment in the early 1980s, it has undoubtedly shaped the course of Asian American independent media. Yet before CAAM rose as a flagship organization, Asian American independent film could be seen as a more informal, grassroots affair. It had direct roots in the larger movement to carve out Asian American studies and identities in the ethnic studies strikes in the 1970s. For instance, in 1968 the student-led ethnic studies strike at San Francisco State University (SFSU) led the way to the building of the College of Ethnic Studies in order to reflect the diverse histories and issues experienced by people of color on campus. This generated a wave of student protests, which in turn established academic departments and centers for ethnic studies that prioritized the inclusion of students of color in previously marginalizing or exclusively white academic programs. At this time, filmmaking and film studies were also emerging as academic disciplines in their own right. Following suit with the work of the student strikers at SFSU, students at UCLA's School of Theatre, Film and Television established the Center for EthnoCommunications in 1968 to similarly address the dearth of students of color in filmmaking. Many successful students emerged from this program, including Black LA Rebellion filmmakers such as Haile Gerima, Charles Burnett, and Julie Dash among others, in addition to the founders of the first nonprofit Asian American film collective, Visual Communications (VC). In the early 1970s, VC's founders, Robert A. Nakamura, Eddie Wong, Duane Kubo, and Alan Ohashi, were among the first to forge a politicized collective approach to filmmaking that led the way to the model for CAAM.

Films produced by VC in its early days reflected and shaped the ethos of the ethnic studies strikes in affirming resistance, rawness, experimentation, and independence. The LA Rebellion filmmakers made low-budget, often black-and-white narrative features in the vein of a kind of pure realism, combining the lo-fi aesthetics of the long take and a looser poetic meditation on Black life in the 1970s. In the same way that the LA Rebellion filmmakers rebelled against the tired and racist stereotypes both in Hollywood films and in radical commercialized responses to them in genres like Blaxploitation, Asian American filmmakers of VC were drawn to experimentations that blurred the boundaries of documentary, memoir, avant-garde, and narrative techniques to make such films as *Wong Sinsaang* (Wong 1971) and *Manzanar* (Nakamura 1976). *Wong Sinsaang* is a black-and-white, twelve-minute experimental short film chronicling the harsh day-to-day reality of the filmmaker's father working in a laundromat and the casual racism he experiences. Both impressionistic and critical of institutionalized racism, the film provides a model for early expression in Asian American film. *Manzanar* is also a film that details its filmmaker's past as it reveals present-day images of a Japanese internment camp and the experiences and memories that emerge from the sense of place.

Asian Cine Vision: Against the "Boring" of Asian American Films

The security that was finally achieved through the formation of the Minority Consortia was a resounding victory for independent producers, including Asian American independent filmmakers. Yet there was also backlash. In particular, while PBS backed CAAM and its supporters, who mostly worked on the West Coast, East Coast filmmakers and activists within Asian American media circles promulgated criticism about PBS-sponsored films. They claimed that these films seemed to adhere to a state-sponsored agenda to represent a prescribed Asian American identity that was at odds with the free artistic enterprise of filmmaking. Art critic Daryl Chin from Asian Cine Vision in New York wrote that many of these seemingly agenda-driven films were "noble and boring" (Chin 1988).

One way of more deeply investigating this clash between "noble and boring" institutional filmmaking and a more artistically independent style is to compare two films that exemplify each style—Visual Communication's sole feature narrative film, *Hito Hata: Raise the Banner* (Kubo and Nakamura 1980), and auteur filmmaker Wayne Wang's classic noir-esque indie film, *Chan Is Missing* (Wang 1982). As mentioned, VC was instrumental in the building of a community infrastructure for the production, distribution, and exhibition of films. The films that it did produce tended to be nonfiction, experimental, or short subjects. In many ways, the Hollywood-style narrative feature film was the stylistic and ideological opposite of VC's communal, low-budget ethos. Yet in 1980, VC did produce a feature narrative film, *Hito Hata: Raise the Banner*, a lavish epic story spanning decades that chronicles the lives of Japanese Americans from their arrival in California in the early twentieth century, their internment during World War II, and their evolution into the 1970s. Directed, produced, and financed by VC, it starred veteran Japanese actor Mako, and included TV actor Pat Morita in a costarring role, as well as members of the LA Asian American theatre group East West Players. It was produced in a thoroughly communal fashion, involving the people and places that made VC and the Little Tokyo community that the film was about. Yet the film was an ambitious effort on all fronts—narratively, cinematically, and especially fiscally. Its distribution and exhibition plans were equally bold, taking the film nationwide, starting with a premiere at "the city's most prestigious cultural venue, the Dorothy Chandler Pavilion, and from there it left for a national road tour with benefit screenings held in New York, Sacramento, Seattle, Denver and Honolulu" (Chin 1972). Indeed, as this exhibition history suggests, *Hito Hata* seemed in many ways to depart in essential ways from the socialist, communal impulse of VC's early days as a grassroots organization suspicious of Hollywood pomp and circumstance. The fact that *Hito Hata* was a feature-length narrative film requiring a large budget, as well as distribution and exhibition requirements that were more costly than short films, challenged and transformed the terms of VC's mission as a nonprofit media organization.

On the other end of the spectrum was Wayne Wang's low-budget, black-and-white feature film *Chan Is Missing*, which was produced and released at around the same time as *Hito Hata*. Unlike the communal circumstances of the VC-produced *Hito Hata*, *Chan Is Missing* followed the path of auteur cinema similar to other American indie feature films. After the demise of the old Hollywood studio system, the 1970s saw the era of New Hollywood and the rise of American auteurs who were greatly influenced by the postwar European auteur cinema that preceded them. Directors like John Cassavetes, Martin Scorsese, Francis Ford Coppola, and later David Lynch, Jim Jarmusch, Spike Lee, and many others inaugurated a new aesthetic language of cinema that borrowed from past American genre cinema but also invented innovative ways to transform them to suit contemporary concerns. Though propped up by Asian American media community members as an important contributor to their communal cause, Wayne Wang was as much a member of the larger coterie of the post–studio system American independent filmmakers as he was of Asian American film and video.

As Peter X Feng (1996) has written, *Chan Is Missing* is the postmodern, Asian American neo-noir par excellence, expertly yet subtly mixing the aesthetics of classical Hollywood cinema with the very present-day concerns of Asian American identity. The film follows two protagonists, San Francisco cabdriver Jo and his nephew Steve, in their search for a missing man named Chan Hung, whom they had entrusted with the money needed to get their own independent cab license. What Jo and Steve find through their amateur detective work is a portrait of Chan that is both mysterious and contradictory. Their explorations of China-town and encounters with other Asian Americans on the diverse streets of San Francisco become a metaphor for Chinese American bicultural-ism and a cinematic meditation on Asian American identity. The film won an award for Best Experimental/Independent Film from the Los Angeles Film Critics Association in 1982, showing for the first time that an Asian American feature narrative film could be viable beyond the Asian American film community.

Chan Is Missing exposed Asian American film and video to a wider public and began to integrate Asian American narratives into the con-temporary language of American independent cinema that references a universal past in Hollywood genre cinema. It's true that contempo-rary American cinema was forged through a reworking of the past in meaningful ways. For instance, Scorsese critically reworked America's most venerated genres, the Western and film noir, into a twisted night-mare vision of the present-day gritty streets of New York in one of the most influential films of the 1970s, *Taxi Driver*. That film utilized the mood of noir while reworking the narrative dynamics of the rescue narrative of the Western to create something familiar, yet entirely new. Similarly, Wang utilizes the influential visual look of noir while cri-tiquing the Orientalist detective serial par excellence, Charlie Chan. The fictional character Charlie Chan was the protagonist of numerous detective novels and sixteen film versions starring white actor Warner Oland in yellowface. Chan was the inscrutable yet benevolent Chinese other, what Frank Chin and Jeffery Paul Chan (1972) famously term an example of "racist love" and a precursor to the model minority ste-reotype. *Chan Is Missing* is a direct rebuke to the offenses of the past, giving us instead a Chan who cannot be defined. Wang's film offers an open-ended definition of Asian American identity that is at once cin-ematic, global, and full of possibility.

The defining tension of Asian American film and video during the institution-building phase was between the communally produced film and the auteur film. Each style bore its signature style and created diversity, but there was also disagreement about the merits of each. Daryl Chin describes how the collision of these approaches shaped Asian American film and video:

> In the 1981 festival, two Asian American features were programmed. One was *Hito Hata: Raise the Red Banner*, produced by the Visual Communications group in Los Angeles, and it's very much a "group" project: it's worthy and noble and uplifting and boring as hell. It doesn't have a whiff of "personality" or of genuine artistic vision. The other was Wayne Wang's *Fire Over Water*, which was to have been shown in a rough cut. . . . Some of us were (again) excited by the movie, but a lot of people involved with the festival hated it. We are talking pure hatred. Well imagine their surprise when, the following year, Wayne Wang reedited the movie, made the structure far less complicated, toned down a lot of the "new talkie" audio-visual dissociation, synched it up and showed it straight and came out with *Chan Is Missing*. . . . Here, all along these Asian American media activists thought that something like *Hito Hata* was going to be the Asian American "breakthrough," and it wasn't, it was that damned quirky oddball personal experimental *Chan Is Missing*. Put that in your peace pipe and smoke it! (Chin 1988)

What Chin suggests is that Asian American film and video evolved out of two different impulses—the communal and the auteurist. This dichotomy has become a hallmark of Asian American independent film. On the one hand, filmmakers and activists have continued to champion politics of identity-driven work made in a communal spirit. On the other hand, critics have also championed Asian American directors and films that tried to steer away from a more overtly institutional model to one that would fit in more easily within other modes of cinema like art house, especially with Asian auteur and genre cinema that was gaining in global popularity in multiple modes. Hence, toward the end of the 1990s, combining Asian American and Asian cinemas became a more viable model for the dissemination of Asian American independent film and video.

SDAFF: Hybrid and Global Asian American Media

One such model, the San Diego Asian Film Festival (SDAFF), represents an interesting departure from the larger narrative of state-sponsored Asian American film festivals. SDAFF provides a study in contrast to this previous narrative because of its essentially entrepreneurial origins. Specifically, San Diego ABC news anchor Lee Ann Kim began SDAFF in order to address the lack of a venue and community around Asian cinema, not out of a need to address the needs of artists. Describing SDAFF's origins, she says, "I was speaking at a tech company here, and overheard a bunch of Caucasians talking about their favorite Asian movies, how they'd get together, eat dim sum and talk over films. At the same time, I was head of the Asian American Journalists Association (AAJA) local chapter, and thinking how we could engage a larger audience with our issues" (D. Elliott 2007). Kim did not have a film background, unlike those involved in CAAM, but she and her team of expert associates inaugurated a film festival in 2000 as an event of the San Diego AAJA held at the University of San Diego. Based on the success of this first event, the festival established itself as a nonprofit called the San Diego Asian Film Foundation and continued to expand in future years. Part of its success, as its programmer Brian Hu (2018) mentions, "has a lot to do with its big annual gala awards dinner, which was unique to the Asian American film festival circuit, as well as the fact that Lee Ann, whose background was not in film, poached festival organizers from other festivals, including the founders of the DC APA Film Festival and the Dallas Asian Film Festival, to be her deputies."

The markedly different way SDAFF began demonstrates the potential for Asian American film festivals to depart from the political values of its founders and to ride the neoliberal wave of DIY content creation and delivery that has become the zeitgeist. First, the so-called "success" story of Kim's single-handed production of this very successful film festival and the way it has been marketed belies the bedrock foundation of Asian American independent media movement that supported those who came before it. It is telling, for instance, that the first Filipinx American feature narrative film, *The Debut* (Cajayon 2001), opened SDAFF in its inaugural year. Like Kim, the film's director was not plugged into the existing bureaucratic system for the distribution and exhibition of Asian American independent films via CAAM. Instead, Cajayon hand-distributed his feature film from multiplex theatre to multiplex theatre. Going against the grain of the independent film market, he chose to gain a more mainstream audience to show his genre picture, explaining that "the core audience is teenagers . . . and they don't go to art houses. I have nothing against Landmark (the art-house chain), but if we played our film there, kids would get the wrong idea about us. They would think we're this arty-farty movie from the Philippines" (Graham 2001). Called the first English-language Filipinx American feature film, *The Debut* is a family comedy about a young Filipinx man torn between his desire to become an artist and obligations to his family. Although *The Debut* was the opening or closing film at many Asian American film festivals, Cajayon's unique style of exhibition defied the overly structured model created by CAAM. It also showed a desire for mainstream exposure that had been lacking as a result of the Minority Consortium system. Ultimately, it would be the breakthrough Asian American independent feature film *Better Luck Tomorrow* (Lin 2002), a high school crime drama taking its cue from Hong Kong crime films, that would break through the institutional ceiling for Asian American films wanting to become mainstream.

SDAFF departs significantly from CAAM, and in this way, reveals how Asian American independent film and video have evolved, for good or ill. Indeed, SDAFF coincided with the rise of the Internet, which brought the crowdsourcing boom in independent filmmaking and helped create Asian American online stars like Wong Fu Productions, Anna Akana, Kevjumba, NigaHiga, and others. In the spirit of *The Debut*, these online content creators have forged a completely new path in content creation by uploading self-made videos onto YouTube, discarding many of the communal aspects of production that distinguished VC and CAAM in the 1970s and 1980s. At the same time, SDAFF has also distinguished itself by embracing global Asian cinema and relegating Asian American independent films to a smaller role. As a festival driven by Asian Americans who desire the presence of all kinds of Asian culture and faces on-screen, it has loosened the divide between "Asian" and "Asian American" and is geared toward the global cinephilia that Asian films reflect. Hu says that only half of the festival's films are English-language Asian American films, and the other half are international Asian films. He says, "For better or worse, we've been called the 'spring break of the [Asian American] film festival circuit,' but that's because we celebrate [Asian American] filmmaking by having fun with it. Which nobody would ever accuse the stately CAAM for doing."

This explication of the tensions between different forms of Asian American filmmaking and film festivals demonstrates the diversity of Asian American independent film and video production, distribution, and exhibition. In between the extremes of "noble and boring" documentaries and comedic YouTube videos lies a world of possibilities, styles, modes, and genres—which continue to grow despite the evolution of Asian American independent media increasingly outside the institutions in which they originated. This history shows that although there remains a struggle to reach wider audiences, the legacy of Asian American independent film and video will always remain with community, whether it be among filmmakers, activists, or audiences. But what is more, and perhaps even more critical, is the discussion of the effect of nonregulated DIY content on the significance of Asian American independent media. If some see Asian American film and video as the struggle against racist, classist, and sexist exclusionary practices of Hollywood, the original profit-driven media industry, what does it mean to replicate this system on YouTube and film festivals? Does the essence of Asian American independent media get somehow lost? Or does the freedom enabled by the new global content and delivery systems and the DIY spirit enlarge and embrace more and sometimes contradicting elements represented by those involved in the creation of Asian American films?

10

Remediating Trans Visuality

AMY VILLAREJO

trans* | remediation | performance

Scholars of digital media have given many names to practices whereby viewers and users transform media texts and objects to uncover new meanings, excavate subjectivities that seem marginalized, or reframe the political valences of a media text for a new moment. Remixers, meme authors, slash fiction writers, hackers, DJs, and vidders are among the new forms of digital readers, writers, and editors who recirculate and recreate media. They show us that media objects, even those lodged in the most corporate environments, are not stable but open to the manipulation of fans, who might seize upon ways to generate new meaning and new stories out of the slightest detail. Media texts and objects are thus revealed as historical, malleable, and open to creative intervention.

Media remixers share with the idea of "trans" a process of transformation, but trans emphasizes how *gender* is likewise historical, malleable, and open to creative intervention. In the wake of decades of activism and life experiences under the rubric of "transsexuality" and "transgender," "trans," or "trans*" now designates space for experimentation in gender and embodiment.[1] As the scholar Jack Halberstam (2018) puts it, "When logic that fixes bodily form to social practice comes undone, when narratives of sex, gender, and embodiment loosen up and become less fixed in relation to truth, authenticity, originality, and identity, then we have the space and the time to imagine bodies otherwise" (xii). For Halberstam, as for many others, the asterisk after "trans" generates room for openness and transitivity: not a transition *to* something fixed or stable, but gender variability in all of its forms, whether identitarian or anti-identitarian.

In this chapter, I bring together practices of media transformation with practices of embodied trans performance in order to understand movement across different platforms and artforms. These practices help to illuminate the relationship between Black gay social movements in past decades and contemporary Black trans expression. I begin by describing a live dance performance entitled *A Meditation on Tongues* by Ni'Ja Whitson. Whitson runs a small dance company in New York, and this work has traveled only a bit. Because such artworks often reach few critics, they become marginalized or ignored in favor of more accessible objects, such as those we can find online. In recounting my experience of the dance performance, I combine my embodied response to the work with publicity and documentation in order to give the fullest account I can offer so that we can see how it questions, mines, and rewrites the works and experiences on which it is based. After describing the performance, I consider some alternative concepts or theories for transformation other than those I cited above, namely, *remediation* and *meditation*. These help me map some remarkable transformations in trans aesthetics, such as a dancing body commenting upon a filmed poet. I close by gesturing to a larger field of art and media that open questions of trans politics.

A Meditation on Tongues

I sit on a gray plastic chair on black wooden risers in a dark flexible theater. A spotlight draws a circle to my right, including part of my shoulder in its bright glow. On the riser just next to me, a dancer named Kirsten Flores-Davis contorts in raw pain, shivering, convulsing, slithering, shuddering. In flexible camouflage pants with diamond-knit reinforced knees, bare feet, a striped cotton tank top, a sports bra, with closely cropped hair, Flores-Davis is so close to me that I can feel their breath, smell their sweat, and it seems to go on forever.[2] As this movement finally comes to an end, the dancer reaches to the audience member one row above me, behind me, to help them rise, hand in hand, breath by breath. We all release, although I can't help but feel that my body, in its sheer proximity to the performer, has been especially implicated in this pain, this performance of suffering. I am on the verge of tears.

This is but one moment in *A Meditation on Tongues*, an extraordinary piece by the NWA Project, a collaboration between artist Ni'Ja Whitson and Flores-Davis. In promotional materials, they describe the performance this way:

> Part abstract, part performance ritual, part live and historical document, this rigorously layered interdisciplinary project (re)images Black and Queer masculinities. It struts. It snaps. It frames new questions about loss at the height of the AIDS pandemic, while challenging constructions of Black love of/as revolution. A bold deconstruction of Riggs' collectivist aesthetics and a raw invocation that shape shifts gender, sexuality, and the body, *A Meditation on Tongues*, remixes historic and embodied invisibilities, spilling between the spaces of mourning and celebration.

The performance is a remediation of Marlon Riggs's groundbreaking film *Tongues Untied*, an experimental documentary from 1989 that depicted the experiences of Black gay men. In this opening section, I read *A Meditation on Tongues* as a way to frame new questions and new media aesthetics around Black and queer masculinities. In its program notes, the NWA Project describes the performance as asking "what an investigation into Black masculinity for gender nonconforming people, women, and trans-identified people brings up." It offers a way in but not an end point. It serves as a provocation that helps me think about what matters and what feels urgent in our fragmented mediascape.

The piece begins before the audience enters the theatre. Performer and dancer Leggoh LaBeija (from the ballroom scene's legendary House of LaBeija) welcomes the audience to a lobby space with spoken word and recorded musical numbers before voguing through the gathered throng. Here, too, the audience feels intimate with the performer, stepping aside to make room for LaBeija's floorwork and receiving the gestures thrown by LaBeija's hands. (On the night I was there, LaBeija's wig accidentally fell off, and, weirdly, an audience member put it back on their head, so implicated did s/he apparently feel in pulling off the performance.) In this brief prelude to *A Meditation*, the audience encounters both a history of performance and a history of transgender—from the Harlem balls by what were then called drag queens in the 1960s to the modern dance form of vogue practiced by multiply gendered folks in the ballroom scene starting in the 1980s profiled in films like Jenny Livingston's *Paris Is Burning* (1992) and Sara Jordenö's *Kiki* (2016).

In the second movement of *A Meditation*, the audience follows La-Beija's instructions and LED lightlines along hallways to enter a "bus," a narrow corridor where they are met by Whitson and Flores-Davis. They perform a story, which might be understood variously as a duet or as a spoken word performance, about a bus ride on the S2 in Washington, DC, in which a rider overhears a conversation between two queens in the back seat, volleying about who is whose "bitch." It's funny and poignant. Whatever one calls it, however, this is pedagogy: Whitson and Flores-Davis offer a primer on snaps, on throwing shade, and on the right of marginal people like these bus riders to define *themselves* as carefully and systematically as anyone else. Getting off the "bus" into the theatre and entering a more somber and structured space of performance, the audience passes a shrine lit with candles, featuring photographs of queer icons like Riggs and Essex Hemphill (whose poetry is featured in *Tongues Untied*), alongside Audre Lorde and other queer ancestors, many of whom died young from AIDS but also from cancer and other ravages.

I understand these two movements preceding the main performance of *A Meditation on Tongues* as a rigorous map of trans politics that enacts at the very least four significant transformations. First, Leggoh La-Beija secures an unbreakable link between art and popular culture. The ballroom scene, its kinship and movement traditions, becomes not just connected but essential to what feels like a contemporary dance performance at home in the art and academic worlds, with technique familiar to trained dancers from a range of styles. In the production of *A Meditation*, a respect for what the voguing world calls "effect," the whole ensemble of handmade costumes and accessories that undergird performances such as those that coalesce in LaBeija's appearance in this prelude, likewise collides with a precisely executed lighting design and elaborate series of lighting and video cues that indexes the world of contemporary art. This may be part of what the NWA Project description alludes to as interdisciplinarity, as it reaches from different sites, scenes, and traditions. I address it as fundamental to remediation.

Second, the passage through the "bus" establishes a different relationship to identity than that elaborated in Riggs's film, as much as the performance pays homage to Riggs and to the strong claims for voices against silence that the 1989 film gave us as its gift. Whitson and Flores-Davis locate political speech and its legacies in everyday public spaces and actions rather than (or maybe in addition to) the realm of poetry, and they offer a lesson in recognizing that speech as it emanates from social actors who may remain fluidly understood in terms of gender, race, and sexuality, even as they lay claim to agency. On the one hand, to put it more baldly, Whitson and Flores-Davis find their genealogy in Black queens throwing shade through snaps; on the other, they refuse to delimit the field of what concerns them in this piece as "Black gay identity," a label that seemed appropriate to Riggs's film and its moment. The category that feels under the most pressure here is, in fact, "men." The subtitle of *Tongues Untied*, after all, is *Giving a Voice to Black Gay Men*, and in the opening montage, under the layered and memorable refrain of "brother to brother," you can see only recognizably Black men. This is in contradistinction to what I would say is the queerer imagery of Isaac Julien's more impressionistic film, *This Is Not an AIDS Advertisement*, made only a year before Riggs's film. There is something wild and exciting about opening this archive and genealogy to the category of "woman," a gesture I'll address in the next section more explicitly.

Third, this sense of a destabilized and inclusive trans project finds articulation in the shrine, which makes absolutely clear the indebtedness of NWA's vision to African and diasporic ritual and resistance. While few of the audience members with whom I saw the piece at my university knew Riggs's film (although some knew *of* it), they nonetheless all began their journey into the heart of the performance as mourners invited into a collective experience. And while aspects of the performers' subsequent movement indexed loss and grief around AIDS, these affects were summoned mostly by the projections of Riggs's film and other images that screened behind or below (on the theater floor) Whitson and Flores-Davis. Although it is difficult to translate abstract movements and utterances (many of which were sounds rather than words) into ritual narrative, it seemed to me that the ritual vectors exceeded mourning to encompass more inchoate but no less palpable experiences of pain, suffering, invisibility, desire, and power. These were not yoked *only* to Black gay men, but they were grounded and articulated by the performers' homage to those who came before us through images in the film and through a Black queer aesthetic forged in the present of the performance.

That these experiences are marked as Black and queer returns us, finally, to the centrality and capacity of bodies in this performance. If *Tongues Untied* fused speech with the visibility of Black gay bodies, this performance uses live queer bodies as vessels and vectors for remediation. While Whitson and Flores-Davis recite some of Riggs's and Hemphill's poetry from *Tongues Untied*, including fragments of the "brother to brother" opening poem from the film, the citationality of their performance raises questions. When they become the speaking subject, the "I" of the poems, they become the "Black gay man" of that speech; in their expressiveness and embodiment, however, they are trans, queer, or nonbinary, so that they both perform *as* Black gay men and refuse the boundaries of that descriptor in their embodied performance presentation. Likewise, as the performers depart from the language of the film into something more like pure presence, often in silence, they realign the political project of the film into the present space and audience, asking those who are gathered together to cross boundaries of identity and affiliation *in the very moment of performance*. In the immediacy of their embodiment, as I describe in my opening account of my experience, the performers solicit affective responses through the endurance and performance of pain as well as joy, and these affects fuse with the political and aesthetic history of struggle and resistance that takes place in the re-screening of Riggs's film. When the performance concludes with a long clip from *Tongues Untied*, the audience ritually exits past the shrine again, a repetition with the significant difference of having lived the past hour together with Whitson and Flores-Davis.

Remediation as Inheritance and Transformation

Aside from wanting to honor one of the most powerful artistic works I've seen in years, I begin with *A Meditation on Tongues* in order to emphasize remediation as a process of inheritance and transformation. The term "remediation" comes from Jay David Bolter and Richard Grusin's (2000) book called *Remediation: Understanding New Media*, in which they argue that the current digital media environment evidences a double or contradictory logic whereby we want to multiply our media, toward hypermediacy, where we are acutely aware of the medium. Yet at the same time, we are moving toward immediacy, where we want to erase all traces of mediation. I share their interest in historical affiliations and resonances rather than origins, in a kind of Foucauldian genealogy that traces how knowledge was constituted through contradictions and interworkings of power. If we understand the long histories of remediation, what Jane Feuer (1983) elsewhere called the "ideology of liveness," we can then better situate so-called "new media" in relation to old ones. While Bolter and Grusin acknowledge the importance of context, so that remediation is neither an ahistorical nor a universal process, their archive is so resolutely Western and white that it is difficult to imagine how they would make sense of the remediation of African rituals, AIDS work, therapeutic dance, voguing, Black trans embodiment, and cinema that I have just described. Nevertheless, their account helps me to think of remediation as a necessary aspect of all mediation, not as a linear march of progress, say from analog video to mixed media performance or back again, but as an entangled and contradictory process. Why is this useful? It helps in the very specific context of trans media to remember the dead, to enliven the complexity of the living moment, to counter youthful orthodoxy and claims to novelty, and to enrich a sense of form.

Remembering the dead is not a simple act of ritual revivification but a complicated forging of genealogy and belonging. Queers live in chosen families, often claimed through complex disavowals of families of origin, by which I mean simply that it's not easy to give up on the pain or the attachment to pain that brings many queers to kin. Where I have been admiring the NWA Project's capacity to make boundaries porous, I have appreciated the ways their performance brings forward the unknown and risky lurking within the present—a present understood as an overdetermined space of liveness and a liturgy and record of loss addressing their implications. Together this brings forth what I am calling remediation. Through it, the NWA Project establishes its ancestors, its kin, its political inheritance, and its future.

As I've said, the NWA Project explicitly remediates Marlon Riggs's film *Tongues Untied*, a film that deserves some further exploration in order to see how it becomes a vehicle for Black trans expression. Riggs's film might be best understood as an experimental documentary, one that blends Riggs's own account of his experience as a Black gay man with the recitation of poetry, footage of stereotypes of Black gay life (including a homophobic comedy routine by Eddie Murphy), and images drawn from the civil rights movement. Using these sources, Riggs shows how queer communities are nonetheless crucibles for complex forms of racism whereby Black gay voices are excluded but Black gay bodies are sexualized for white consumption. He also ties his crushing account of the loss of his friends due to HIV/AIDS (from which Riggs himself eventually died in 1994) to Black historical records of loss.

Tongues Untied is acutely aware of Black gay men's bodies. Riggs combines spoken word vignettes with highly stylized bodies in performance and in gesture in order to explore the range of Black gay identities. In settling upon his own personal story as the central element of the film, Riggs performed what he describes as a catharsis, expunging the pent-up rage he felt as a young man exposed to vicious racist and homophobic slurs. In this sense, he puts his body at the core of the film to promote a positive identity for Black gay men. His camera lovingly admires other Black gay bodies, too, as it brings Riggs into conversation with the poet Essex Hemphill and writer/activist/poet Joseph Beam.

Through its altar and mourning rituals, the NWA Project pays homage to Riggs, Hemphill, and Beam: three beautiful Black gay men who died from AIDS. And yet *A Meditation on Tongues* also raises questions about the positive Black gay identity that Riggs advances in his documentary. Thirty years after the film's release in 1989, NWA asks what role *Tongues Untied* can play in a Black trans* archive of experience and embodiment. In particular, *A Meditation on Tongues* explores how different forms of art remediate trans aesthetics so that the category of "gay male" is no longer at the center of inquiry and so that nonbinary gender codes persist through performance. Using different terms but very much in the same spirit, Eliza Steinbock (2019) describes this process as reclamation rather than remediation: "transgender studies reclaims space from gay and lesbian studies that often co-opts representations of gender variance (e.g., tomboy and sissy) into discrete categories of sexual identity" (19). Through the dancers' expressive resources—including gesture, voice, choreography, and proximity to the audience—this reclamation fuses and complicates discrete genders and sexualities in order to produce a new assemblage of trans*.

Readers attuned to the queer valences of this process may also hear echoes of Eve Kosofsky Sedgwick's idea of reparation in remediation, from her richly influential 2003 essay "Paranoid Reading and Reparative Reading, or, You're So Paranoid You Probably Think This Essay Is about You." I don't see reparation as synonymous with remediation. As Heather Love (2010) has noted, the keywords associated with the reparative align with the affective and ethical field I've been nudging against and convey a largely positive charge: "*multiplicity, surprise, rich divergence, consolation, creativity,* and *love*" (238). Associated with the paranoid position (mastery, one-upmanship, critical distance, and aggression) are more negative terms: "*rigid, grim, single-minded, self-defeating, circular, reductive, hypervigilant, scouringly thorough, contemptuous, sneering, risk-averse, cruel, monopolistic,* and *terrible*" (238). Of course the appeal is to land on the side of love! But if Sedgwick's essay through Love's reading helps us to think about the ways negativity and aggression are nonetheless not only at the heart of psychic life but resources in the worldmaking activity that is, for her, reading literature, then *both* the reparative and paranoid positions inhabit us, haunt us, call us, structure us. And yet, as much as the queer theory inspired by Sedgwick and Love wants to propose nuanced, attenuated, deidealized, and resourceful stagings of critical investments and reading practices, they remain for me at some distance from trans remediation's popular, everyday, ritualistic, embodied reprocessing of art and identity.

Black Gay Histories

Popular, everyday, ritualistic, embodied: these terms return us to the opening of *A Meditation on Tongues*, the voguing performance by Leg-goh LaBeija. The past several years have witnessed a resurgence of inquiry into the history of New York's ball culture, through films that trace the lives of activist artist ancestors. In addition to *Kiki* (Sara Jor-denö 2016), an American-Swedish co-production mentioned above, the films *The Death and Life of Marsha P. Johnson* (David France 2017) and *Happy Birthday Marsha!* (Tourmaline and Sasha Wortzel 2018) revisit AIDS and early queer politics before trans identity and trans activists of color were abandoned in favor of a white politics of respectability. In their homages to Marsha P. (which stands for "pay it no mind") Johnson and Sylvia Rivera, we witness remediated history.

If we excavate that history in the spirit of the NWA Project, we find that it begins in a snippet of film that precedes Marlon Riggs by decades: a 1968 documentary film called *The Queen*, directed by Frank Simon and narrated by Jack Doroshow, a.k.a. Flawless Sabrina. It follows the competition of the 1967 Miss All-America Camp Beauty Contest, a drag queen contest at whose core are three contestants: Miss Sabrina (our narrator), Miss Crystal (of the House of LaBeija) and Miss Harlow, who eventually is crowned the winner. In a moment near the end of the film, we witness Crystal's eruption over the supposition that the contest was rigged in favor of the white contestant Harlow. "I have a right to show my color, darling," asserts Crystal. "I am beautiful, and I *know* I'm beautiful."

In the following years of the 1970s, Crystal extends this affirmation into the building of an institution, the House of LaBeija. In ball culture, a house becomes a gathering of kin (presided over by a mother and father), a specifically queer space for young people seeking support, shelter, mentorship, and even medical care. The House of LaBeija (like the later creations the House of Xtravaganza, the House of Pendavis, and the House of Ninja) was created to combat the racism Crystal experienced in ball competitions and to showcase trans of color style and accomplishment. It is this history that Jennie Livingston documents in her 1991 film *Paris Is Burning* and that more recent films seek to include explicitly as part of a trans archive or trans inheritance.

Paris Is Burning left a trail of controversy, with some alleging that Livingston's gaze on the ball culture was voyeuristic and anthropological. Structural racism and white privilege within the trans and LGBTQ activist communities ensured that the film was often shown in contexts that were divorced from the realities of their trans/queer/people of color subjects. And trans people of color continue to be subjected to violence and murdered at alarming rates. At the same time, ball culture flourishes and nurtures new forms of queer culture, most notably the enormously popular television show *RuPaul's Drag Race*. Frank Ocean celebrates the House of LaBeija by sampling Crystal's voice in "Ambience 001" on his video album *Endless*, and Jill Soloway remixes Crystal's image into the opening credits to her television series *Transparent*.

The politics of opening *A Meditation on Tongues* with Leggoh LaBeija now become more apparent. The voguing performance cements the ties between this piece and the histories of trans defiance of anti-racist kin-building that have sustained trans communities even in the most dire times. It announces links between high cultural dance and popular practices. It remembers all of the LaBeija ancestors, all of those bodies who died from HIV/AIDS, and allows us to mourn together as a broader trans/queer/POC formation. Through embodied performance and recorded sounds and images, Leggoh LaBeija remediates representations that took shape in the 1960s and asks the children of the new century to watch out: trans* is beautiful and we *know* we are beautiful.

PART III

Digitizing Race

11

Intersectional Distribution

AYMAR JEAN CHRISTIAN

Internet television | distribution | intersectionality

Is the Internet revolutionizing TV? Or is it like twentieth-century "leg-acy" TV, dominated by corporations that will continue to lag in cultural innovation? The Internet allows producers to develop and release TV programming at almost any budget, lowering barriers to entry and let-ting new, independent voices speak their stories to potentially massive audiences. TV is not just a technology, it is an interconnected system that adjust to cultural shifts. This chapter shows how the Internet has opened opportunities to disrupt the TV system through diversity and innovation, but how tech companies are failing to catch up. Despite modest interest in cultural representation, "Internet TV" looks a lot like broadcast and cable. Yet if we look at independent, digital producers *and* distributors (channels), we can see hope for change.

The roots of this potential for change began in 2000 when the United States saw a TV boom following the introduction of new distribution technologies: the Internet and cable. In media, distribution is power. Distributors, or channels and networks, secure financing (advertising or subscription), "pick up" shows (productions), and release them to audiences. Television distribution of original narrative series used to be limited to three heavily regulated networks—ABC, CBS, and NBC. Throughout the 1970s and 1980s, TV was deregulated alongside the in-troduction of cable and loosening of program and channel ownership rules. One of the results was more channels distributing TV to more specific audiences (e.g., CNN for news, Lifetime for women, BET/UPN for Black people, MTV for youth). The number of programs and the cultural specificity therein exploded in the so-called "post-network" or "networked" era. By the time the Internet saturated the U.S. market, cable channels had accumulated enough wealth from subscribers and advertisers to make big-budget, high-quality narrative series. By 2012, the Internet distributors had done the same. Distributors from Netflix to Amazon started to buy up projects left and right, committing to hundreds of hours of programming every year. Feeling the heat of competition, researchers at the channel FX tracked the peak TV trend and counted 487 series in 2017—a record high, more than twice the 182 shows distributed in 2002 (Otterson 2018). Streaming services accounted for most of the increase from 2012 to 2017, increasing their buys sixfold, from 15 to 117.

Yet as tech companies move into the TV world, we still see a failure to remedy diversity problems. They continue to overlook great talent among those who have been historically excluded from Hollywood. Consider YouTube, the most popular online video site for many years after its debut in 2005. In 2017 YouTube's chief business officer, Robert Kyncl, said that he lamented what had happened with Issa Rae, a Black female creator who had risen to fame on YouTube through her show *Awkward Black Girl*. Rae's next project, *Insecure*, was picked up by HBO rather than YouTube Red, the company's premium subscription network for big-budget TV. Kycl said, "Literally, if her life cycle was shifted by three years, if she came through and pitched us the show and her success on YouTube, we'd be like, Yes! Done! Makes total sense. . . . There's just nothing that would stop us from doing it." Yet this is disingenuous, as YouTube has consistently failed to develop its own talented creators.

Indeed, there are many YouTube creators aside from Issa Rae who have broken into mainstream film and TV since 2007, when more people started taking the platform seriously. YouTube was not interested in developing any of them. This list includes Abbi Jacobson and Ilana Glazer (*Broad City*), Hannah Hart, Franchesca Ramsey, Grace Helbig, Todrick Hall, Rhett James McLaughlin, Charles Lincoln Neal III, and Lucas Cruikshank (*Fred*), Felicia Day, Trixie Mattel, and Katya Zamolodchikova (*Unhhhh*), Jen Richards and Laura Zak (*Her Story*), and Cecile Emeke (*Ackee & Saltfish*). These are just a few of the creators who have gone on to make bigger-budget, long-format shows and films or achieve mainstream acclaim. Several other creators who initially published their shows on Vimeo and later published on YouTube—including Adam Goldman (*The Outs*), Ingrid Jungermann (*F to 7th*), and Sam Bailey and

Fatimah Asghar (*Brown Girls*)—all landed bigger development deals on other web TV and legacy channels. All of these are missed opportunities. If YouTube Red's programming slate included these stars, it could be positioned next to Netflix as a leading innovator in TV development for its ability to advance cultural knowledge.

The Marginalization of Intersectional Talent

It is not surprising that most of these creators are "intersectional," meaning they identify with multiple communities marginalized by their race, class, gender, sexuality, ethnicity, religion, disability, or citizenship status. The framework of intersectionality was developed throughout the twentieth century by Black feminist and women of color writers such as Sojourner Truth, Audre Lorde, the Combahee River Collective, Kimberlé Crenshaw, Patricia Hill Collins, and many others to describe the interlocking nature of oppression and the specificity of being both Black and woman (and often queer). As Audre Lorde (1984) writes, "Ignoring the differences of race between women and the implications of those differences presents the most serious threat to the mobilization of women's joint power" (117). Marginalized by feminist and sexual justice movements for their race and by racial justice movements for their gender, intersectional writers could not deny the ways oppression—but also strength and innovation—is interconnected. Intersectionality has tremendous value in helping us understand how to represent specific experiences across individual, interpersonal, and institutional contexts.

YouTube has consistently failed to value the work of women, LGBTQ people, and people of color because their subscriber numbers tend to be lower. Yet this is in part because YouTube inconsistently promotes them.[1] For years, many in the industry excused YouTube's inconsistent development of its own talent because the platform was not making money. It was not until the mid-2010s that YouTube became profitable. In 2018 it was valued at upwards of $70 billion, and Google bought it for $1.6 billion in 2006. I argue that the platform could have reached that valuation faster, and might be even more valuable now, had Alphabet (the parent company of Google) invested earlier and taken more risks.

Instead, YouTube made decisions that led to exclusivity, rather than support for its creators. In 2012, as Netflix acquired *House of Cards* by shelling out $100 million to beat out HBO for the series, YouTube was spending roughly the same amount of money. Yet this money was not being spent on homegrown creators. Rather, it spent money across more than a hundred channels, most of which were mainstream media corporations and celebrities without a demonstrated track record of getting consistent online attention or telling interesting stories. In the wake of the platform's disregard for its own talent, multichannel networks (MCNs) stepped in, signing up hundreds and sometimes tens of thousands of creators to give YouTube better targeting and monetization tools, representation in Hollywood and with brands, and occasional investments in original production. Investor interest in MCNs skyrocketed, eventually reaching the many billions Google had invested in YouTube itself. But creators had a number of complaints with MCNs, most notably that the networks invested only in the top 2–5 percent of its creators, leaving everyone else with minimal support. YouTube's subsequent development plans involved relying almost entirely on quantitative data to decide which channels were worthy of investment and preference in marketing. The company gave the top 5 percent of channels in each category preferential treatment in representation on its advertising networks and algorithms.

This quantitative perspective on cultural development replicates legacy media's desire for "mass audiences." It limits the value of specific ("niche") experiences and misses the cultural value of narrative series for branding a channel. Every channel needs at least one "hit" series or franchise with fan bases across communities, but series are valuable to networks beyond their popularity. Channels develop series to get attention from specific, passionate communities, critics, and the industry as well. For instance, HBO developed *Girls* for six seasons despite it never being particularly popular. The same is true with FX for *Louie* and NBC for *Community*. These series attracted fan dedication and made the networks culturally relevant, thereby inviting other viewers who weren't necessarily fans of those shows to remember to check out what the channel was offering.

The other tech companies who have pledged billions in original TV programming, including Amazon, Apple, and Facebook, should take notice. They have all gone into TV development by hiring mainstream media or corporate development executives and hoping that algorithms and scale will make them relevant. But the lesson of YouTube is that algorithmic targeting and scale are not enough to make a platform stand out. Automating development organization through technology will only get them so far. If they are trying to "brand" their platform and give it an identity, they must first consider the identities of the people they invest in. They should consider their ability to tell complex, longer stories and not only their ability to get lots of views and comments—as well as consider the strengths of intersectional producers.

Indie Channels Forge New Paths to TV

While there are more TV shows than ever before, there has not been a rapid rise in diversity in television. Most channels use diversity to gain attention for their new original programming slates but find sustainable development a challenge. In the 1990s Black TV shows rapidly rose and fell on broadcast channels, which developed those shows to secure new audiences as cable siphoned away White viewers who could afford to pay for TV (H. Gray 1995). Cable picked up the slack in the late 1990s and early 2000s: HBO kicked off its ambitious programming with *Oz*, Showtime with *Soul Food* and *Resurrection Boulevard*, then *Queer as Folk* and *The L Word*, Logo with *Noah's Arc*, and so on (Fuller 2010). Diversity also helps revive stale program slates, like when *Chappelle's Show* reinvigorated Comedy Central or *Empire* and *Scandal* brought new life to stale old broadcast networks FOX and ABC. New TV platforms have caught on to the trend, with Netflix's greenlighting the queer *House of Cards* and intersectional *Orange Is the New Black*, Amazon with *Transparent*, Facebook with *Quinta vs. Everything* and *Loosely Exactly Nicole*.

Series creators take risks by helping channels brand themselves and diversify, as corporations quickly lose interest when the money comes in (or does not come in fast enough). The cancellations of *Sense8* and *The Get Down* by Netflix, *Underground* by WGN and Amazon's queer/feminist comedies *One Mississippi* and *I Love Dick* sent shock waves through diverse communities of TV fans (Adalian 2018). After years of demanding greater representation of queer people, women, and people of color in expensive dramas, fans were shocked to learn that the competitive TV environment was making networks risk-averse. Research from the Writers Guild of America and the University of Southern

California all show representation lagging behind and in front of the camera (Hunt 2016; Smith, Choueiti, and Pieper 2016). Without a solid base of producers, talent, and executives in Hollywood, sustainable development remains a challenge for creators large and small.

Fortunately, indie studios and networks have been creating new distribution opportunities and pipelines for talent. From popular online channels to newer networks and studios, the field is slowly opening for creatives who were historically locked out of the system. Simply put, straight, White, cisgender, middle-class able-bodied characters are everywhere on TV, and audiences looking for those stories have plenty of options. To get fans who are loyal to a channel's brand and stand out from the pack, the channel has to offer something different—and diversity fits the bill.

Signs of tides shifting are everywhere, starting with the success of studios developing intersectional programming—series about folks who share multiple non-normative identities along lines of race, gender, class, sexuality, disability, and so on. Issa Rae has been making waves outside HBO and *Insecure*, continuing to release new programs on her YouTube channel, producing an original queer podcast called *Fruit* with the podcast app Howl, and partnering with Columbia Pictures to bring new writers to Hollywood. There has also been evidence of studio interest in intersectional stories. Former talent agency executive Charles King started a production company called MACRO to create a pipeline for cross-platform multicultural programming. Perhaps more exciting is the presence of small indie networks operating outside the mainstream studios that are focused on helping creators build audiences for shows to speed the process of development by bigger players. Women and people of color working in Hollywood are starting their own channels to bring new writers to development. Director Ava DuVernay started a film collective called ARRAY for Afrodiasporic film. The LGBT film distributor Wolfe Video transitioned from distributing VHS and DVD to creating an online streaming platform called WolfeOnDemand. Comedians Horatio Sanz and Fred Armisen started Más Mejor, a digital comedy studio that focuses on cultivating Latinx voices. Actress Elizabeth Banks started a digital platform for female comedians called WHOHAHA, and actress Erika Alexander started a production company called Color Farm.

Outside the industry's supply chain, channels are often more explicitly intersectional. Not content to wait for production funds from corporate-backed networks and celebrities, indie entrepreneurs are starting their own channels and winning over subscribers with programs they can't get consistently on bigger platforms. Black&Sexy TV was among the first. An outgrowth of Dennis Dortch's debut feature *A Good Day to Be Black and Sexy*, the channel was one of the biggest subscription channels on Vimeo's OTT ("over the top") platform, which creates an app for channels across connected TV devices. Black&Sexy consistently put out new programs, many of them with twenty-minute episodes and with characters who show up across different series. SLAY TV launched, courting queer and trans viewers with new and existing series. Joining SLAY are Revry TV, which has been doggedly working to produce and license diverse LGBT programming, along with Dekkoo, Between Women TV, and Tello films.

It remains to be seen whether new indie distributors can stick around. Historically, indie distribution online is much harder than indie production, because fans want access to libraries with syndicated series and movies, which are expensive. Netflix spends billions of dollars on licensing Hollywood movies and TV shows each year to keep its subscribers. Most indie networks can barely cover production of original programming and license series (many of which are already online free) for a cut of revenue or minuscule fees. Moreover, Hollywood historically sees diversity as a "fad," a way to generate buzz and interest in periods of media transition, as scholar Jennifer Fuller has argued. The Black sitcoms from the late 1980s and early 1990s mostly premiered on broadcast networks as White viewers "fled" to cable. Now diversity is back again as networks slowly transition from linear cable to on-demand networked distribution.

Indie Producers Forge New Paths to TV

Another important shift allowed by digital media is that individual producers no longer have to wait for channels and incubators to take notice—they are able to organize their own productions, take them directly to audiences, and even orchestrate a network pickup. To learn more about what it takes to find success through this difficult route, I share the story of Fatimah Asghar and Sam Bailey producing and releasing *Brown Girls*, an intersectional web series.

Some of their insights can be generalized to broadly help underrepresented communities take control over their media. These include: Tell a story that has never been told on TV and make sure it reads as sincere to the people represented and cuts across identities. Represent community in front and behind the camera. Treat production, writing, directing, design, and music as crafts in conversation with the everyday lives and artistry of the communities you're representing. Keep fans updated on social media from production through release. Solicit coverage in publications relevant to that community. Premiere in the city or cities where there is demand to see your story and plan to engage viewers on social media by watching the story with them in real life.

Yet there is also much to be learned from the specifics of their story and the decisions these two women made each step of the way. After premiering on February 15, 2017, on *Elle* magazine's website and in over a dozen cities worldwide amid a torrent of advance press, *Brown Girls* was sold to HBO in one of the fastest acquisitions I had seen in ten years researching web TV. It proved how developing artists at small-scale can position them for big-scale development. OTV | Open Television, an intersectional platform I started in Chicago, helped Sam develop two seasons of her first series, the Gotham Award-nominated *You're So Talented*, contributing production funds through non-exclusive licensing (allowing Sam to keep her intellectual property), organizing screenings in Chicago, and assisting with online marketing. As Sam grew into her position as a director, producer, and marketer of her work in Chicago and online, she was able to put these skills to great use with *Brown Girls*. They didn't need much of my help. The *Brown Girls* sale is clear evidence of the power of telling diverse stories in a "peak TV" market. Most of the work of indie production is hidden, as Stuart Cunningham (2013) writes of cultural innovation generally. Intersectionality makes this work even more difficult to know. This is how they did it.

Financing and Pre-Production

Fatimah invited me and Sam to a reading of the script in early 2016. I could instantly hear how Fatimah's natural, humorous, and crisp dialogue would translate beautifully on-screen. With Sam in the room as a potential director, I knew that the series would be gorgeous. Already I could see Fatimah making a crucial decision that eventually helped the show when it was released: all characters with speaking roles had to be people of color. There are so many great actors who rarely have the chance to play complex characters, and the series would showcase them in an act of solidarity with communities who have been excluded from Hollywood. A number of media outlets picked up on this and it became a selling point of the show.

Financing is always a challenge, but they used every available resource in their cities. *Brown Girls* was primarily funded by a grant from the Voqal Fund, which is administered by Chicago Filmmakers and specifically supports digital work made in Chicago. The team crowdfunded almost all the rest of the budget, with OTV offering minor financial support.

Production

Another selling point was that most of the crew were women, queer, or POC-identified. When *NowThis Her* covered *Brown Girls* right before its release, it mentioned this fact, and the video was seen over 2 million times on Facebook ("New Web Series" 2016). Sam has spoken extensively about how behind-the-camera diversity actually improves the artistry of what is being made, not only because there are tons of talented crew but also because it can help bring out great performances. As Sam told *Okayplayer*, "To the best of my ability, I try to make sure the people in my production crew mirror the story they're helping to tell in front of the camera. . . . I wanted the actors to feel like they were entering a safe space to tell this story without being exoticised or judged" (K. Clark 2016). Because of this, they emphasize the importance of getting the word out about production before and during shooting. *Brown Girls* had just a temporary title card before shooting, but armed with this and a strong pitch, they were able to crowdfund for the remainder of the budget. Crowdfunding is never easy, but it allows producers to identify key supporters and fans before the release.

During production, Sam and the team worked to create a distinct world. They shot in Pilsen, a predominantly brown though rapidly gentrifying neighborhood in Chicago. The wardrobe, from Vincent Martell of VAM, and production design, from Suzannah Linnekin, specifically and artfully represented the complex lives and worlds of the two leads.

Post-Production

The music of *Brown Girls* is intimately tied to the story and the artistry and narratives of women of color. The central friendship is loosely based on that of Fatimah and Jamila Woods, a Chicago-based poet and singer whose album *Heavn* comprises the bulk of the soundtrack. Jamila's stunning album, named one of NPR's fifty best albums of 2016, serves as the perfect score as it is rooted in Black feminism. For the trailer, which dropped in the fall of 2016, Jamila collaborated with Indian artist Lisa Mishra for an original theme song that perfectly reflects the bond between Black and brown women that is the core of the story. Indeed, the team knew in pre-production that they would be able to add Jamila's music in post-production, allowing the show to feel integrated.

Marketing and Exhibition

When the team released the trailer, they reached out to writers from publications specifically focused on brown people and women. From those few articles in outlets like Black Nerd Problems, Role Reboot (a feminist site), and Remezcla (a Latinx site), the mainstream press started to pick it up. *Brown Girls* eventually gained coverage from over fifty publications, including *Time* and the *Guardian*. Filmmakers always seek mainstream press, but after seeing where the views were coming from, I can say that targeted press is helpful in many ways. Sites like Remezcla, as well as queer publications like *Out* magazine and *Autostraddle*, drove more traffic than bigger sites like Vice and NBC.

Indie creators innovate in how they handle press. OTV has had a lot of success coordinating exclusive premieres with various sites, where trailers and episodes are viewable only on specific websites for a limited time. With so much competition for attention online, media outlets want exclusive content, and indie creators need viewers who come from their communities. *Brown Girls* premiered a scene from one episode exclusively with *Out* magazine, and premiered the first episode exclusively on *Elle* magazine's website. After releasing the trailer, Fatimah also reached out to her personal network and asked friends to help spread the word. The result was that artists hosted screenings in sixteen towns and cities internationally on the night of its release—including premieres in New York, Los Angeles, Atlanta, Seattle, Rincón, and London. *Brown Girls* premieres showcased the talents of brown women, with artists across disciplines of dance, comedy, and music performing and attracting crowds. The premieres also featured local vendors who were women of color selling jewelry and T-shirts.

The premieres helped #BrownGirlsTV soar to the number two trending Twitter hashtag in Chicago on the night of its release, beat out only by tweets about the TV show *Star* on FOX. The creative team asked a couple of friends to live-tweet the day of the premiere, notably poet and University of Chicago professor Eve Ewing. Recruiting fans who were already known among the communities being represented to talk about the show the day of its release was key, but many of the tweets for *Brown Girls* also came from everyday fans who connected with key moments in the show and expressed their enthusiasm by posting GIFs and pics.

Conclusion: Measuring Success in Intersectional Storytelling

While all of this was happening, Sam and Fatimah were taking meetings in Hollywood. As we can see from their story, their success can be connected to a number of factors. First and foremost, I credit their success to their incredible talent and artistry, but it was also clear that they very intentionally worked to serve communities that are underrepresented. In a "peak TV" environment where hundreds of TV series are being released every year by major corporate networks, serving the underserved is a viable strategy for calling attention to these works. It is also a critical practice at a time when so many communities with intersecting struggles are fighting for their legitimacy and right to exist.

Their story helps us to see what can happen when filmmakers and creative people—whatever their race, gender, sexuality, class, citizenship status, or ability—support one another. It truly takes multiple communities to advance the art and business of TV. We need new stories from new writers who have been excluded, and media industries desperately need to diversify intellectual properties by investing in new writers. Diversity programs are one way to prevent complete exclusion, but only pipelines with funding can help television distributors survive the competitive TV landscape. In an ever-diversifying America, this is a smart move not only for achieving long-term success, but also for combating our hate-filled political climate.

12

Podcasting Blackness

SARAH FLORINI

podcasting | technological affordances | social enclaves | sonic media

Technological devices, software, and platforms are often conceived of as static and unified objects of study. Designers intend certain uses when they create a device or platform, and they deliberately craft it accordingly, producing a set of materialities and functionalities that facilitate those uses. But users are creative and unpredictable. They often perceive and use the features of technology in unintended ways, not only changing the uses of technology, but also transforming their very nature (Miller and Slater 2000). Hardware, software, content, user practices, and interpretations of technology all emerge from complex social processes (Sweeney 2017). Not only can technologies be used to create and circulate culturally specific content and achieve diverse communicative outcomes, but core conceptions of what a given technology *is* and what it should be used for are deeply shaped by culture.

This chapter examines this process through an analysis of an informally networked group of independent Black podcasters. I begin by explicating the term "affordances," providing a theoretical framework for thinking through how user practices shape technology. Then, after a brief description of the podcasts analyzed here, I argue that this network of independent Black podcasters uses podcasting and social media in culturally specific ways to transform what is normatively considered mass media into a space for enclaved Black sociality. Finally, I outline how they employ the mobile technologies of headphones to produce a sonic recreation of Black social enclaves on-demand.

The Social Construction of Affordances

The term "affordances," which has become commonplace in the study of digital technologies, refers to the set of characteristics that enable and constrain particular behaviors. It was coined by James Gibson in his book *The Ecological Approach to Visual Perception,* where he explored the affordances that were created through the interaction of animals with their environments. Applying this principle to digital media, the interaction between the user ("the animal") and the technology ("the environment") facilitates or hinders certain ways of using technology. Affordances are not stable characteristics of technologies, but arise in the interaction between users and technology. For example, a visually oriented social media platform like Instagram will have different affordances for a user who is blind than for a user who has sight. The characteristics of each user—in this case, having sight or not—alters the affordances that emerge when each interacts with the platform. Instagram isn't very useful for keeping in touch with friends and family if you can't see the pictures they post. The affordance of visually based social interaction is available to one user, but not another.

Affordances are not just about physical and material characteristics, but are also tied to perception. That is, affordances must be perceived to emerge as affordances (Norman 2013). Peter Nagy and Gina Neff (2015) argue that affordances arise at the intersection "between users' perceptions, attitudes, and expectations; between the materiality and functionality of technologies; and between the intentions and perceptions of designers." They use the term "imagined affordances" to highlight the element of social construction in the production of affordances. Affordances are constituted by the attributes of the technology itself, which were created by designers who made choices based on their particular intentions. But users bring with them their own perceptions, beliefs, and practices, which differ from user to user. While designers shape the materiality and functionality of a given technology, users may bring cultural practices and epistemologies that cause them to *perceive* the technology differently, thereby leading to the emergence of affordances.

Lori Kido Lopez's (2016b) work on Hmong communities in the United States offers a compelling example of this process. She analyzes how Hmong living in the United States have developed what she calls "teleconference radio," the use of conference call software and mobile phones to create radio-style programming. Bringing their own perspectives and expectations, they imagine a different set of affordances and transform technologies designed for one-on-one and small group communication into a broadcast-style format. The materiality and functionality created by the intentions and choices of the designers combine with the cultural practices and perspectives of the Hmong to allow them to access a set of affordances that non-Hmong users might never anticipate.

This dynamic is why many advocate for diverse design teams in technology industries. Designers with different perspectives will likely bring new insights into the design process. Moreover, the tripartite construction of affordances reveals that we cannot think of any given technology as a singular unified object, but should instead think in terms of multiplicity. There is not one Twitter that offers the same affordances to all users. There are many Twitters, offering different affordances to various groups of users.

Independent Black podcasts offer a useful example of how a given group of users can elicit an unintended set of affordances. I focus on a group of Black independent podcasts that are tightly but informally networked together. These podcasts, with a few exceptions, are noncommercial and largely labors of love.[1] The oldest podcasts in this network—including *Insanity Check, The Black Guy Who Tips, Where's My 40 Acres?, Blacking It Up!* (produced by This Week in Blackness)—were started between 2008 and 2010, with the network rapidly expanding between 2012 and 2014. Several of the podcasters have formed podcast networks that offer a variety of shows under one franchise name, which is often the same as the name of their primary podcast. These include This Week in Blackness (TWiB!), The Black Guy Who Tips (TBGWT), Movie Trailer Reviews (MTR), the Cold Slither Podcast Network (CSPN), and the Black Astronauts Podcast Network. All of these Black independent podcasts produce talk-based programming but vary greatly in their production value and the regularity of their output. Due to their irreverent approach and eclectic topics of conversation, many are categorized as comedy by podcatcher services such as iTunes or Stitcher. Some podcasts are ostensibly focused on one topic or theme. For example, *Where's My 40 Acres?* (WM40A?) began as a hip-hop podcast, and *Spawn on Me* and *Gaming and Then Some* cover video games. But it is not uncommon for these podcasts to cover a range of topics, ranging from television to politics to the latest social media dustups.

Podcasts are often thought of as merely radio programming made on-demand for asynchronous listening. Many popular podcasts are National Public Radio (NPR) or Public Radio International (PRI) shows made available for download. But a network of independent and largely noncommercial Black American podcasters has cultivated their podcasts to serve as loci of interaction for a large networked community. After a brief description of these podcasts, I outline how the podcasts utilize Black linguistics and communicative traditions to cultivate digital iterations of Black social spaces that function like the barber/beauty shop or church. Such spaces have long served important social and cultural functions in Black American communities. Combining these communicative traditions with high levels of digital interactivity—between audience and podcasters as well as among the audience—the podcasts allow listeners to become interlocutors in the conversations. Mobile technologies, particularly smartphones and headphones, allow for these sonic simulations of Black sociality to be on-demand anywhere. Many Black listeners use this digital assemblage as they navigate the predominantly white spaces of their workplaces, allowing them to insulate themselves with the sounds of Black sociality in environments in which they feel alienated.

Podcasts and/as Social Networks

The Black independent podcasts I focus on in this study are held together by many forms of informal affiliations. In many ways, this network of podcasts resembles the "horizontal" approach described by Richard Berry (2006) in his work on early podcasting in the early 2000s, where "producers are consumers and consumers become producers and engage in conversations with each other. . . . There is no sense of a hierarchical approach, with podcasters supporting each other, promoting the work of others and explaining how they do what they do." While podcasts have become more popular and more professionalized, these podcasts have retained their communitarian ethos. The podcasters listen to and appear on each other's shows, and they share heavily overlapping audiences. Many of the same people in the chatrooms of various podcasts are leaving reviews and listener feedback for multiple podcasts. Additionally, these podcasters and their audiences are also deeply connected on online platforms such as Twitter, Facebook, Instagram, and Twitch. They combine long-standing communicative practices that have until recently existed primarily in Black social spaces with use of multi-platform channels for audience interaction. In this way, these podcasts simulate an experience of Black sociality, making them markedly different from the predominantly white podcasts.

The interconnectedness of these podcasters and their audiences is in line with what we know about the listening habits of podcast consumers. While the average American consumes roughly four hours of audio per day, podcast listeners consume an average of six hours and six minutes and can be categorized as "super-listeners" (Edison Research 2012). Of weekly podcast listeners, 37 percent consume five or more podcasts a week, with an average consumption of six per week (Edison Research and Triton Digital 2014). However, the podcasters examined here and their audience seem to be not only consuming podcasts at a "super-listener" rate, but also choosing podcasts that are connected in order to build and maintain the network.

Moreover, while legacy radio programs are often tightly formatted, these Black independent podcasts opt for an approach that more closely resembles informal social interactions. They embrace a free-flowing, flexible, and conversational approach, including a wide range of vernaculars. They also employ significant use of phatic communication, interactions that are solely for creating and maintaining social connection rather than conveying information. Though the hosts have topics or news stories they are prepared to cover, they do so via free-form conversation that is generally not limited by time constraints. It is not unusual for shows to be two or three hours long, with hosts moving from topic to topic through organic conversation, rather than predetermined segments. The shows receive little to no editing, presenting the discussions in their entirety. At most, discussions are cut into more than one episode, an approach commonly taken by *WM4oA?* The podcasts embrace a range of Black vernaculars and regional accents. The irreverent, humorous, and conversational nature of the podcasts makes heavy use of Black American cultural commonplaces, thereby marking the space as Black through linguistic practices, communicative norms, and a reliance on cultural competencies.

Another way that Black independent podcasts depart from mainstream conventions is by employing an informal conversational style. One comment left on iTunes by a listener described the discussions on *3 Guys On* using the term "chop it up," a vernacular expression common in Black communities that refers to friendly, informal conversation. Rod from *TBGWT* describes their podcast format by saying that it's "kind of just talkin'. But it's organized talkin'." Often shows depart from the formal introduction that offers listeners the name of the podcast and the names of the hosts. It is not uncommon for *WM4oA?* to get so wrapped up in conversations that they get twenty or thirty minutes into a show before introducing the hosts. Some podcasts never introduce the hosts, leaving listeners to glean their names only through consistent listening.

As a result, it is not uncommon for listeners and podcasters to compare these podcasts to iconic spaces of Black sociality like the barber/beauty shop or the church. For example, one early episode of TWiB!'s *Blacking It Up!* was explicitly titled "Barbershop." Comments left on iTunes by listeners of *TBGWT*, *3 Guys On*, and *The Black Astronauts* reiterate the assertion that the shows are reminiscent of the barbershop. One review for *TBGWT* was even titled, "Barber shop (or beauty shop) talk for you [sic] iPod and MP3 player." One *3 Guys On* review, titled "am i [sic] in the barber shop?!" began, "Cuz that's how i feel when i listen to y'all." Similarly, *What's the Tea?* has been compared in iTunes reviews more than once to going to church. One review says that the hosts, Nic and Reggie, "come together each week to take you to pod church and you would do well to attend service regularly." Another simply states, "They remind me of folks I went to church with and had great conversations with."

The Sound of Black Social Enclaves

Such enclaved social spaces serve important social and cultural functions. Melissa Harris-Lacewell (2004) argues that important ideological work, such as the construction of worldviews and collective identity, happens in everyday talk and interactions occurring in these Black social spaces. Vorris Nunely (2011) demonstrates that such enclaves are crucial to the development and maintenance of Black epistemologies and subjectivities. He describes them as "lifeworlds" where Black political rationality is privileged and where "the unsaid in the public sphere gets said; where the unhearable gets heard; and where the filtering of American and African American culture and life occurs through African American hermeneutics." These camouflaged spaces produce and maintain what Nunely terms African American Hush Harbor Rhetoric (AAHHR), which contains and conveys Black epistemes and rationalities and takes Black experience as normative. This is more than cultural difference and identity; it involves the construction of worldviews and serves as an arena in which to form and maintain Black subjectivities. Thus, he asserts, enclaves and AAHHR do not just challenge mainstream white American perspectives and worldviews politically or socially. They dispute dominant discourses of what it is to be fully human.

Podcasting's commonalities with radio strengthen the medium's ability to convincingly reproduce the feeling of enclaved Black social spaces. Scholars have argued that radio is a deeply intimate medium. Susan Douglas (2004) has pointed out this phenomenon, asserting, "Listening often imparts a sense of emotion stronger than that imparted by looking [because] . . . while sight allows us some distance, . . . sound envelops us, pouring into us whether we want it to or not, including us, involving us" (30). This sense of being immersed in sound allows listeners to feel transported into the conversation they are listening to, feeling as if, as one iTunes review for *Straight Outta LoCash* describes it, they are "chilling with the homies and kicking it and having a good time." With a network of podcasts whose content closely mimics the kinds of conversation that traditionally happens in Black social spaces like the barber/beauty shop or churches, the sound that "envelops" the listeners is that of Black enclaved sociality. The podcasts provide listeners with a downloadable, mobile, sonic recreation of these Black social spaces. While it is not the same as being physically co-present, the podcasts preserve enough of that experience to invoke it in the minds of listeners.

However, these podcasts are not always simply mimicking Black sociality—the digital and social media network in which the podcasts are embedded also creates numerous avenues for listener participation. These Black independent podcasts maintain various combinations of real-time chatrooms accompanying their live streams, a strong social media presence, and multiple avenues for listener feedback, including email, comment sections, and voicemail. Often shows will live-stream during the workday, allowing many listeners working in offices to interact with the show and other listeners in real time. Often comments in the chatrooms or on Twitter are inserted into shows' discussions, allowing listeners channels for synchronous interaction and participation. To varying degrees, these feedback channels, particularly the chatroom, allow the audience members to become interlocutors in the conversations as they unfold on-air. Thus, they are not merely listening to a sonic recreation of Black enclaved sociality, but actively participating in the construction of discourse there.

Mobile Listening as Sonic Enclave

This portable recreation of enclaved Black social spaces is intensified by mobile listening practices, which allow listeners to reproduce a sense of these spaces on-demand wherever they are. This is not the traditional way that we have understood personal listening practices, as there are many ways sound is used to produce a sense of private space (Weheliye 2005). Podcast listeners who wear headphones can create a "sound bubble" around themselves as a means "to claim a mobile and auditory territory for themselves through a form of 'sensory gating'" (Bull 2014, 115). Headphones are often sold as a means of sonic personalization by their manufacturers and used as such by consumers (Hosokawa 1984). Mack Hagood (2011) describes Bose's QuietComfort noise-cancelling headphones as "*soundscaping devices*, carving out an acoustically rendered sense of personal space" (574, emphasis original). Soundscaping offers the normative subject a "sense of physical and psychological space" despite their surroundings.

Yet Black listeners challenge this norm by using their headphones to participate in Black sociality and community formations. Many listeners have reported via feedback channels like iTunes and Stitcher reviews that they listen to these Black independent podcasts while commuting to work and while at work, often listening in their cubicles or offices through the use of headphones. Oftentimes they are one of a few or even the only Black person at their place of employment. Mobile consumption of these podcasts allows these listeners to soundscape their daily lives with sounds of Black sociality. These podcasts let Black listeners take the spaces of enclaved Black social interactions with them and give them the chance to feel insulated by Black enclaved sociality as they navigate the world.

More than simply feeling cocooned in the sounds of Black sociality, such listening aids in the reproduction of Black subjectivity constituted through AAHHR. Nunely (2011) argues that the spaces of AAHHR are "spatialities where Black meanings can be found, where Black folks go to rebaptize themselves in Black culture in ways often unavailable in the public sphere" (156). He argues that Black cultural commonplaces can exude "massive concentrations of Black symbolic energy. This symbolic energy moves African American audiences because it taps deeply into African American terministic screens, experiences, memories, and meaning" (47). Mobile listening allows for this process to become portable and on-demand. Through the use of Black epistemes and discourse, the podcasts produce the listeners' subjectivity in opposition to the dominant racial discourses that work to produce them as racialized and therefore marginalized subjects. They are able to sonically shut out the dominant discourse and cocoon themselves in sonic landscapes that hail them as fully human Black subjects.

Further, these podcast listeners demonstrate how users' cultural practices, expectations, and subject positions interact with the materiality of technology and the designers' perceptions and intentions to shape the imagined affordances of a technology. Such Black podcast listeners are inarguably using the practice of soundscaping to claim an acoustic space and insulate themselves from their surroundings. But their strategy is the inverse of the businessmen who populate Bose's advertisements. Hagood points to the underlying neoliberal logic of the Bose headphones' branding and advertising campaigns, which heavily feature white male business travelers attempting to find respite from the unwanted noise of jet engines, crying children, and women's voices while in transit. He argues that QuietComfort headphones are designed as technologies of individualization built on the neoliberal logic "that problems must be solved individually and within the market rather than addressed as systemic issues" (582). Yet these Black podcast listeners soundscape with the sounds of Black sociality, cultivating not individualism, but collectivity. They do not seek to isolate themselves, but rather to ameliorate their isolation in a white milieu. Their simulated private space is not one of individual privacy, but of the collective private spaces of Black enclaves.

Conclusion

This group of podcasters and their audience use podcasts and their associated technologies in ways that diverge from normative practices. This is because, as Black Americans, they possess a culturally specific set of communication practices and life experiences that allow them to perceive different affordances than the designers intended or that other users might recognize. They imagine different affordances and use technologies to achieve goals that not only differ from but also resist normative uses of the technology. The most common understanding of podcasting is as a mass medium, with many of the most popular podcasts being radio shows that have been made available for mobile asynchronous listening. For this network of Black independent podcasters and their audience, podcasts serve the dual function of mass media content and social interaction. Combining culturally specific modes of communication with a prioritizing of audience interaction, they create a space that recreates historically important modes of Black sociality. Similarly, while headphone makers and many users perceive headphones as a means of producing individualized sonic spaces, the podcast listeners discussed here employ them to insulate themselves in the sounds of Black collective culture.

This network of independent Black podcasters and their audience is not unique in its reimagining of affordances. Such an analysis could focus on any marginalized group or population that has historically had to make do with technologies not intended for them. Attention to the role of user perception and practices in the production of affordances offers insight into the possibilities of technology beyond those currently imagined by engineers. This could provide information about the social and cultural functions of technology, and, if incorporated into the design process, could lead to new and innovative technologies.

13

Black Twitter as Semi-Enclave

RAVEN MARAGH-LLOYD

Black Twitter | semi-enclaves | cultural boundaries

While families across the United States gather around their decorated Thanksgiving tables, a group of users online anticipates the holiday for altogether different reasons. For years, African American users have deployed the hashtag #ThanksgivingClapback to share their own traditions and experiences that often run counter to dominant narratives of family, food, and culture. Among its many functions, Black Twitter interrupts widely held assumptions of a unified social-national experience that African Americans have long had to reimagine for themselves. Created by Twitter user @KashmirVIII in 2015, #ThanksgivingClapback provides a connected way to share hilarious, real-time celebrations of African American family traditions. With their particular cultural insider knowledges, individual users add to a collective that expertly highlights and archives black traditions around food and family, as well as important linguistic traditions regarding language and communication.

By tapping in to the linguistic tradition of "playing the dozens," where African Americans playfully and artfully exchange insults, Black users discursively employ the clapback to real or imagined scenarios at Thanksgiving gatherings: "'Aunt: You know how we hate it when you bring your phone to the table.' 'Me: Funny I was going to say the same thing about your potato salad' #thanksgivingclapback." Tweets such as this one implicitly reference several layers of African American cultures, such as the "know-it-all" auntie and the foods prepared at black Thanksgiving dinners in contrast to the dominant culture.[1] Such references allow Black users to easily commune online through cultural markers as well as display and develop individual and collective self-definitions.

In turn, #ThanksgivingClapback shapes Black Twitter and the users therein who are able to culturally enter, understand, and respond. As one Twitter user summed up, "I be looking forward to the #thanksgivingclapback every year." Moreover, by highlighting African American traditions during Thanksgiving, users in this space do the work of decentering the mainstream ideas that form a dominant (read: white) American experience. In this chapter, I explore the ways #Thanksgiving-Clapback and similar online discourses function to contest cultural appropriation, or the taking and profiting from marginalized bodies and cultures. I argue for the concept of "semi-enclaves" as they allow Black users to maintain their own cultural spaces while also engaging with the mainstream in intentional ways. In the case of #ThanksgivingClapback, I argue that Black users protect against digital iterations of cultural appropriation by crafting culturally specific posts that rely on intertextual understandings of black cultures and linguistic play while also engaging with outsiders by authoring and controlling the narrative of black culture(s) more broadly. Through discourses such as #Thanksgiving-Clapback, Black users decenter interlopers' ability to colonize the space and bodies therein, as well as work to amplify black experiences more broadly. These two seemingly conflicting strategies demonstrate Black publics' long-standing cultural and technical expertise in adopting new technologies toward the goals of protection *and* celebration.

I begin by defining Black Twitter and the ways scholars have understood its contributions. Next, I analyze #ThanksgivingClapback as a semi-enclave and explore instances where Black users protect against iterations of cultural appropriation. I draw from Racquel Gates's (2018) theorizations of negativity to show that Black users strategically deploy stereotypes and "negative" images so as to define and secure the cultural boundaries of Black Twitter. These foundations allow me to argue that online traditions and linguistic practices like #ThanksgivingClapback demonstrate a distinct way that Black users foster culturally discursive skills that center and protect blackness and marginality more broadly.

The Subgenre of Black Twitter

The term "Black Twitter" is used to describe a heterogeneous group of Black users who have self-selected into a culturally discursive subgenre of Twitter. As African Americans and others in the Black diaspora have done for centuries, Black Twitter showcases the need for marginalized people to exist within their own space in order to build and maintain self-defined cultures, often without the mainstream gaze. The disproportionately large number of African American users on Twitter only begins to tell the story of the importance of this subgenre for millions of Black users. In 2017, studies showed that around 69 percent of African Americans used at least one social media site (Pew Research Center 2017). More specifically, 26 percent of Twitter users were Black; in comparison, Whites made up 24 percent and Hispanics 20 percent (Pew Research Center 2018). The technological nuances of Twitter more importantly highlight the untethered relationship between Black publics and technology. First, Black Twitter provides a separate networked space for millions of Black users who self-select into the group based on topics, linguistic strategies, and identifiable cultural markers. Second, Black Twitter showcases the technological dexterity that Black users have wielded to suit their needs and desires, contrary to "digital divide" arguments focusing on deficits. And third, Black Twitter broadens black political and cultural discourse toward the goals of solidarity and justice. These non-exhaustive illustrations not only highlight the important work being done about Black publics and technology, but also foreground my argument about the ways we might think about race, marginality, and technology as strategically protective and celebratory.

Following the way that Catherine Squires (2002) understands the existence of multiple marginal public spheres, Catherine Knight Steele (2016) theorizes the ways that Black publics form separate spaces, or enclaves, that elude the mainstream gaze. Here, Black Twitter functions as a culturally accessible network whereby Black users are able to negotiate political and social identities, such as positions within black feminism. One of the ways these enclaves are able to function is through the deployment of humor, which for marginalized groups has often been toward the goals of social critique (Sharma 2013). I extend these theorizations of enclaved Black publics by proposing a semi-enclave that protects against cultural appropriation and simultaneously engages the mainstream in strategic ways.

Black Twitter also highlights Black users' long-standing ability to assess and reinvent technology toward their own goals. In this vein, André Brock (2016) writes,

> Thanks to Twitter's availability in an Internet-enabled communitarian-device alongside the lowered barrier of adoption, thanks to familiarity with a pre-existing ritual mode of computer-mediated, community-oriented communication, the CTDA analysis used inductive reasoning to argue that Blacks were able to retrofit Twitter's brevity, ephemerality and performativity to signifyin' discourse. (13–14)

Here, Brock argues that Black users "retrofit" the technological affordances of Twitter, such as character limitations, to already existing cultural practices that rely on such brevity. I rely on Brock's argument here to demonstrate that we can analytically understand discourses such as #ThanksgivingClapback beyond a one-dimensional framing of jocular comments about Black families during the Thanksgiving holiday. That is, I argue that Black users tap into long-standing linguistic strategies in order to protect and celebrate Black culture using these particular affordances of Twitter.

The hashtag, for instance, allows users to easily find and join a particular discussion in real time as well as archive important political and social discourses and communities (Bonilla and Rosa 2015). Other affordances such as trending topics make particular discourse communities visible to broader publics. Although Twitter does not make its exact algorithm publicly available, the site's trending topics feature generally highlights the most popular conversations across users (T. Gillespie 2011). Brock (2012) argues that trending topics make Black Twitter visible "as an intervention on 'White public space'" (541). Among other functions, hashtags and trending topics allow Black Twitter users to "look for" each other within the discussion of #ThanksgivingClapback while also interrupting mainstream understandings of holiday traditions more broadly.

Lastly, Black Twitter extends beyond its users to engage with "outsiders" who are also interested in, for example, the advancement of social justice. In their work on the political progress of online hashtags, Deen Freelon, Charlton McIlwain, and Meredith D. Clark (2016b) analyzed and tracked the movement of the hashtag #BlackLivesMatter into the mainstream. They found that this particular social-political movement, which was born online after the shooting of Trayvon Martin in 2012, elicited "elite responses" from politicians and other policy makers as a unique form of activism and engagement online. In a similar vein, Rachel Kuo (2018) demonstrates the individual and collective power of counterpublic movements that were created through hashtags such as #NotYourAsianSideKick and #SolidarityIsForWhiteWomen toward the outward goals of visibility and justice for women of color. These theorizations of Black and marginal publics as they mobilize and interact with outsiders both on- and offline allow us to see how Black Twitter might simultaneously act as an enclave *and* an outward expression of Black cultures and identities.

Inside the Semi-Enclave: Protection from Cultural Appropriation

I define #ThanksgivingClapback and similar discourses as a semienclave to signal both the outward-facing possibilities and the private practices that Black users engage in online. In building on Catherine Squires's (2002) theorization of multiple marginal public spheres and its extension to the digital, I argue for a "semi-enclave" as simultaneously a culturally cordoned-off space and a discursive strategy that strategically engages mainstream culture.

In her theory on multiple marginal spheres, Catherine Squires (2002) describes enclaves as clandestine spaces where marginalized groups were historically forced to exist separately from the public sphere. These spaces then became a site of reprieve by incorporating both discursive and physical means of survival. That is, though Black publics were denied public access and a voice, the enclave provided forms of resistance through physical spaces and hidden discourse.

This kind of enclaving maps onto digital spaces as well, as Catherine Knight Steele (2016) has demonstrated. In her analysis of Black women bloggers' engagement with entertainment and lifestyle content, she finds that blogging can allow for a historically necessitated separation from dominant culture through everyday talk that is simultaneously personal, political, and communal. Similarly, André Brock, Lynette Kvasny, and

Kayla Hales (2010) found that Black users' engagement with online content fosters separation from the mainstream gaze. As they state, "Online environs such as *Racialicious* and *Essence* have become new 'third places' and *(reasonably) safe spaces* within which women of color can reflect upon their discursive construction in media and in policy" (Brock, Kvasny, and Hales 2010, 1051; emphasis added).

Although #ThanksgivingClapback is publicly accessible via Twitter's search and trending topics functions, the discursive play and specific cultural references between users cordon off outsiders from taking part online. That is, Black users tap into linguistic practices and social humor in ways that directly and exclusively speak to each other. The historical linguistic practices of signifyin' and playing the dozens have allowed for Black publics to artfully play with language in ways that hail and maintain their "extended fictive family" (Gilyard and Banks 2018, 93). Humor has also long been a tool for African Americans to critique dominance while maintaining cultural collectives and survival techniques (Haggins 2007; Watkins 1999).

Signifyin' is a linguistic tactic meant to obscure language and allow for community and social critique for Black Americans. Influential thinkers Henry Louis Gates Jr. (1983) and Zora Neale Hurston (1935) trace black oral traditions, such as playing the dozens, to West and Central African cultures who then adapted language to the North American context during their forced migration. Gates (1983) explores signifyin' as a linguistic strategy employed by Africans and African Americans, which turns language on its head. Gates writes that Black subjects dwell "at the margins of discourse, ever punning, ever troping, ever embodying the ambiguities of language, . . . repeating and simultaneously reversing in one deft, discursive act" (Gates 1983, 686). Sarah Florini (2014) has since understood the multiple layered meanings of signifyin' as "a powerful resource for signaling racial identity, allowing Black Twitter users to perform their racial identities 140 characters at a time" (224). I understand #ThanksgivingClapback as an example of signifyin' that provides a way for Black users to align themselves with a long history of Black traditions and cultural practices. Moreover, I contend that the semi-enclave is, in part, fueled by practices of signifyin' as layered discursive meanings misdirect outsiders and make it difficult to duplicate content.

Figure 13.1. #YouNameIt video, which Black users layered on top of #ThanksgivingClapback to deepen discursive and cultural recognition among Black Twitter users.

One such example of the semi-enclave as protection against cultural appropriation came in the form of the #YouNameIt video. This video originally featured a black choir and the famous gospel singer Shirley Caesar before being remixed to fit the theme of black Thanksgivings (see figure 13.1).[2] The 2016 video, which many have since dubbed the "Thanksgiving Anthem," shows Caesar emphatically and in short bursts singing about a farmer and his "abundance of produce and livestock" (Tristan 2018). Caesar's "beans, greens, potatoes, lambs, hams . . . you name it" was then remixed and put into context of black Thanksgivings as "grandma's response to 'what's for Thanksgiving dinner'" (Tristan 2018). Many Black users' familiarity with their grandmothers as the center of family cooking functions as well as the recognition of gospel music and its style of emphatic singing create a culturally rich and easily referenced and replicated text within Black Twitter. Furthermore, these layered discursive elements fashion a culturally separate arena that conceals the intended meaning of the message from outsiders. In other words, in the context of #ThanksgivingClapback, the references to this video simply read as a lighthearted replication of a singer that is remixed online to highlight foods at the Thanksgiving table. The layers of meaning regarding Black cultural traditions of gospel and specific foods remain visible only to Black Twitter users, given the multiple layers of meaning packed into one post. In a signal to the understanding of meaning between these users, one user writes, "*You already know* what it is. Had to bring it back for the holidays. #YouNameIt #Thanksgiving #thanksgivingclapback" (emphasis added).

Because of the cultural specificities of #ThanksgivingClapback and similar discourses within Black Twitter, interlopers—or those who become involved in a space that is not meant for them—are hindered from not only entering the semi-enclave but also profiting off Black users therein. Writing about surveillance and profit, Keith Gilyard and Adam Banks (2018) assert,

> Some cases of appropriation and outright erasure persist and speak to large tensions in digital cultures that have been at work since the earliest eras of the Internet: a communitarian ethos of sharing vs. intellectual property and commercialization, and the viability of Black cultures in online spaces designed and built with little involvement by Black people or attention to Black interests. (97)

This is similar to what Lisa Nakamura (2002) has termed "identity tourism" in her discussion of cultural fetishizing in the digital world. This strain exists between a "communitarian" Internet and tenets of intellectual property as well as the particular historical legacies of appropriating U.S. black culture(s) for profit.

The act of appropriation is one that attempts to take from Black bodies, fetishizing and exoticizing them in a process bell hooks (1992) calls "eating the other." E. Patrick Johnson (2003) examines this "cultural usurpation" of black forms as one way white, dominant culture keeps the non-white "in their place" (4). Here, racist appropriations of blackness, such as language, dress, and music, associate black culture(s) with denigration, always situating it as "Other." "Black performance," writes Johnson, "becomes the site at which people and behavior are construed as 'spectacles of primitivism' to justify the colonial racist gaze" (7). Whiteness, as an engrained and produced structure, uses the essentialized view of blackness—to talk, walk, dress, and act—to its advantage. Johnson's reading is worth quoting at length here:

Figure 13.2. Example of intertextuality within
#ThanksgivingClapback where Black users pull
from popular television shows, such as *black-ish*.

For their part, whites construct linguistic representations of blacks that
are grounded in racist stereotypes to maintain the status quo only to
then reappropriate these stereotypes to affect fetishistic "escape" into the
Other, to transcend the rigidity of their own whiteness, as well as to feed
the capitalist gains of commodified blackness. (5)

#ThanksgivingClapback features protection from such cultural appro-
priation by circulating texts, such as the #YouNameIt video, that signal
several layers of Black cultural practices and traditions that become difficult to parse out and usurp. These tweets are often accompanied by
visuals from highly circulated texts, such as Internet memes and screen
shots of television shows including *T.I. and Tiny: The Family Hustle* and
black-ish (see figure 13.2). Here, Black users cordon off their own discourse by tapping in to the referential skills of intertextuality as well as
the wit required to "clapback," which signifyin' and playing the dozens
linguistically encourage. Within Black Twitter, #ThanksgivingClapback
allows Black users to continue to escape mainstream audiences and
ward off cultural appropriation.

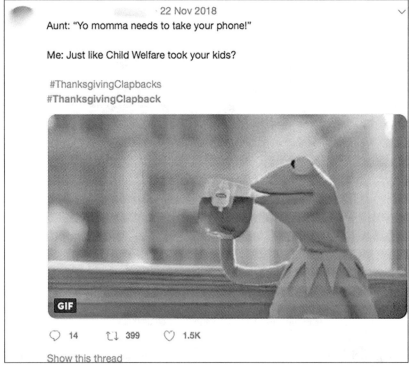

· 22 Nov 2018

Aunt: "Yo momma needs to take your phone!"

Me: Just like Child Welfare took your kids?

#ThanksgivingClapbacks
#ThanksgivingClapback

GIF

14   399   1.5K

Show this thread

Figure 13.3. Example of "negative" representations within #ThanksgivingClapback.

Beyond the Semi-Enclave: Visibility to Outsiders

I have argued thus far that conversations like #ThanksgivingClapback operate as a semi-enclave by creating a linguistic space that discursively prohibits participation from those outside the community. Yet we must still recognize that Black Twitter functions within the mainframe of Twitter, and that public accounts and discourses are fairly easily accessible to the general public. This is particularly the case given that popular tweets rise to visibility through trending topics. Thus, while #ThanksgivingClapback operates as a semi-enclave by cordoning off discussions, we can still nonetheless consider what it means for this kind of conversation to be encountered by users who are outside Black Twitter.

For instance, those who do not regularly participate in Black Twitter may witness Black users poking fun at their real and/or fictive family members using seemingly negative representations. Using Racquel Gates's (2018) framework regarding the productivity of "negative" representations, I argue that the semi-enclave allows outsiders to view #ThanksgivingClapback while still making Black discourse online culturally impenetrable through the deployment of "negative" representations.

Because representation is a contested space that guides the reality of audiences, the representational terrain of Black people and families has seen quite a bit of debate (H. Gray 1995). There are some, for instance, who decry reality television as disposable and argue that it does little to advance audiences' perceptions of Black women, in particular. Regarding #ThanksgivingClapback, many of the posts reference uncles getting evicted and aunts having too many children, which on the surface, might seem counterproductive to the idea of outsiders getting a glimpse into black cultures vis-à-vis the public mainframe of Twitter (see figure 13.3). Wrapped up in this discussion of "negative" images is a long-standing desire to control the representations of Black people to propagate the respectability of middle-class African American families. Historically, many Black elites felt that the entire race had to "prove themselves" in the face of morphing oppressions (Levine 1977). That is, for many African Americans, there was no room for representational behavior that would lead dominant groups to see African Americans as less than human. Many Black leaders and community members have thus tried to combat negative representations with positive portrayals of black family life, such as (at the time) *The Cosby Show*. Of course, regardless of these arguments, activists and critical cultural scholars have urged for the need to interrogate oppression and dominance itself, rather than one's desire to assimilate into it (Hall 1997b).

Racquel Gates (2018) most recently challenges this assumption that there is no place for what we might consider "negative" images of Black families. She writes, "Negative spaces can exist as havens for topics deemed outside of the boundaries of respectable texts, particularly when those topics have to do with matters of identity" (25). Gates argues that negative texts, such as reality television, often escape critical attention in ways that miss, for example, the work that Black women do to reframe cultural narratives about themselves. As I assert, although stereotypes deployed online through #ThanksgivingClapback might seem counterproductive regarding the representation of African Americans, these "negative" texts function to precisely define the boundaries with outsiders. That is, while the deployment of stereotypes within #ThanksgivingClapback allows those outside Black Twitter to perhaps view the hashtag and users therein, any replication and engagement by interlopers become culturally insensitive and problematic.

Stuart Hall (1997a) has written that simply replacing negative representations with positive ones does little to upend and critique the creation and maintenance of negative texts in the first place. This discussion of the role of negative representations is important here, as Black users not only celebrate Black families through #ThanksgivingClapback, but also poke fun at each other in ways that might seem stereotypical and regressive. For instance, one user writes, "Mom: 'when you gonna bring your girlfriend home?' Me: 'The same time you bring my dad home' #ThanksgivingClapback #singleparentprobs." Another user adds, "Aunt: 'didn't your son get suspended?' Mom: 'he sure did! Didn't you get evicted?'" The nod in the former tweet refers to broader (mis)conceptions about the predominance of Black female-headed households (Sudarkasa 2007), while the latter points to failures in education and housing. Yet as Gates reminds us, such notions are not necessarily politically or ideologically regressive—they can provide a necessary reprieve from the need to constantly prove oneself, particularly when the barriers to success are the result of racism and systemic oppression. Thus, Black Twitter allows users a moment of humorous reprieve through the long-standing linguistic tradition of ritualized verbal contests while also speaking truth to broader social experiences of some Black families in the United States.

Rather than simply cast off these historically damaging tropes, Gates (2018) argues that "the idea of negativity offers . . . a mode of analysis for *seeing* the work that these texts are doing in the first place" (19). Here, the "negativity" of the clapback teaches outsiders that if they engage in and attempt to take from conversations and bodies involved in #ThanksgivingClapback, they would certainly invite criticism. Posts like "Uncle: You know a lot about politics but you still failing your classes. Me: You know a lot about the law but you still ended up in jail #thanksgivingclapback" showcase the learned linguistic style of the clapback as Black users construct a technologically discursive community that makes reproduction and appropriation by outsiders automatically problematic.

Figure 13.4. #ThanksgivingClapback as "talking back" to one-dimensional representations of blackness.

Thus, not only are users playing the dozens with each other, they are demonstrating to outsiders that "If you clap, 'we gon' clap back'" (Gilyard and Banks 2018, 93).

Users encountering these conversations from the outside may also be able to learn about the diversity of black cultures and the different political battles that wage on within black communities. For example, one user highlights the intersection between race, sexuality, and black linguistic traditions in the semi-enclave: "#ThanksgivingClapback Homophobic Uncle: You still telling everyone you're gay? Me: You still telling everyone you're employed?" Another post read: "Aunt: All these girls out here and you still decided to be gay. Me: All these men and you still ain't got one? #ThanksgivingClapback" (see figure 13.4). Here, Black users deploy the clapback in a way that fosters a broader discussion about homophobia and the harmful realities of many queer people of color, particularly during the holidays. Some Black women also tapped into the resistive functions of the clapback by speaking to issues such as natural hair. Posts like "Aunt: Your natural hair lookin a lil dry. Me: Just like your Mac n cheese #ThanksgivingClapback" were highly circulated by natural hair bloggers, such as @naturalhairrule, who has about forty-four thousand followers. These posts challenge the essentializing and reductionist effects of seeing Black Twitter—and people—as a monolith. Moreover, as the natural hair post demonstrates, the hashtag also allows Black women in particular to negotiate, resist, and make visible common microaggressions, such as those having to do with hair and skin tone. Here, Black users online can wield the more public functions of Twitter in order to (re)present blackness in its diversity by skillfully making stereotypes work against themselves.

Through the deployment of a host of "negative" stereotypes, ranging from the unemployed uncle to the auntie with several children, #ThanksgivingClapback enters into the realm of contestation from within. While fetishism and other forms of stereotypes turn the "Other" into an object, Black users rewrite and diversify the intersectional representations of black culture(s) online. Thus, in tandem with the linguistic and cultural specifics of the enclave, the visibility of these conversations can also contest dominant forms of racial and sexual representations.

Conclusion

As we can see from these examples, the subgenre of Black Twitter adapts traditional forms of black linguistics and culture to allow users the space to retreat from the mainstream even as it has the potential to shift racial representations. I have argued that the semi-enclave is a lens through which we might be able to better understand the complexities of black discourse online. Through online discussions such as the ones surrounding #ThanksgivingClapback, we are able to glean how Black users protect against tenets of cultural appropriation by incorporating the linguistic strategy of playing the dozens as well as specific intertextual references that protect communities from interlopers. Further, while we may disparage "negative" stereotypes within the conversations, I argue that they have political potential for Black users who dare outsiders to appropriate this space. Together, the digital activities of Black users work within popular stereotypes to expose the hidden glaciers of oppression. Whereas blackness is always already marked with "difference," Black users online employ humor to discursively work to both protect themselves and counter dominance within the semi-enclave.

14

Arab Americans and Participatory Culture

SULAFA ZIDANI

YouTube | comedy | metalinguistics

The first thing you hear on the debut episode of the YouTube show *Punny Pun Times* is Fahed Zoumot's laugh—an iconic feature of the show. The episode opens with two friends, Tarek Al-Jundi and Fahed Zoumot, sitting on a couch with part of a painting showing on the wall behind them and a yellow towel casually resting on Al-Jundi's knee. An off-screen voice says words to them in English, to which they respond with puns by putting these words into sentences with similar-sounding words. What is unique about these puns is that they are often not in the same language, but instead the comedians create cross-linguistic puns that mix similar-sounding phrases in English and Arabic. *Awakening*, for example, turns into "*Ah, wen kaynin?!*" (So, where were you?!), *water* into "mit*water*" (nervous), and *melodic* into "eid *meladik*" (your birthday).

While mainstream representations of Arab Americans on film, television, and news media have been locked within a limited set of narratives primarily centering on terrorism, videos such as these show us the possibilities that are opened up by online participatory cultures. When everyday citizens have the ability to make and share their own content, they do not need to subscribe to industrial norms around genre and narrative; indeed, these humorous videos defy genre as well as expectations around Arab American identity. In this chapter I investigate the cross-linguistic pun videos made by *Punny Pun Times* as a way of challenging the definitions of what it means to be Arab American. Through analysis of their video content and interviews with the producers, I argue that *Punny Pun Times* puts forward a new articulation of Arab Americanness that challenges the binary between Arab and American and exposes the significance of a global framework in understanding Arab American culture.

Who Is Arab American?

The year 2018 ended with a milestone in representation for Arabs and Muslims in America—the election of the first Arab and Somali women to congress; Rashida Tlaib in Michigan, and Ilhan Omar in Minnesota. The image of the Palestinian thobe worn by Tlaib in Congress and Omar's hijab (for which a rule from 1837 banning head attire in Congress was scrapped) became symbols of this accomplishment, marking the arrival of Arab Americans into this historically White governmental space. NBC TV news anchor Ayman Mohyeldin commented on this, saying, "As the son of a Palestinian mother, it's a milestone for Palestinian Americans to see their heritage and culture reflected in their elected officials" (Zogby 2019).

For Arab Americans, the climb toward social mobility rests on a history of mistreatment and misrepresentation. To better understand why the election of Tlaib and Omar to Congress is significant and the landscape in which *Punny Pun Times* is operating, we must first look at how Arabs and Muslims saw themselves portrayed in U.S. media and their underrepresentation in U.S. government. Part of this problem is related to one of identification, as the definition of "Arab" has changed over time. Zachary J. Foster (2017) traces the definition of "Arab" throughout history and finds that since as early as the seventh and eighth centuries, the meaning of the word "Arab" changed regularly depending on who was doing the defining. This has continued into the United States as well. Since the first significant groups of Arabs began arriving in the United States in the late 1880s, they have been classified in different ways by the U.S. federal government—from Turkish Asians, to Syrian, Lebanese, then White (Naber 2012; Gualtieri 2009). Although acquiring the label of Whiteness was considered a success in the early 1900s because of the social status of Whiteness in the United States, this category does not represent the issues that are unique to the Arab population. Moreover, since Arabs are not socially seen as White, they do not gain any social benefits from this categorization (Gualtieri 2009). In January 2018, Arab American advocates and organizations backed by experts and census officials pushed to add a

Middle East and North Africa (MENA) category to the census. The U.S. government rejected the suggestion, meaning that Arabs in the United States would continue to be categorized as White (Harb 2018).

Beyond issues with definition and classification, Arab Americans are also plagued with the continued conflation of Arab identity with the Muslim religion. Some Muslims may be Arab, but there are many non-Arab Muslims from all around the world, including Turkey, India, Pakistan, Indonesia, and the Balkans. Likewise, when it comes to religion, Arabs may be Muslim, Christian, Druze, Baha'i, or Jewish, among other religions. They may have ancestry from any number of countries from the Middle East, the Persian Gulf, or North Africa. As Evelyn Alsultany (2012) argues, "This conflation enables a particular racial Othering that would not operate in the same way through other conflation, such as, for example, Arab/Christian. Arab/Jew, or Indonesian/Muslim" (9).

Due to these and other instabilities, it is impossible to reach an all-encompassing definition of who exactly is Arab American. In their attempts to find a stable and concise definition for Arab American, scholars have resorted to connecting Arab American identity to ancestry in countries that are members of the regional political organization known as the Arab League, but connecting an identity to a political entity has multiple disadvantages. First, political entities may have interests that are not necessarily tied to culture, and second, political entities change based on shifts in political relations between governments and not on culture or heritage. At the time of writing this chapter, for example, the Arab League members do not include Syria or Libya, but this does not mean that people with ancestry from these countries are no longer Arab.

Portrayals of Arabs in U.S. Media

These disagreements about who is Arab American and the conflation of Muslim and Arab have been reinforced in contemporary media representations as well. In Alsultany's extensive investigation of the portrayals of Arabs and Muslims in post-9/11 media, she finds that film, TV, and news media participate in creating this conflation and attaching it to negative ideals that seem the inverse of America. This serves to legitimize racial profiling, despite it being an "unrealistic endeavor" (Alsultany 2012, 10). But there are many other problematic portrayals of Arabs and Muslims throughout the history of U.S. media. While in the early twentieth century Arabs were depicted as lazy sheikhs with harem girls who live in faraway exotic and magical lands, these portrayals shifted after 1945—a year that marked the decline of European colonies, the end of World War II, the beginning of the Cold War, and the creation of Israel. Arab men started being shown as royal sheikhs with oil money threatening the U.S. economy, or terrorists threatening U.S. security. Arab women went from being portrayed as harem or belly dancers to being invisible until the 1970s, when their portrayal changed to dangerous terrorists with a degree of sex appeal, and in the 1980s to veiled women oppressed by misogyny and Muslim religion.

This is not to say that all portrayals of Arabs and Muslims in U.S. media are exoticizing or negative. Sympathetic portrayals have proliferated as well, often in response to political circumstances. For example, after the election of President Barack Obama, sympathetic representations of Arab and Muslim Americans could be seen in roles such as loving family members and patriots, innocent victims of hate crimes, and government agents working to prevent terrorist attacks. Alsultany argues that these portrayals may be comforting, but they effectively deflect attention from "the persistence of racist policies and practices post 9/11" (Alsultany 2012, 12) as part of the War on Terror. Moreover, even these so-called sympathetic representations serve to uphold the idea that Arab and Muslim Americans can be understood only in the context of terrorism and threats to U.S. national security.

As a result, many Arab Americans and Arabs across the globe grow up with an imagined dichotomy between two terms of identification: they learn that being Arab and being American are identities that are mutually exclusive and cannot overlap or intersect. This dichotomy was historically constituted through Orientalist discourses that reinforced hierarchies of difference between "the East" and "the West" (Said 1978). But it is shored up within contemporary Arab American communities, as well as by the education system and media in the United States (Naber 2012). The result is that many Arab Americans themselves began to view the ideals of Arabness and Americanness as separate. Nadine C. Naber argues that this Orientalist binary creates a divide between "a gendered and sexualized notion of an inner-familiar-communal (Arab) domain and an external-political-public (American) domain" (Naber 2012, 8). Based on the wide variety in the assemblages of visions that constitute Arabness, Naber suggests using the term "articulations of Arabness" (8) to refer to stories of Arab Americans.

Drawing on Naber, I use the term here to emphasize that there is not only one version of Arabness, but rather a collection of varying articulations. In this chapter, I look at how *Punny Pun Times* uses participatory culture and puns to push forth a particular articulation of Arab identity that is tied to a transnational framework. One way of understanding articulations of Arabness and the negotiation of these aforementioned dichotomies is to assess media representations created by and for Arab Americans, such as those made by Tarek Al-Jundi and Fahed Zoumot in *Punny Pun Times*. Beyond the content of their videos, it is also important to consider the digital platforms on which the content is shared— including Instagram, Facebook, and YouTube, each of which offers opportunities for Arab Americans to produce and share content, as well as for audience members to engage with their videos and share their own insights about Arab Americanness.

Punny Pun Times as Participatory Arab Americanness

Punny Pun Times was created in 2016. Their Facebook page description reads, "Tarek and Fahed, two lifelong friends with a skill to twist words in a bilingual stupid fashion are now making videos to share the laughter with the world" (*Punny Pun Times* n.d.). Their videos are typically set in a living room with Al-Jundi and Zoumot sitting on a couch, sometimes with special guests (see figure 14.1). Throughout each video, Tarek Al-Jundi's brother Rami Al-Jundi (referred to as "the voice," because he is not seen in the video) tosses out English words that are then transformed into Arabic sentences. This creates a cross-linguistic pun in every response, since the sound of the English word has to match another word in Arabic. For example, in episode 3, in response to the word *phenomena*, Al-Jundi yells out "Isma'a, ana ta'abaan, *fe nam ana?* Walla ma *fe nam ana?*" (Listen, I'm tired, can I sleep, or not?). In episode 5, they have two consecutive puns when Al-Jundi responds to *obsess* by saying, "Fe kteer klab *o bsess* fe hadak el ma7al" (There are many dogs

Figure 14.1. Fahed Zoumot and Tarek Al-Jundi in the classic *Punny Pun Times* setting.

and cats over there), and then Zoumot responds to *beggar* by saying, "W *bagar* w khirfan w . . ." (and cows and sheep and . . .).

In a video interview about their launch, Al-Jundi and Zoumot explain that creating these puns was an activity they were already doing as friends, and Tarek Al-Jundi's brother Rami suggested they record it (BaselMeets 2018). This spontaneity has been important to *Punny Pun Times*, especially in their early days. In an interview I conducted with Al-Jundi, he said that they did not give much thought to their branding decisions like choosing the name *Punny Pun Times*. Yet after seeing their videos rapidly rack up thousands of views, Al-Jundi and Zoumot decided to focus on their comedy. They developed a presence across platforms and collaborated with media companies such as YouTube, Facebook, Uber, Asli Content, and others, expanding *Punny* into a variety of genres. These include the classic videos of Al-Jundi and Zoumot creating puns on their couch, videos of their travels around the world, and competition videos where they invite others to participate.

The videos produced and shared by Al-Jundi and Zoumot can be seen as part of a global Arab American online participatory culture. The concept of participatory culture is premised on the idea that consumers are not merely passive audience members, but rather individuals who make choices about how to take an active part in the cultural system. According to the definition created by Henry Jenkins et al. (2009), participatory cultures are marked by the ease with which users can express themselves, the strong support that participants feel when sharing their creations, and the opportunity to build social connections where their contributions matter. In becoming active producers and manipulators of meaning, users transform the experience of consumption into something productive: "Consumption becomes production; reading becomes writing; spectator culture becomes participatory culture" (Jenkins 2005, 60). By participating in the creation of these YouTube videos, Al-Jundi and Zoumot weave their personal experiences into the texts, employing existing material around them as they explore their own status. The work of *Punny Pun Times* fits into Jenkins et al.'s (2009) different forms of participatory culture by facilitating *affiliation* with online communities on different social media websites, creating new *expressions* and creative production, supporting *collaboration* and teamwork, and *circulating* content to shape the direction of media flows. There are many potential benefits from participatory culture, such as creating opportunities for learning and a diversification of cultural expression. Indeed, given the ease with which consumers can become producers through digital tools, online participatory cultures also have the potential to disrupt the power dynamics that have historically shaped media production and consumption. Thanks to increasing access to cultural production and circulation, there is more room for everyday citizens to participate in power negotiations (Banet-Weiser et al. 2014).

Moreover, Al-Jundi and Zoumot utilize participatory culture as a way of taking part in the articulation of Arabness. Christopher Kelty (2013) argues that "participation is no longer simply an opening up, an expression, a liberation, it is now also a principle of improvement, an instrument of change, a creative force. It no longer threatens, but has become a resource: participation has been made *valuable*" (5). Through the creative videos of *Punny Pun Times* and their wide reach on social media, Al-Jundi and Zoumot share their take on culture and their experience of it. They also invite their viewers to take part by incorporating their suggestions and engaging with them on their Facebook and Instagram pages. The popularity of *Punny Pun Times* has translated into a number of contracts and sponsorships that Al-Jundi and Zoumot have used to increase user engagement. This includes the creation of quizzes that invite viewers to guess the pun, and opportunities for collaborations with other social media celebrities and comedians who are connected to the Arab experience in different ways. In this way, *Punny Pun Times* uses participatory culture to invite others to share in articulating Arab American identity and connecting that identity to a global framework.

Yet there are also limits to what participatory cultures can accomplish. For instance, there is a potential for creating a cultural divide based on resources, as the amount of time, money, and knowledge regarding this new cultural system can determine who will be part of the cultural elite and who will be in the cultural underclass. Since we are not yet at a point where everyone can participate equally, participatory culture is more of a utopian ideal or aspiration than a reality (Jenkins and Carpentier 2013). Jenkins (2016) suggests substituting the term "participatory culture" with "a more participatory culture" to emphasize that participation is to be understood as a matter of degree, and to call attention to those with fewer resources for participation in the cultural system. Participatory culture, therefore, reflects not only the opportunity for grassroots participation in online discourse, but also the complex power dynamics that are imbricated in that online participation.

Making Puns and Collapsing Dichotomies

One way of understanding the specific kinds of linguistic jokes made on *Punny Pun Times* is to look at their audience—in particular, asking who is attracted to these videos and how they engage with them. In an interview I conducted with the video producers, Al-Jundi argues that puns are not only funny, but can also serve as an effective educational tool for people who are trying to improve either their English or their Arabic. He says, "We want to see if we can use them to educate people who are weak in either English or Arabic, hone their skills by increasing their vocab capabilities." In explaining the success of *Punny Pun Times*, Al-Jundi says,

> The reason why we think it did so well is because of relevance. Everyone has that silly friend. And in general, people love comedy that messes with perspective, taking a word that triggers a certain impression in your head

and seeing it, beyond all expectations, be twisted into a whole other word (and hence, impression), is a perception play. Add the bromance and silliness of the chemistry between Fahed and I, and it went viral.

Al-Jundi's description evokes Limor Shifman's (2012) work on memetic videos, or videos that invite viewer participation and the production of derivative videos. Shifman finds that there are six primary features common to videos that go viral and generate further video production: a focus on ordinary people, flawed masculinity, humor, simplicity, repetitiveness, and whimsical content. Each of these attributes is evoked in Al-Jundi's explanation—including his portrayal of himself as an ordinary person or "that silly friend" everyone has, the flawed masculinity that becomes evident in his "bromance and silliness of the chemistry" that does not meet the hegemonic expectations of masculine behavior, the emphasis on humor and loud laughter, the simplicity of production design that communicates an accessibility to their audience, the repetitiveness of words that become puns and general predictability of their format, and the deployment of incongruous humor that contributes to a sense of whimsy. In their particular style of humor, they continually join unexpected pairs, creating a nonthreatening surprise or unexpected juxtaposition defined as incongruous humor (Meyer 2000; Perks 2012). Given that their videos might otherwise be seen as extremely culturally specific and thus limited in their potential reach, these attributes clearly serve to make their Arab American style of humor and language-play accessible and inviting to their digital audiences across the globe.

Beyond contributing to their popularity, the kind of pun creation that Al-Jundi and Zoumot engage in also has political meaning. Cross-linguistic puns are a specific category of puns that rely on the similar sounds of words from different languages. Ibrahim Muhawi (1994) categorizes cross-linguistic puns as a speech event that is a "metalinguistic joke" (155). Despite being a play on language, these jokes are not merely about language, but more importantly about the social life of the community that they come from. Metalinguistic jokes draw on the complexity of the contact between two or more languages and use phonological similarity or difference to make a cultural or political statement. In its metalinguistic jokes, *Punny Pun Times* brings together two languages, both of which represent two sides of the culture to which the hosts belong. In their experiences, English and Arabic continually cross each other and neither one subsumes the other. In *Punny* videos, English is not an imperialist force that erases Arabic; likewise, Arabic is not exoticized or portrayed as a lesser language. The cultural hierarchies, dichotomies, and negative depictions discussed in the beginning of the chapter are not seen in these videos. What the videos reinforce is the sense that both of these languages are indispensable.

Through this linguistic merging, *Punny Pun Times* is able to disrupt the dichotomy of Arabness and Americanness that has limited Arab American identities. Al-Jundi and Zoumot's online videos challenge perceptions of Arabness and Americanness as separate and opposed to one another by arguing that they can be effortlessly joined. Their message even extends beyond the boundaries of Arab America, since they often incorporate additional different languages or accents such as Japanese, Spanish, or North American accents versus immigrant accents. For example, in an episode titled "Watch! Arab Amigos and Spanish Puns," the show's guest Vanessa Arturo is given the Spanish word *madre* (mother) and yells out, "*Madre*! Wallah, uqsim billah, wallahi fakkart fil mawdoo'a bas *madre*" (I don't know, I swear to God, I thought about it, but I just don't know). By inviting other languages and voices to their show, they broaden their participation to include immigrant narratives in America at large and not just the experiences of Arab Americans. This joining together of immigrant voices further bolsters the breakdown of familiar dichotomies.

Global Arab America

Alongside the deconstruction of binaries between Arab and American, *Punny Pun Times* videos are also an expression of the complexity of Al-Jundi and Zoumot's own multilayered identities as products of transnational ties: Tarek Al-Jundi is Jordanian Palestinian American, and Fahed Zoumot is Jordanian Lebanese but works in Dubai. The videos of *Punny Pun Times* can thus be seen to evoke a global diaspora that expands Arab American identity beyond the borders of the United States. Ramesh Srinivasan (2006) writes that "with advances in networked technologies, diaspora now maintain social and political ties that are transnational, including fellow communities in other host countries and the homeland" (503). *Punny Pun Times* evokes a playful expression of these ties, utilizing cross-linguistic puns and humor to connect different accents of English, different dialects of Arabic, and sometimes other languages like Spanish or Japanese. In addition to the classic videos of the two of them on a couch in a living room, they have created *Punny Pun Times* videos in Jordan, Dubai, and Nepal. Play—or, specifically, word-play—is central to creating these ties through their videos. By bringing in different languages and non-Northern American accents in English, they create a connection between Arabness and Americanness, between Arabness and other immigrant communities within the United States, and to cultures outside the United States.

Moreover, these videos expand definitions of Arabness by showing the wide range of individuals who identify as Arab. For example, there are three different episodes featuring Wonho Chung, a stand-up comedian born in Saudi Arabia and raised in Jordan. Chung has said that although his father is South Korean and his mother is Vietnamese and he may not be Arab on the outside, he is, "on the inside, Arab all the way" (Chung 2010). Bringing voices like Chung's into their episodes reinforces *Punny Pun Times*' role in disrupting the ideals of what counts as Arab in a world characterized by transnational cultural ties.

This is not to say that the videos of *Punny Pun Times* cannot be criticized. For example, the comedians themselves say they would like to increase their female viewership and acknowledge that comedy is still a male-dominated space (BaselMeets 2018). They sometimes make jokes that might come at the expensive of other marginalized groups. There is also much to unpack in terms of the duo's economic sponsorships and relationships with social media companies. However, within the scope of this chapter, my aim is to focus on the generative cultural push of their videos to help create linguistic and cultural connections that are rare within the mainstream media landscape.

The videos of *Punny Pun Times* create new modes of expression that show how Arab American identities are tied not only to Arabness and Americanness, but also to other immigrant communities within the United States, and to cultures outside the United States. Al-Jundi and Zoumot utilize resources such as time, money, and knowledge to participate in connecting these different communities and call existing cultural hierarchies into question. In a moment where American popular culture is increasingly being understood in relation to its transnational positioning, this study helps us to consider what we gain by analyzing Arab American popular culture through linguistic, multicultural, and global frameworks.

15

Diaspora and Digital Media

LIA WOLOCK

diaspora | solidarity | blogs | archive

As global migration has boomed and identity has become less connected with place, the term "diaspora" has been taken up by a variety
of populations making claims to many kinds of community (e.g., racial,
ethnic, linguistic, religious) at many scales (e.g., regional, global). The
word "diaspora" was coined over two thousand years ago. Combining
dia- (across) and *-spora* (seed, to spread), early Greek translators of the
Hebrew scriptures used the word to describe the forced exile and dispersed connection of the Israelites. Spread apart and carrying the seeds
of their culture in their teachings and their sacred texts, many Jewish
people today continue to claim that they are part of the Jewish diaspora
and that their cultural inheritance is defined by their being spread apart
yet connected. In this chapter, I analyze the increasing resonance of a
solidarity-oriented diasporic consciousness for South Asian Americans
in the United States and how multiple, sometimes competing versions
of South Asian American identity are actively constituted through digital media. I do so to highlight how diasporic identifications are always
constructed in relation to transnational migrations and imaginaries, as
well as in relation to other racialized groups. This work is important to
consider because transnational migrations, diasporic communities, and
the strategic use of media have been crucial to the problematic maintenance of racial hierarchies in this nation since its founding.

First, I offer a brief history of South Asian migration to the United
States and sketch the mainstream racialization of South Asian Americans. Next, I consider how South Asian Americans have used media and
communication technologies to manage their relationship with identity,
highlighting a shift over time from a diasporic consciousness focused on

longing for a distant homeland and its internal divisions, to imagining new identities and coalitions. As part of this, I consider the affordances and cultures of the web as a space for identity work. Finally, I use a blog called *Sepia Mutiny* and the South Asian American Digital Archive as examples of sites where some South Asian Americans, in spite of strong internal and external pressures, are forging new, social justice–oriented visions of being South Asian American. Unpacking the conflicting understandings of diaspora and identity at play in this complex set of communities and media reveals the processes by which racial categories get constructed, reconfigured, and stabilized, as well as the active role some marginalized and diasporic communities have taken up online to reconfigure race, solidarity, and belonging.

Coming to South Asian America

South Asian American is a coalitional identity label that encompasses people who live in the United States and Canada and trace their cultural heritage to the nations of the South Asian subcontinent: India, Pakistan, Bangladesh, Sri Lanka, Bhutan, Nepal, and the Maldives. Some consider Afghanistan part of South Asia as well. South Asians have been migrating to North America from as early as the sixteenth century (Priyadarshini 2014), with a notable population involved in agriculture, railroad construction, and lumber in the Pacific Northwest at the start of the twentieth century. However, at that time large-scale migration was blocked informally through acts of prejudice and violence, and formally through xenophobic immigration laws. South Asian America today is deeply shaped by a major influx of professional, educated, and highly skilled workers who came after the passing of the 1965 Immigration and Nationality Act. The policy shift favored highly skilled labor, as well as family members of those who had already immigrated. From 1965 to 1977, 83 percent of South Asian migrants to the United States entered with advanced degrees (Prashad 1999, 186) and from 1980 to 2013, the Indian immigrant population in the United States increased from 206,000 to 2.04 million, doubling every decade (Lee 2015). This new body of South Asian migrants, markedly different from the Asian (including South Asian) populations that had arrived before it, entered into an already complicated racial field.

By 1966, East Asian Americans had been recast by mainstream America as the "model minority" (Petersen 1966) whose success could be used as a weapon against other minority communities fighting for their civil rights (Osajima 1988). With smaller long-term South Asian populations in the United States than East Asian groups, the racial position of the post-1965 South Asian migrants was less stable. Stereotypes of South Asians as dangerous, dark-skinned hordes, sly colonial underlings, and mysterious spiritualists conflicted with the simultaneous fantasy of South Asian Americans as a "less troublesome" model minority. In some ways, the lack of stable categorization and the surplus of meanings projected by mainstream populations onto South Asian Americans became another reason to consider people of South Asian heritage suspicious. Even with such wide variation, the common understanding most often returned to for South Asian Americans for the last several decades has been that of the model minority—educated and skilled, politically pliant, and culturally insular.

The place of East Asians and South Asians in the United States can also be understood within the larger context of U.S. racialization and what Claire Jean Kim (1999) calls the "racial triangulation of Asian Americans." Kim argues that the current categories of Asian, Black, and White in the United States were developed together, and can be understood only in relation to each other. For over two hundred years, essentialized notions of identity have been mobilized to produce and maintain a field of racial positions that reinforces White racial power as natural and inevitable, and excludes other categories from full civic, economic, or social participation in the American body politic. Asian Americans are relatively valorized as "dependable," "successful," "hardworking" laborers above Black communities, but are kept in check using civic ostracism, which positions Asian-heritage people as apolitical and permanently culturally foreign (Kim 1999, 107; Lowe 1996, 5).

Because Asians are perceived as industrious and controllable, the civic arrival of Asians as Americans is always deferred while their labor is consumed, even celebrated. Refusing Asian Americans full cultural citizenship while using their lauded and exploited economic performance as a tool to rebuke other minority communities, the racial structures of America are stabilized (Nishime 2014). Threats to this vision of U.S. race relations are met with confusion, and often hostility. For example, no matter how many generations of family have lived in the United States, Asian Americans are still marked as indelibly alien—as is suggested by the intensity and repetition with which they are perpetually asked, "Where are you from?" The question implicitly asserts that they *cannot* be from *here*. Indeed, any answer that locates them as American is deemed insufficient, and the question is repeated, with increasing frustration and aggression, until an answer that locates them *elsewhere*, as foreign in their very essence, is obtained.

The Techie and the Terrorist

Over the last thirty years, two major developments reoriented the mainstream image of South Asian Americans. The rise of technology jobs starting in the 1980s called for a massive reorganization of national and global labor that some South Asian populations were poised to utilize. The potential for certain Asian Americans to access a more flexible, transnational, and economic citizenship (Ong 1999; Visweswaran 1997) owes a great deal to inequalities of migration and capital accumulation informed by centuries-long histories of colonization and commerce. Both on- and off-shore, South Asians came to represent the promise of skilled technology labor and the threat of outsourcing the American Dream (Hashmi 2006). From fictional characters like the sweet yet nerdy Raj Koothrappali (*The Big Bang Theory*) to successful foreign students decried by then-radio host Steven Bannon as taking American jobs (Fahrenthold and Sellers 2016), the mediated figure of the techie was competent but asocial and inhuman.

Separately, the aftermath of 9/11 caused an even greater seismic shift in popular understandings of South Asians and South Asian Americans. In a continuation of robust histories of Islamophobia, Orientalism, racism, and xenophobia, brown bodies at home and abroad became the playground of national insecurities, new surveillance technologies, and banal regimes of terror. While the trope of South Asians as invading hordes that must be stopped by vigilantes has a more than one-hundred-year pedigree in the United States (Lal 2007), the post-9/11 rise in hate crimes against South Asians and Muslims was stark. In the week after 9/11, for example, there were 645 bias incidents recorded in the United States, ranging from harassment to arson to murder, all directed against

Americans perceived to be of Middle Eastern or Muslim origin. Eighty-one of these attacks were conducted against people of South Asian heritage (Mishra 2001), and such incidents have persisted in the years that followed, growing particularly numerous in the charged atmosphere surrounding the 2016 presidential election.

In the wake of 9/11 and the tech boom, the images of the techie and the terrorist have become two enduring poles around which mainstream understandings of South Asians and South Asian Americans orbit. Their power draws many into an unproductive, binary conversation, where they feel they must argue for the (supposedly good, certainly better) image of the techie over the image of the terrorist. In truth, both misconstrue the internally diverse and complicated reality of South Asian American communities. Worse, both are based on and reinforce the mainstream American conception of South Asians as permanent foreigners. Some of the most problematic and enduring depictions include the brain-eating cultists from the movie *Indiana Jones and the Temple of Doom* and the caricatured, accented voice of Apu Nahasapeemapetilon on *The Simpsons*. Whether taking White hostages, eating brains, "taking" American jobs, or speaking in a mocking accent, these mainstream images implicitly and explicitly deny that those of South Asian heritage can ever be fully American.

Even those mainstream depictions that avoid these tropes, such as many of actress Mindy Kaling's characters or the videos of YouTube stars like Liza Koshy, tend to sidestep deep cultural questions altogether. Such roles emphasize the troubling idea that it is better to treat racial difference as colorful adornment than to step into the quagmire of race relations and cultural authenticity, and thus have to fight against a set of well-worn, interrelated stereotypical tropes and roles. While for some these whitewashed stories read as universal and relatable, they are actually dependent on ignoring racial struggle. This stunted range of popular imagery, however, has always been supplemented by community media created by and for South Asians.

South Asian Diasporic Communication

As identifications within the South Asian American diaspora have become increasingly complex, so too have interpersonal relationships with communication and technology use. Earlier South Asian migrants often identified themselves strongly in relation to nostalgia for a homeland left behind, whether national (e.g., Pakistan), religious (e.g., Sikh Khalistan), or linguistic (e.g., Tamil Eelam). This "lost" homeland was directly accessible only through long physical journeys, crackling phone wires, and worn airmail letters, all of which were cost- and time-prohibitive. More sociable and entertaining options included enjoying records and cassettes that had been lovingly carried across oceans, attending community film screenings, and listening to or watching public access radio and TV shows in metropolitan areas. Over time, technologies for personally keeping up with a distant homeland became faster and more accessible. By the 1990s, South Asians abroad discussed things like culture and classical music and organized meet-ups through Usenet forums, an early precursor to Internet bulletin boards.

Second-generation (and later) South Asian Americans increasingly understand themselves in relation to a constellation of interacting regional, national, and transnational identifications. Many South Asian Americans who were born in the United States come of age feeling distinctly both South Asian and American. Some describe this as not a desire for return, since a place like Nepal might never have been one's homeland, but a pull to meaningfully "re-turn" to one's cultural inheritance (Brah 1996)—to explore it, process it, and claim it. These feelings are often visible within digital discourse as South Asian Americans (like so many other communities) have taken to the web to produce, remix, curate, and discuss images of themselves. The most recent era of digital diaspora highlights a new potential relationship with identity, one based on connection-in-dispersion.[1] In this version, being spread apart may be generative of an entirely new, potentially positive experience, no longer marked by lack, but rather by an excess of meaning, new identities, and new cultural practices created through interaction. Combining neoliberal fantasies of self-empowerment with very real access to complex connection, each person is a site of interconnection and meaning-making (Massey 1994, 154). Although we cannot fully control all the meanings that collide in this intersection, there is opportunity for people to accept, prioritize, and strengthen some of these connections over others.

Yet the Internet is not, as it is so often depicted, a utopian space or a blank slate where everyone can freely articulate and spread new visions of solidarity and identity. The potential of Internet technologies and digital media might be open-ended, but their creation and use are shaped by issues of access and culture as much as they are by technological innovation. Safiya Noble (2018) and André Brock (2011) argue that a normative Whiteness is implicitly and constantly reified in and through technoculture. For example, Noble (2018) systematically unpacks the centuries of racist and eugenicist "knowledge" and cultural baggage that undergird the Google search result, revealing how the Google search algorithm and apparatus are products and promoters of a racist society that masquerade as neutral technology. Sarah Florini (2017) further highlights how the inherent Whiteness of technoculture shapes and is shaped by an overwhelming belief in networked individualism as the new "social operating system" of society (Rainie and Wellman 2012).

Coalitional South Asian America

The state of contemporary popular and political culture in the United States—gripped by White angst, engaged in acrimonious immigration debates, and entering an era of computer-assisted global surveillance—combined with the colorblind, individualist bent of technoculture, provides fertile ground for the continued racial triangulation of South Asian Americans as permanently foreign techies or terrorists. In both cases, the ordinariness and possibility of simply being a brown American and enjoying a normal life are foreclosed. These dominant visions of South Asian Americans ignore the internal complexities of South Asian America, including its multitude of religious, linguistic, national, ethnic, classed, and caste-based communities. In addition, overly simplistic imaginaries of South Asian America work to foreclose meaningful solidarities with other marginalized racial and religious communities in the United States by placing them in hierarchies and oppositions, and by erasing the internal diversity that could be a bridge for cross-cultural understanding. For example, in 2014 nearly one in every twenty of the roughly 11.1 million unauthorized immigrants in the United States were from India (Passel and Cohn 2016). Yet national debates about immigration make it appear as if "undocumented" migrants only come from Mexico and Central and South America.

Seeking new ways of being South Asian American in the early 2000s, a generation of activists, authors, educators, and everyday citizens came together to build new connections within the community and outside. Rather than a convenient catchall name, South Asian America became, for them, a call to action, to build a community based on deep, politically conscious, internal and external solidarities.[2] Whereas other prominent ideas of South Asian American diaspora were and are based on holding on to something lost and far away, or divisions between those who trace their heritage to different South Asian nations or religious communities, this concept of identity considers both individuals and communities as generative sites of interconnection. At these interconnection points, activism, awareness, and belonging are consciously curated, created, and spread in spite of the dominant individualistic logics of technoculture. One way of viewing this vision of South Asian America is through digitally mediated communities like *Sepia Mutiny* and the South Asian American Digital Archive.

The multi-author blog and forum *Sepia Mutiny* (sepiamutiny.com) played a central role in this constellation of organizations and sites during its run from 2004 to 2012. With more than 60 bloggers, over 5,000 posts, substantive 100-comment discussions, and up to 16,000 daily visitors in the pre-Facebook and Twitter era, the *Sepia Mutiny* community advocated for a South Asian American perspective that was at once radically inclusive and ordinary. With heavy readership in North America and South Asia, its bloggers wrote on national and international topics ranging from the intellectual and political to the deeply personal and popular. This was a far cry from the many narrowly constituted, separate South Asian diasporas that were dominant a generation earlier.

Although started by Indian Americans, the Mutineers, as the bloggers called themselves, came to include people of Pakistani, Bangladeshi, Sri Lankan, and European descent; Muslims, Sikhs, Hindus, Christians, and unaffiliated; straight and queer; Republicans and Democrats; novelists, DJs, tech entrepreneurs, journalists, activists, lawyers, academics, artists, and a rocket scientist. Some of them were indeed in technology-oriented fields, but unlike the stereotype, the techie Mutineers were anything but apolitical. The breadth of blogger backgrounds, moreover, was not by accident, but brought about through concerted effort. The founders actively sought out and supported bloggers with backgrounds different from their own. Critical gaps were acknowledged, such as a lack of bloggers from lower socioeconomic backgrounds, and more bloggers sought. Bangladeshi-American electoral organizer and artist Tanzila "Taz" Ahmed (2012) articulated *Sepia Mutiny*'s formula most succinctly in her farewell post: "I always approached blogging on this site with three things in mind—1) write about the Desi-American experience, the narrative I was yearning for, 2) a 1:1 ratio of pop to politics posts, and 3) find the marginalized Desis and give them space."[3]

Through blogger selection, content choices, and elaborately moderated comment threads, *Sepia Mutiny* curated the complex, coalitional vision of South Asian America the Mutineers hungered for, piecing it together bit by bit. They filled their blog and its community with the images and voices that were so painfully missing from mainstream media and so frequently shunned at conservative cultural functions that kept different South Asian American communities separated by "nation of origin," religion, language, caste, and so on. Instead of asserting an essential identity, the blog cultivated a reflexive, conversational, politically oriented community. Accumulating more than 250,000 substantive comments in the pre-Twitter era, *Sepia Mutiny* fought against the closure of identities and meanings, and instead pushed for community participation, political engagement, and multidirectional solidarities. To make space for productive conversations in the face of dominant American technocultural trends such as trolling and bad-faith arguments, the bloggers and administrators spent countless hours meticulously moderating comment threads, paying special attention to the posts of women and Muslim contributors, who received the most vitriol. While sites like *Sepia Mutiny* heavily cultivated internal community formation and dialogue, others worked to capture and promote this vision more broadly.

Since 2008, the South Asian American Digital Archive (SAADA, saada.org) has worked to collect and digitize artefacts of South Asian American history, contextualize them and make them accessible, and legitimize them as pieces of American history. Starting with its digital archive, it later activated interest, investment, and awareness through multiple practices and digital platforms. The digital archive, which boasts nearly 4,000 items as of this writing, specializes in uncovering, connecting, and sharing artefacts from overlooked aspects of South Asian American culture and history, such as political activism and organizing against imperialism and bigotry stretching back to the early 1900s. In 2011 SAADA began producing engaging articles that combine archival materials with personal narratives and political insight in its slick online magazine *TIDES* (saada.org/tides). Some articles add historical depth to analysis of current events, such as Sherally Munshi's (2018) "Beyond the Muslim Ban," which connects current U.S. policy to a hundred years of xenophobic exclusionary immigration law. Others use personal stories to examine complex community issues, as with Jessica L. Namakkal's (2017) musings on her multiracial identity and contingent racialization, titled "Peanut Butter Dosas: Becoming Desi in the Midwest." Still others promote outward-facing solidarities, like Manan Desai's (2014) "What B. R. Ambedkar Wrote to W. E. B. Du Bois." Taken together, *TIDES* and the archive provide a specific kind of access to a history and reality long obscured. This history is both radical (surprising, different, politically progressive) and highly curated, leveraging the utopian promises of digital media for pro-social aims.

While accessible to a wide audience, the archive and *TIDES* centrally reach South Asian Americans. Projects like the forthcoming crowd-funded, multi-authored textbook *Our Stories: An Introduction to South Asian America* bring together a wide South Asian American community to contribute, ostensibly in the hopes of helping expand education about South Asians to American school children. Yet with 407 crowdfunding "backers" and over 65 author contributors, *Our Stories* mobilizes escalating digital and participatory practices to implicitly argue that this community must understand itself and be understood as internally diverse.

Even more outward-facing, SAADA's stand-alone site the First Days Project (firstdaysproject.org) invites any immigrant to the United States to record and share their experience of arrival. The stories then produce clickable pins on a timeline or world map visualization. This project reflects an active shift on the part of SAADA to argue for South Asian American history as American history *because* the experience of South Asians in America is part of and revealing of the commonly invoked "American immigrant experience" more generally. After the launch of the First Days Project in 2013, a discussion emerged about whether the project should be actively restricted only to the stories of immigrants of South Asian heritage. In response, the SAADA board of directors revised its mission and goals to read: "We envision

American and world histories that fully acknowledge the importance of immigrants and ethnic communities in the past, strengthen such communities in the present, and inspire discussion about their role in the future" (saada.org/mission). SAADA's various ventures offer sites of carefully curated participation in American history. Together they leverage techno-utopian hopes and discourses of American multiculturalism toward the pro-social end of reconceptualizing diaspora, minority identity, and the nation.

Taken together, *Sepia Mutiny*, SAADA, and similar sites work to produce and engage a specific vision of South Asian American diaspora—coalitional South Asian America—through community building and imaginative, digitally mediated labor. This conception of South Asian America is internally diverse, ordinary, fun, politically active in conjunction with other marginalized communities, and quintessentially American. Mobilizing a generative sense of diaspora as miraculous connection-in-dispersion, those invested in producing coalitional South Asian America work to enhance or build politically conscious yet everyday connections. Internally, they do so among South Asian America's diverse communities, and externally, they work to connect with other marginalized communities in the United States and around the world. They fight the racial triangulations that oversimplify South Asian American identity and isolate marginalized communities, setting them against each other when they have so much in common. The internal and external forces that push to simplify South Asian American identities and isolate communities of color, which facilitate racial hierarchies and intolerance, depend, at least in part, on ignoring the global and historical trajectories that have produced the specific racializations each minority community in the United States faces. Such regressive and isolating forces also depend on the unquestioned, implicit Whiteness of technoculture and mainstream media culture.

While there is much inertia to overcome, new digitally mediated experiences of diaspora allow space for such communities to build or strengthen novel connections, imagining new configurations of identity, solidarity, and belonging. Many South Asian American activists are working to produce coalitional strategies of domestic solidarity, community sociality, and global decolonization. Identities are always experienced personally and locally, but they are forged out of the transnational movement of people, ideas, capital, goods, and, increasingly, data. The proponents of coalitional South Asian America are mobilizing a generative model of diasporic identity alongside countercultural digital media practices, and in the process they are reframing their understandings of and engagements with race.

PART IV

Consuming and Resisting Race

16

Disrupting News Media

MEREDITH D. CLARK

journalism | Black Twitter | #BlackLivesMatter | social justice

August 9, 2019, marked the five-year anniversary of Mike Brown's slaying at the hands of Ferguson police officer Darren Wilson. For nearly two years after Brown's death, #BlackLivesMatter stood as a symbol for the pursuit of racial justice using a multi-method approach to political organizing for racial justice. The hashtag and its corresponding movement were developed by Alicia Garza, Patrice Cullors, and Opal Tometi, three Black women with extensive experience with grassroots campaigning for Black liberation. The phrase was invoked as a part of a repertoire of contention, which Charles Tilly (1986, 2008) defines as the entire set of tools a subordinate group has for making claims against a dominant one. With the advent of social media, protest repertoires have extended into digital networks, directly contributing to hashtag-assisted social movements such as #ArabSpring, #MoralMondays, and #Occupy-WallStreet. In previous protest eras, the dominant media technologies of print and broadcast equipped movement actors with the ability to publish newsletters and newspapers, as well as produce broadcasts to connect with, develop, and mobilize groups. We now see the use of social media tools like Twitter in "online direct action" designed to draw attention to mainstream media's exclusionary reporting power, and promote specific outcomes championed by marginalized groups.

Yet five years after the height of the Black Lives Matter movement, I see a missed opportunity to direct networked civil disobedience toward a target of opportunity—the journalistic practices that contribute to the deviant framing of Black people and Black bodies. Such practices normalize the underlying narratives about Black criminality used in attempts to justify extrajudicial killings and an overuse of force. Notice,

205

for instance, my use of the word "slaying" rather than "murder" at the opening of this essay. The word choice is a lingering effect of the *Associated Press Stylebook*'s preference for using "slay" to describe an extrajudicial death committed by a perpetrator who is legally acquitted. The *Stylebook*, colloquially known as the "journalist's Bible," is part of a system of unchecked reporting norms and practices that privilege the corporate interests of media owners over the lives of disenfranchised people. In the world created by news media narratives, Michael Brown was not murdered, even though his community says otherwise. And until news media's mechanisms of control are called into account by anti-racist actors for this and other subjugating practices, social media's democratizing potential will never be truly fulfilled.

Perhaps this target was overlooked by movement leaders as they focused on the immediate goals of attaining legal justice and civic accountability—a focus that left creating and circulating counternarratives as merely by-products of their use of digital and social media tools. But if Tilly's observation that protest participants "generally innovate at the perimeter of the existing repertoire rather than breaking entirely with old ways" (1995, 2), I find merit in making the connection between mediated resistance practices of earlier eras and ones formed in the digital age. Further, I offer that consideration of the relationship between social movement actors and mainstream news media, linked by social media, as an opportunity to use academic inquiry to suggest ways future movements may disrupt dominant media narratives that undermine their causes.

This chapter proposes a few ways to imagine how historically subjugated communities and groups, particularly Black people, can use digital and social media tools to introduce a shift in normative ideals about how news media portray us. With an eye on the future and a perspective informed by critique of movement platforms from the past, I advocate using radical imagination—a concept Shawn Ginwright (2008) describes as living in the world as it should be, not as it is, as a means of identifying targets of opportunity for future democratic media activism via digital and social media tools. Informed by digital intersectionality theory, "a resource grounded in the offline and online subjectivities of participants" (Tynes, Schuschke, and Noble 2016, 26), I argue that there is a historically informed mandate for Black people to harness contemporary media technologies and use them to demand accountability and participation from the press in reconstructing the value of Blackness as part of a normative narrative.

In the nineteenth century, *Freedom's Journal*, the first newspaper published by free Black men in the United States, encouraged Black people to pursue agency by controlling news media narratives about Black people. In 1967, the Black Panther Party for Self-Defense Ten-Point Platform and Program also espoused self-definition through creation, control, and support of media channels. A similar directive, however, is conspicuously absent from the 2015 platform of the Movement for Black Lives, a policy document created by activist groups, including members of Black Lives Matter. This omission may be a reflection of the perception that mainstream news media's influence is in decline as media outlets close, merge, and consolidate. It may spring from a sense of overconfidence in citizen journalists' ability to participate in creating and disseminating news in real time via the modern affordances of Web 2.0. But as we consider new directions for digital media and critical race studies, we should also recall that none of the existent media technologies of prior eras are defunct; in fact, some of the older ones—print news, analog broadcast stations, and others—are still being used by marginalized groups as conduits for productivity. And the infrastructures of these "legacy" media forms, which are often replicated in digital news media systems, still remain influential in contemporary struggles for racial justice in the digital age. Thus, while social movement actors continue to refine their media-use tactics in the Information Age, I exhort participants to consider direct, intentional, and strategic engagement of digital and social media use targeting mainstream media norms and operational practices in the fight for just representation and the fullness of Black humanity. Mainstream media, particularly news media, must be considered as a multifaceted target of opportunity for anti-racist work. These sites—including legacy newsrooms and their products—are tactically accessible and valuable to digital and social media information campaigns against racial injustice.

From Unrest to Uprising

There is a direct line to be drawn between historical and contemporary media depictions of Black civil unrest. Scenes from street protests during the Black Lives Matter movement evoke comparison to news media images captured during the civil disorders that roiled in Black enclaves across the country as frustrations with extrajudicial violence and white aggression boiled over in the late 1960s. In 1967, acting on an assignment from President Lyndon B. Johnson, the eleven-member Kerner Commission assessed the influences of major U.S. institutions, including government, law enforcement, schools, and the news media, and produced a report that warned that the country was moving toward "two Americas: one Black and one White; separate and unequal." The report criticized the news industry for its failure to integrate both personnel and coverage as a contributor to the public unrest within Black communities, remarking that despite its efforts to report without sensationalizing events, it had failed in its social responsibility to serve an American public that was equitable in its inclusion of Black perspectives:

> By and large, news organizations have failed to communicate to both their black and white audiences a sense of the problems America faces and the sources of potential solutions. The media report and write from the standpoint of a white man's world. . . .
>
> Slights and indignities are part of the Negro's daily life, and many of them come from what he now calls "the white press"—a press that repeatedly, if unconsciously, reflects the biases, the paternalism, the indifference of white America. This may be understandable, but it is not excusable in an institution that has the mission to inform and educate the whole of our society. (*Kerner Report* 1968)

The exclusion of Black editorial perspectives among producers of mainstream news media, and the resulting mischaracterization of Blackness are persistent problems. *Freedom's Journal* was founded in 1827 as a means to allow Black people to tell their own stories. Publishers John Russwurm and Samuel Cornish noted that white publishers had a tendency to generalize about Black deviance, casting suspicion on all Black people based on the criminal actions of an aberrant one. In the nearly two hundred years that have passed since the paper's initial run, Black publishers have adopted a publishing ethos that accounts for both structural and dynamic influences of race and power at multiple levels (Bobo 2000; Conwell 2016). By owning and operating their own outlets, the

Black press of the 1950s and 1960s circumvented white editorial control to chronicle the civil rights movement, while mainstream news media ignored and/or scandalized it. But as the children of professional Black news workers eschewed the family business in favor of jobs in the private sector in the 1980s, and digital technology gave affordance to a different type of publishing in the 1990s, the widening information and access gap of the so-called "digital divide" coincided with the shuttering of Black community newspapers throughout the country, and the number of Black journalists being added to and promoted within mainstream media newsrooms failed to grow at an adequate pace.

Statistics on newsroom demographics published annually by the News Leaders of America (formerly the American Society of News Editors) since 1978 indicate that the problem persists among mainstream print and digital media outlets. As of 2018, Black people made up only 9.02 percent of the full-time journalism workforce, while comprising 13.4 percent of the U.S. population. This employment gap contributes to the empirical evidence surrounding narratives of Blackness-as-deviancy that characterized coverage of the 1967 civil disorders, the uprisings of 2014 and 2015, and a host of points in between. Tara Pixley, a photojournalist, documentarian, and scholar, recounted one instance in which her news judgment was the sole force intervening on troublesome coverage of Ferguson. In 2014, as editors deliberated between two photos to feature in a gallery of the most compelling images of the week, they focused on a set of contrasting images. One was of a Black man, his face shrouded by a T-shirt, staring at the camera as an area gas station was being looted. The other depicted protestors on the street, mid-shout, some of their hands raised to punctuate their cries of "hands up, don't shoot." Pixley, the lone Black person in the room, cautioned that leading with the former would communicate to the world that crime, not protest, was the uprising's central narrative. She detailed her experience in a 2017 column for *Nieman Reports*, making the stakes of such intervention plain in an appeal to other professional newsworkers:

> Through the professional ethics and practices of objectivity in journalism, we have consistently found ways to humanize most members of American society, from convicted rapists to murderous white supremacists. Depictions of black Americans rarely receive such treatment in

news media, however, whether in images or the written word. We must commit to challenging all prevailing and easy narratives, affirming a desire to do both good, accurate, ethical storytelling and to take into consideration a multifaceted perspective with which we may be entirely unfamiliar. This originates with the journalists on the ground and continues with the editors making choices in the newsroom.

Yet the public response to coverage of the Ferguson uprising indicates that this task is no longer up to professional news workers alone. The restless observers of racial injustice have a critical role to play in actively decertifying mainstream media's power to extend these tropes any further.

A Historical Mandate for Collective Action on News Media Narratives

The importance of being free to speak for ourselves, and to circulate narratives informed by a multiplicity of Black perspectives, is a theme that links pro-Black policy platforms from the age of abolition to the civil rights movement to the era of affirmative action, and is finding maturity in this day. As part of its work for Black liberation, the Black Panther Party (BPP) produced and distributed its own newsletter from 1967 to 1976, which eventually became a newspaper with circulation throughout the Black diaspora. Through rhetorical and journalistic use of words and images, the BPP addressed a void in storytelling about Black life and Black power that mainstream media sometimes declined to acknowledge, and was often inclined to villainize. As Thy N. Phu (2008) states, "From the time of its inception, the Black Panther Party achieved prominence as the visible icon of black power, underscoring the urgency of community programs as well as self-defense, by playing—in often skillful ways—with photography" (168). Though the efficacy of that play has been contested by scholars both inside and outside the movement— particularly by Black women who challenged the utility of the BPP's symbolic use of images—the BPP recognized the importance of harnessing media technologies to tell its own stories. While the party's central policy statement, published in 1966, does not directly speak to pro-Black media, it contains an implicit reference to its utility via the platform's first, fifth, and tenth demands, which call for "power to determine our own destinies," "education that teaches about our true selves," and "community control of modern technology," respectively.

However, the BPP platform lacked the nuance modeled by the Black Lives Matter movement and its related policy statements. Created by women and informed by the experiences of gender nonconforming individuals, the movement:

> affirms the lives of Black queer and trans folks, disabled folks, Black-undocumented folks, folks with records, women and all Black lives along the gender spectrum. It centers those that have been marginalized within Black liberation movements. It is a tactic to (re)build the Black liberation movement. When we say Black Lives Matter, we are talking about the ways in which Black people are deprived of our basic human rights and dignity. (Garza 2014)

Claiming and centering difference was critical to the creation of digital counternarratives that advocated for considering the intersectional existence of the Black people whom the movement sought to free. This includes the Black mothers who were impacted not only by racism, but by sexism, and the Black transgender women who had to contend with both of these these, as well as transphobic fears within their own communities. Thus the importance of having many speakers was emphasized in the movement's development, as each perspective contributed something to the collective narrative developed via a series of tweets, blog posts, vlogs, and other born-digital media. While it lacks the cohesion offered by formal media routines, this collective use of media does what many news organizations—due to budget constraints, time, and/or size—simply cannot do: it presents a multiplicity of voices and perspectives on an issue, and offers narratives that are more broadly reflective of the range of experiences often missing from news coverage of Black communities.

By drawing on insights from the contemporary democratic digital media and social media activism strategies modeled by the most recent era of Black media activism, we can develop dynamic efforts to diversify coverage about Black people, both from within and outside the newsroom. We can critique the contemporary accommodation/assimilation model espoused by the news industry itself, which continually pursues an additive approach to rectifying Black exclusion in editorial decision making. This approach places intentional racial uplift on the back burner in favor of an idealistic embrace of meritocracy—the belief that given enough time and training, more Black journalists will simply assimilate and ascend into editorial roles within mainstream media. Its fatal flaw is common to progressive proposals for integration across fields, including technology, education, and business: a merit-based approach such as the accommodation/assimilation strategies the news industry has pursued for the last fifty years fails to examine how whiteness is considered normative, and that the cultural values created in spaces that privilege white-dominance-as-normative cannot be dislodged or dismantled by simply adding Black people to the mix.

Why Mainstream News Media Still Matter

In her foundational critique of the reproduction of racism via public discourse, Teun A. van Dijk (1992) notes that talk and text about people on the margins—specifically people of color—has wide-ranging ability to function as cultural influence with social and political outcomes. This claim is historically supported by the Kerner Commission's observations, as well as by contemporary research that indicates a persistent bias about Black people's tendency toward criminality (Holt 2013; Dixon 2006, 2008), the absence of Black fathers and their perceived lack of involvement in the home (Reynolds 2009; Harrison and Brown 2017), and the perception that Black bodies are impervious to pain (Hoffman et al. 2016). More specifically, Robert Entman and Andrew Rojecki's (2000) seminal examination of race-centric reporting highlighted that media norms and practices have concrete consequences for Black lives. During their data collection and analysis in the early 1990s, the researchers found that news media framed affirmative action debate in a way that positioned it as an issue of Black advancement at the expense of white self-preservation, leading them to conclude that such news media routines contribute to an inability to develop the majority group's collective understanding of the struggle for racial equity. Visual cues of inflammatory figures like Louis Farrakhan evoked schema that interpret Black empowerment as a radical notion, the researchers found.

Those same reporting practices are still at work in framing contemporary movements, where the most widely watched cable network in the country, FOX News, irresponsibly reported on Black Lives Matter as "a terrorist movement," funded by domestic and foreign actors with anti-American agendas. Even supposedly nonpartisan media are implicated in problematic framing of the most recent movement for Black racial justice, as a Black reporter for the *New York Times* negligently described Michael Brown as "no angel" in a front-page profile that ran alongside one of the teen's killer. The development and repetition of criminality and deviance frames contribute to moral panics fueled by anti-Black racism, a phenomenon so recurrent that David J. Leonard (2014) calls it America's national pastime.

Despite the efforts that diversity programs and high-profile hires have had in attempting to reshape existing media structures into spaces that are more inclusive, news media will always exist as an arena of contention for racial and social justice movements. They are spaces in which domination and subjugation are narrative cues with the ability to shape the literate public's perceptions of power, and they remain largely controlled—both symbolically and dynamically—by elite white men. Investigating news media infrastructures via digital intersectionality theory, which places the perspectives of the disenfranchised at the center of its analysis, we must consider questions of where and how historically subjugated individuals and groups can systematically address the industry's practices and how they contribute to public perceptions of Black deviance. This includes considering what tools are most effective in the project of dismantling the narratives they produce, and how these approaches should be formed. Critical race and digital media studies of how Black publishers used earlier media technologies to introduce counternarratives of Black lived experience, and examinations of how contemporary social movement actors have used social media tools to do the same, lead me to suggest that an *activist-inclusive* strategy that targets legacy news media infrastructures is a viable tool for denuding and dismantling reporting practices that reify white supremacy and Black subjectivity through the production and dissemination of mainstream media news.

John T. Barber and Alice Tait (2001) urge Black leaders to "form a global agenda for establishing policies that will aid Blacks in gaining a foothold in the Information Society" (341). Emergent technology, the authors write, presents both opportunities and obstacles for Black communities (specifically African Americans) to move from information-processing and distribution roles, such as data-entry and machine operators, to more influential positions of information creation and editorial judgment. The collective work enabled by social media, which challenged dominant narratives during the Black Lives Matter era, and in digital protest theaters before it, identified a few potential avenues for addressing Barber and Tait's challenge.

For instance, the plurality of narratives arising out of the online racial justice movements underscore the inherent deficiency in limiting Black perspectives to newsroom quotas and traditional journalism styles. Hashtag campaigns like #IfTheyGunnedMeDown critiqued common news-gathering practices by juxtaposing two photos of the same person—one signaling Black respectability, taken from participants' graduation days, in their military service uniforms, or at church; the other, signaling Black deviance with participants clutching liquor bottles, making profane gestures at the camera, or simply goofing off with friends. While reporting on Brown's murder, reporters frequently grabbed photos from his social media accounts, which were then highly circulated and subjected to uninformed analysis on major news stations. In one, the college-bound teen wore the requisite senior photo props—a green cap and gown with a red sash draped around his shoulders. In the other, Brown stood tall on his grandmother's front porch, yards from where he was gunned down, his fingers extended in a gesture that some reporting interpreted as a peace sign, while others wondered aloud whether it was a gang sign. Newsmakers often left the ambiguity of Brown's gesture open to interpretation—their job was simply to provide a photo of their reporting's subject, and they did.

#IfTheyGunnedMeDown called out the damaging effect of this practice, a reporting strategy that had evolved from relying on mug shots or state ID photos to save reporters time. It may have been legal and within the bounds of the social networking platform's terms of service, but that does not mean that these practices are justified in the newsroom. Indeed, such legally defensible but morally questionable practices reinforce white dominance as normative in the social construction of news. Using radical imagination to think about the impact of breaking-news decisions like photo selection is an opportunity to improve on such practices. When we look at how scores of participants in #IfTheyGunnedMeDown demonstrated just how damning the reporting practice could be, and how procuring a more representative photo was just as easy, we find opportunities to privilege the perspective of the communities who have the most to lose as a result of shoddy reporting. In future instances, news gatekeepers could use digital intersectionality by putting the perspectives of the affected community at the center of their choices, and making the effort to understand how even one questionable photo selection makes their outlet complicit in perpetuating frames of Black criminality. It may not have happened in the case of #IfTheyGunnedMeDown, but as the online discourse made clear, the practices that perpetuate these frames will not change without the intervention of a dedicated media strategy.

Part of the unrealized task of Black Lives Matter (as well as other social media–assisted racial justice movements) is to form a Black digital diasporic agenda for news media that so forcefully complicates the creation of hegemonic news narratives that producers are forced to reconsider their angles and editorial voice. Potential points of exploitation include news media's reliance on expert sources for information and "color" in their coverage—a need currently being addressed in academia by the public curation of source lists using the hashtags #CiteASister, #BlackTwitterstorians, and #WomenAlsoKnow. Demands for seats, space, and consultation on citizen editorial boards, in which members of the community serve in league with the publisher, executive editor, and other members of an outlet's collective conscious, are additional points of entry for ongoing efforts to situate underprivileged perspectives in mainstream media. Community inclusion in the political endorsement process, such as providing space for Black activists to directly question would-be elected leaders in the more intimate confines of an outlet's offices, could forge connections that complement street-level mobilization. Making a direct contribution within existing media structures is still a worthwhile pursuit for normalizing a more comprehensive and culturally competent narrative about Black life in the United States, a goal the Kerner Commission articulated more than fifty years ago in its report. It will simply require a radical reimagining of what such participation looks like so it becomes less a matter of fixing news media's so-called pipeline project. It must include a commitment to nourishing back to life the damaged relationship between Black communities and the news media that claim to serve them.

There are also opportunities to do corrective and in some cases reparative journalism work. This kind of work has been modeled by outlets such as *National Geographic*, which ran an apology for its racist coverage of non-white people; and the *New York Times*, which opened up lines of editorial inclusion by adding more writers of color to its opinion section, relaunching its shuttered race beat as an ongoing digital project, and including a call for letters to the editor that reflect a "diversity of perspectives." Each of these efforts seems to coincide with renewed attention to racial justice as is discussed in digital and social media spaces outside the control of mainstream newsrooms.

Fulfilling News Media's Promise of Social Responsibility

Mainstream news media are long overdue for an intersectional power analysis of how their structures and routines help maintain structural inequalities as unchecked assumptions about the status quo in the public imaginary. This, I believe, is the next site for compounding the potential of social media use in social justice projects. I encourage media scholars and practitioners to engage in a radical reimagining of how mainstream media has the opportunity to reshape its processes by heeding the voices of marginalized audiences and emboldened activists. Despite shifts in form, delivery, and function, news media remain influential in their ability to shape public perceptions and understanding of Black life. If they are to address their complicity in shaping public attitudes called out by anti-racist activists during the Black Lives Matter movement, news media must meet them along the lines of social media connectivity that have been traced in the emergent body of scholarship on social movements in the digital age.

As a complement, I encourage activist groups and other motivated actors (who recognize mainstream media's potential for change through citizen journalism) to recognize the inherent need for their voices to be included in shaping mainstream media production, and to codify this realization in their list of demands from mainstream media at every level. If journalism is ever to meet the promise of operating from a position of social responsibility to the public, understandings of "the public" must center historically marginalized peoples, rather than the elite class of readers and subscribers who drive the economic engines of the news.

17

Latinx Audiences as Mosaic

JILLIAN M. BÁEZ

audiences | media studies methods | heterogeneity

Although Latina/os comprise 17.8 percent of the U.S. population (U.S. Census Bureau 2017) and media industries clamor to reach this segment of the audience, Latinx media audiences remain understudied in both media studies and ethnic studies.[1] Responding to this dearth in research, a burgeoning body of scholarship is documenting how and why Latina/os consume media. This essay offers a brief survey of the existing research on Latinx media audiences, noting the various theoretical approaches and research methodologies used in this line of scholarship. Drawing from my own experience doing media ethnography, I explore challenges unique to working with Latinx media audiences, such as varying language use and a complex media diet that includes consumption of both English- and Spanish-language media. I also offer suggestions for future research on Latinx audiences. Looking across market research, ethnographic studies, and survey and interview methodologies, this chapter demonstrates that the growing field of Latinx audience studies is dynamic and has much to contribute to media studies' understanding of race, language, generation, and transnational media consumption.

Portrait of a Complex Audience via an Intersectional Optic

There are approximately 58 million Latinx people in the United States (U.S. Census Bureau 2017). As an umbrella term that groups many different ethnicities, "Latinx" includes people from over twenty countries in Latin America and the Caribbean living in the United States. While "Latina/o" is sometimes confused as a race within the popular imagination, most Latinx people are racially diverse (usually a mix between Spanish European, Indigenous, and black) due to the history of colonization in Latin America. As such, Latinx people vary widely in terms of complexion and phenotype. The Latinx population is also a heterogeneous group that varies greatly in terms of generation (contingent upon when one's family migrated to the United States), cultural traditions, and language usage and preferences. To complicate matters, while the Spanish language is often considered foundational to Latinx identity as it is the official language in most Latin American countries, there is currently an increase in Indigenous Latin American migrants who speak other languages, such as Mixtec and Nahuatl (Semple 2014). In addition, recent studies suggest that second- and third-generation Latinx youth are more likely to not only speak English as their dominant language, but also prefer English-language media (Rojas and Piñon 2017; Pew Research Center 2016).

The heterogeneity of the Latinx community has vexed the U.S. Census Bureau since it began collecting data on Mexicans in 1930 (Cohn 2010; Mora 2014). Although U.S. media industries, particularly advertising, have taken an interest in Latinx audiences since the 1980s (Dávila 2012), they have struggled to fully capture this segment of the market. The reason for this is twofold. First, the diversity within Latinx communities, or what Angharad Valdivia (2003) calls "radical hybridity," does not easily fit within the simple categories used in marketing research (Báez 2017a; Chávez 2015). In addition to differences in immigration histories and relationships to the United States (e.g., Puerto Ricans are U.S. citizens even on the island of Puerto Rico), the cultural and linguistic differences across Latinx communities have proven difficult for media industries to grasp (Báez 2018a; Dávila 2012; Westgate 2014). While media companies are beginning to take these differences more seriously, as in the case of Nielsen's motto "No somos todos iguales" (We are not all the same) and Univision's allowance of non-neutral Spanish, English, and Spanglish in reality programming (Avilés Santiago and Báez 2020), the most recent reception studies indicate that Latinx audiences are frustrated with the flattening of ethnic differences in Latinx-oriented programming (e.g., Báez 2018a; Rojas and Piñon 2017).

The second reason that media industries struggle to fully capture the heterogeneity of Latinx cultures is the complex media diet of most

Latinx audiences. Latinx daily media consumption often includes both Spanish-language and English-language media cutting across international, national, and local outlets. In some borderland areas, like San Diego, Latinx audiences can even pick up broadcast signals from both sides of the U.S.-Mexico border (Moran 2011, 2016). Latina/os are heavy media users who are also more likely to be content creators on social media platforms than any other group in the United States (Negrón-Muntaner et al. 2014; Negrón-Muntaner and Abbas 2016). These media habits are challenging to advertisers who often work within specific media markets that are delimited by language. As a result, media industries are gathering more data to comprehend, and hopefully more effectively target, Latinx consumers. For example, in 2018 the premiere audience measurement company Nielsen launched the initiative Latinx Nielsen, and in 2017 the Spanish-language television giant Univision created the website Univision Insights. Both of these outlets claim to provide the latest data on Latinx demographics and media consumption habits.

The existing research on Latinx audiences paints a richer and more complex portrait of Latinx media consumers than market research (Báez 2018a). Early surveys of Latinx audiences indicated that Latina/o media consumers engage with media in unique ways compared to the general U.S. audience, including consuming Spanish-language media as a form of language and culture maintenance (DeSipio 1998; Ríos 2000, 2003; Ríos and Gaines 1998). These early studies also indicated that some Latinx audiences reported dissatisfaction with their English-language media choices. Literature that builds on this research demonstrates that Latinx audiences have an ambivalent relationship to both English-language and Spanish-language media in the United States (Báez 2018a; Dávila 2012; Rojas 2004). More specifically, Latinx audiences tend to be frustrated by the "symbolic annihilation" (Tuchman 1979) of Latina/os in mainstream English-language media outlets. Reception studies also find that Latina/os express disappointment with the racist, sexist, and homophobic content of Spanish-language radio and television in the United States (Rojas 2004). Research on Latina/os' social media usage suggests that Latinx users fill in representational gaps not filled in both general market (English-language) and ethnic (Spanish-language) media (Avilés-Santiago 2018; Báez 2017b).

In order to fully grasp the hybridity of Latinx audiences, we must approach this community as a *mosaic* where individual parts, each with its own uniqueness, make up a larger whole. To address Latinx audiences as a variegated mosaic, most Latinx reception studies adopt an intersectional optic that looks across multiple facets of identity, including race, gender, sexuality, class, age, and generation. In particular, many Latinx reception studies employ a feminist lens of analysis and tend to focus on the specific experiences of girls and women (e.g., Báez 2018a; Brown 2010; Cepeda 2008; Rivero 2003; Rojas 2004; L. Vargas 2009). The scholarly focus on women dovetails with media industries' preference for Latina consumers over male consumers. For example, in recent years Nielsen produced two reports, "The Latina Power Shift" (2013) and "Latina 2.0" (2017), that are widely used across media industries. Both reports suggest that targeting women consumers is more lucrative than marketing to their male counterparts due to Latinas' increasing educational attainment, their cultural hybridity (what Nielsen calls "ambicultural" tendency), and their roles as decision makers of household purchases. Only more recent work is beginning to explore masculinity among Latinx audiences (e.g., Casillas 2014; Cepeda and Rosales 2017). Unfortunately, as of this writing, Latinx trans audiences have not been studied.

Although gender is attended to rigorously within Latinx audience studies (with the major exception of trans experiences), there are other identities and experiences that remain underexplored. For example, sexual orientation is sorely understudied within Latinx reception studies. I touch on non-heteronormative sexuality in my book on Latina audiences in Chicago (Báez 2018a) and work on undocumented queer art circulated via social media (Báez 2017a), but much more research is needed in this area to unravel how LGBTQIA audiences make sense of Latinx-oriented media. How might a LGBTQIA positionality overlap and diverge from the perceptions of heterosexual Latinx audience members?

In keeping with the metaphor of the mosaic, Latinx media studies overall tends to carefully unpack the concept of Latina/o as a panethnicity.[2] Many scholars demonstrate how Latinx-oriented media often fail at representing the diversity in Latinx communities (e.g., Dávila 2012; Valdivia 2010). Reception studies suggest that Latinx audiences

are frustrated with homogeneous representations that do not differenti-
ate among Latinx nationalities such as Mexican, Puerto Rican, and Colombian (Báez 2018a; Dávila 2012). The early and emerging research on
Latinx audiences largely explores the experiences of Mexican Americans
and Puerto Ricans. Although there are reception studies that offer comparative perspectives across different Latinx ethnicities, particularly following Vicki Mayer's (2004) call to "pass the pan" within Latinx media
studies (e.g., Báez 2018a; Cepeda 2008; L. Vargas 2009), few operate
very far outside a Mexican/Puerto Rican binary.[3] In other words, we still
know little about Latinx audiences that are not Mexican American or
Puerto Rican. Notable exceptions include María Elena Cepeda's (2008)
work on Colombians' reception of pop singer Shakira and Keara Goin's
(2017) research on Dominican audiences' interpretations of actress Zoe
Saldaña.

It behooves us to be inclusive about growing segments of the Latinx
audience, including Colombian, Cuban, Dominican, and Salvadoran
audiences. Although Cuban Americans have a long-standing history in
the United States and some research exists on Cuban American media
industries and content (e.g., Soruco 1996), little is known about them as
audience members. Furthermore, several non-Mexican and non-Puerto
Rican Latinx groups are concentrated in various cities (including New
York City, Miami, Los Angeles, and the Washington, DC area) throughout the United States. Each of these enclaves has its own local media
ecosystems, often including newspapers and community radio. Some of
these urban enclaves are transnational media epicenters. For example,
Miami is home to much of the Latin music industry and *telenovela* productions. Studying these local (and sometimes also transnational) media
might reveal new and unique patterns of media consumption.

Curiously, spirituality and religion are not overtly discussed in the existing literature on Latinx audiences. In my own research, especially during my ethnographic fieldwork on Latina audiences in Chicago (Báez
2018a), I found that audiences sometimes talked about their religious
background or their faith of origin. For example, some participants
made reference to religious figures and iconography (e.g., the Virgin
Mary in Catholicism) or strict dress codes for Jehovah's Witnesses. In
general, I did not probe the participants about this facet of their identity
and how it might influence their perception of media. I now view this

as a missed opportunity because religious beliefs and iconography can certainly impact one's media choices and shape perceptions of a given media text (L. Clark 2003). I explore religious subjectivity in my research on undocumented women's use of social media (Báez 2016), but scholars should pay more attention to religion and/or spirituality, as they can be key facets of one's identity and interaction with the world.

Lastly, Latinx audiences' political orientation, particularly as it intersects with ethnicity and religion, also shapes reception. Latinx political orientations range from conservative to progressive, often contingent upon ethnicity and religion. For example, Cubans in South Florida tend to be more politically conservative than other Latinx groups (Krogstad and Flores 2016). In terms of religion, in the 2016 presidential election Latinx pro-choice evangelical Christians tended to vote for conservative candidates (Stewart 2016). In the wake of the 2016 presidential election, where mainstream political analysts were baffled by how President Trump garnered so many Latinx votes (Gomez 2016), it is imperative to investigate how media consumption intersects with religion and political orientation. Federico Subervi-Vélez's 2008 edited volume *The Mass Media and Latino Politics* is currently the only book that explores Latinx audiences from a political communication perspective. More research is needed in this area to make sense of shifting Latinx voting patterns and the overall changing political landscape in the United States.

Latinx Audiences as Activists, Fans, and Content Creators

For decades both mainstream and ethnic media industries have positioned Latinx audiences primarily as consumers (Dávila 2012; Báez 2017a, 2018a). This positioning is endemic of a commercial media system whereby people are valued only for their buying power (or in the case of social media, their "clicking power"). Many Latinx audiences internalize this consumerist optic, calculating their worth vis-à-vis visibility in advertising and marketing (Báez 2017a, 2018a). However, Latinx audiences occupy multiple roles in their relationships to media. As will be discussed below, in addition to consumer, a Latinx audience member might also consider themselves a citizen capable of influencing media, a media activist pressuring media organizations for more inclusive hiring and content, and a creative worker engaged in cultural production such as fan media, podcasts, digital art, and videos.

Latina/os have a long (though often obscured) history of organizing for media policy in the United States (Beltrán 2016; Castañeda 2014a; Noriega 2000). At the same time, Latinx audiences report knowing very little about this history and contemporary media policy issues (Báez 2018b). This is partly because commercial media position Latinx audiences as consumers instead of as citizens who have a stake and say in media representation, particularly in regard to broadcast media that are regulated by the state (Báez 2015, 2018b). To undo this relegation of Latinx audiences as mere consumers, we can expand our understanding of Latina/os as citizens who can demand more inclusive media ownership and representation. In addition to treating Latinx audiences as citizens, we also should remember that some Latinx audiences are media activists. By media activists, I include people who not only formally work in the field of media activism (e.g., an employee at Free Press or the National Hispanic Media Coalition), but also ordinary citizens who advocate for better representation by contacting media companies and producers. In this sense, the scholarship on Asian American media activism (e.g., Lopez 2016a) is instructive in providing a framework to reposition Latinx audiences who seek and demand more inclusive media as media activists.

In addition to positioning Latinx audiences as citizens (and potentially media activists), Latina/os can also be fans. An excellent example of the intersection between media activism and fandom can be found in the social media engagement for the Netflix sitcom *One Day at a Time* (2017–2019). A remake of Norman Lear's 1970s series of the same name, *One Day at a Time* foregrounds a lower-middle-class Cuban American family in Echo Park, Los Angeles. Starring Justina Machado as a single mother and Emmy, Oscar, and Tony Award-winning Rita Moreno as her diva mother who helps to raise her two grandchildren, the sitcom features an almost all-Latinx cast and tackles complicated issues of queerness, colorism, sexual harassment, mental health, immigration, and alcoholism. Following the first and second season, Latinx and non-Latinx viewers rushed to Twitter using the hashtag #saveodaat to demand that Netflix renew the show. After the third season released in early 2019, Netflix announced that it may cancel *One Day at a Time*. As with previous seasons, fans pleaded with Netflix via #saveodaat to fund another season, noting that there are no other shows like this on television. Despite the outpouring of tweets in support of *One Day at a Time*, a tweet from Netflix stated that "simply not enough people watched to justify another season" (Netflix 2019). As of this writing it remains to be seen whether Netflix executives will change their mind or whether the show will be picked up by another platform. This example demonstrates how Latinx fans attempt to advocate for more dynamic media representations via social media. The case of *One Day at a Time* also points to the limited agency Latinx fans hold in the decision-making process of media companies.

Given Latina/os' ambivalent relationship to media so often marked by "symbolic annihilation," most of the scholarship on Latinx reception from a media studies perspective tends to characterize them as dissatisfied audiences. As a result, Latinx fandom, as a pleasurable form of media engagement, is undertheorized (Báez 2017c). Following Stuart Hall's (1980) encoding/decoding model, audience research indicates that Latinx fans have negotiated readings of media texts that can simultaneously include pleasure, discomfort, disgust, or frustration (Aparicio 1998; Báez 2018a; Brown 2010; Casillas 2014; Cepeda 2008; Rojas 2004; Valdivia 2000; Paredez 2009). Scholarship on popular music and *telenovelas* is one of the few academic spaces where Latinx fans' relationships to media are explored (Báez 2017c). Reading scholarship on music and television from a Latin@ studies perspective reveals not only that ethnic studies has studied fans for decades (albeit through different language and frameworks than media studies), but also that Latinx audience studies can deeply inform larger dialogues in fan studies about transnational consumption and cultural hybridity. In Latinx reception studies we are only just beginning to theorize Latinx non-fans, or audience members who vehemently oppose certain media texts, genres, or figures (Báez 2015; Rivera 2019).

Foregrounding Latinx fans requires researchers to deepen their understanding of ambivalence, negotiated and oppositional readings (as per Hall's encoding/decoding model), and deep disappointment or disgust with media texts. It will also prompt Latinx media studies to engage in more direct dialogue with fan studies. In addition to viewing audiences as "producers of meaning" (Hall 1980), fandom scholarship considers audiences prosumers who produce, circulate, and consume fan media content. Recent studies explore Latina/os as prosumers (Báez 2016; Morales 2016) following research indicating that Latina/os are heavy creators of user-generated content in digital platforms (Negrón-Muntaner et al. 2014). Much of the Latinx user-generated content is in the realm of entertainment, but users also use digital media to circulate activist messages (Báez 2016, 2017b) and to foster collective memory and grief (Avilés-Santiago 2018) and transnational relationships (Avilés-Santiago 2014; Mora and Rojas 2017). In more traditional media, Latina/os are very involved in community radio across the United States (Castañeda 2011). Overall, situating audience members not only as consumers but also as producers and distributors is essential for pushing the boundaries of ethnic studies and media studies.

Broadening Methodologies

In order to advance Latinx reception studies, researchers also need to engage with new and multiple methodologies. Following early cultural studies approaches in the 1980s and 1990s that relied on interviews about particular media texts (Nightengale 1996), Latinx audience studies tend to replicate this methodology. While interviewing individuals certainly yields significant findings about how audiences perceive the media text in question, it does not take into account the context in which media are consumed. For example, asking an interviewee what they think of a television show will glean different insights than observing a participant watching a television show at home with their family. I noticed this distinction clearly when I collected data about Latina audience reception of the ABC television series *Ugly Betty* (2006–2010). When I interviewed women about this *telenovela* adaptation, many participants were highly critical of the show, particularly in regard to the two main women characters, Betty and Hilda. Some women asked why Betty needed to be called "ugly" and were dismissive of the show because of the title. Others were angered by Hilda's (Betty's sister) performance of the Latina spitfire with her hoop earrings, urban accent, and form-fitting clothing. However, when I observed audiences watching the show at home with family or friends, frequently participants would find Betty endearing, noting her "good nature" and "wanting to help her family." While watching, viewers also mentioned respecting Hilda as an assertive single mother who worked hard to care for her son. Some audience members also admired how Hilda would protect Betty. Overall, attention should be paid to what audiences *say*, and what they *do*.

Melding interviews with other methods, such as participant observation, will help researchers to more deeply understand Latinx audiences. There are a number of media ethnographies scholars can draw upon to do this sort of work by both anthropologists (e.g., Abu-Lughod 2004) and media scholars alike (e.g., M. Gillespie 1995). There are very few media ethnographies of Latinx communities, with exceptions like Báez (2018a) and Mayer (2003), partly because employing mixed methodologies requires interdisciplinary training and ethnography is a resource-intensive method. However, when time and funds are available, I urge scholars to pursue ethnography as a window into how and when Latinxs consume media, how they perceive media, and moreover, how media play a role in everyday life.

In addition to ethnography, quantitative methods can also play an important role in more fully understanding Latinx audiences. Early research on Latinx audiences (e.g., DeSipio 1998; Ríos and Gaines 1998) utilized quantitative methods, often in the form of surveys and sometimes accompanied by qualitative focus groups or interviews, to measure Latinx media consumption patterns and perceptions of media representations. This early research laid the groundwork for later qualitative studies that more deeply probed into how Latina/os interpret media. In the present, few scholars study Latinx audiences through quantitative methods, particularly in measuring media effects. Key exceptions are the work of Rocio Rivadeneyra (Rivadeneyra and Ward 2005; Rivadeneyra 2006; Rivadeneyra, Ward, and Gordon 2007) on Latinx adolescents' perceptions of television and Dana Mastro's research on the effects of television on racial stereotyping (Tukachinsky, Mastro, and Yarchi 2017; Mastro, Behm-Morawitz, and Ortiz 2007). Considering how richly quantitative and qualitative methods can mutually inform one another (e.g., quantitative studies often lay the groundwork for qualitative studies that gather more nuanced data with a smaller sample), a re-engagement with quantitative audience research is critical for advancing the field. Collaboration between researchers trained in quantitative and qualitative methods could also be very fruitful for triangulation.

Lastly, archival methods are highly underutilized in Latinx audience studies. While media historians have explored audiences via archival materials (e.g., Butsch 2000; Douglas 2004), we know very little about Latinx audiences of the past. Clara Rodríguez's (2007) study of film viewers in the late nineteenth and early twentieth centuries in Puerto Rico stands out as one of the few historical studies focused on Latinx audiences. In particular, more historical research is sorely needed on Latinx print, radio, and television audiences of both English-language and Spanish-language outlets.

Conclusion

In this essay, I provide a brief overview of the most critical interventions of Latinx audience studies. Latina/os are a diverse group in terms of national origin, language use, generation, and race. Latinx media consumption patterns oscillate between English-language and Spanish-language media. In order to capture this complexity, Latinx reception studies offers sophisticated theoretical frameworks and empirical evidence that detail how cultural hybridity and transnational identities are forged and maintained by media. I suggest that we approach Latinx audiences as a mosaic to grapple with the multiplicity of their reception experience.

In addition to highlighting the contributions of Latinx reception studies, I also offer several recommendations for future research to deepen our understanding of Latinx audiences, a demographic that is growing in the United States and consumes media daily in a shifting global multimedia landscape. First, I suggest that researchers deepen their intersectional optic. Existing research on Latinx reception provides sharp analyses of gender, but would benefit from more closely examining sexual orientation, religion, and political orientation. In addition, although Latinx audience studies rigorously analyze Latinidad as a pan-ethnic strategy and identity, more empirical data need to be collected about non-Mexican and non-Puerto Rican Latinx audiences. Second, I call for a reframing of Latinx audiences as citizens, activists, fans, and producers. In this way, I am broadening media industries' insistence on positioning Latinx audiences as passive consumers valued for their buying power. It is paramount that researchers not reproduce this limited consumerist framing of Latinx audiences. Lastly, I urge scholars to engage with new types of methodologies, including ethnography, and revisit old approaches like survey methods, to more fully elucidate the Latinx audience experience.

18

Media Activism in the Red Power Movement

MIRANDA J. BRADY

Indigenous activism | documentary | allies | tactics

The 1960s and 1970s marked an important era for Indigenous activism in Canada, the United States, and globally. Such activism was motivated by a long history of dispossession and was highly influenced by the momentum of other social movements during that era (Mather 1973; Lyons 1978). Indigenous nations had exercised their own self-governance structures for hundreds or even thousands of years before the formation of the United States and Canada in 1776 and 1867 respectively (Bonaparte 2006). However, settler-colonial agendas of resource extraction and territorial dispossession meant horribly oppressive conditions for Indigenous peoples; these agendas were forwarded through policies of assimilation and the intentional disruption of traditional Indigenous governance structures in favor of ones that could be federally manipulated (George-Kanentiio 2011).

One example of the systematic disruption and dispossession of Indigenous lifeways can be seen in the Indian Residential Schools in Canada, which were attended by 150,000 First Nations, Métis, and Inuit students from the 1870s to the 1990s. The Truth and Reconciliation Commission of Canada documents thousands of stories of physical, sexual, and psychological abuse suffered by the students who attended the schools at the hands of church clergy who operated them, as well as underfunding by the government, leading to malnourishment, death, and the spread of disease (Truth and Reconciliation Commission 2015; Milloy 1999). Children experienced harsh corporeal punishment for speaking their native languages, and in some cases, were used as research subjects without their knowledge or informed consent or that of their parents (Mosby 2013).

Indian Residential Schools were just one component of overall systems of white supremacy aimed at assimilating Indigenous peoples into majority culture in Canada and paralleled in the United States. Another example occurred between 1945 and 1960, when the United States processed 109 termination cases through which the government ceased to recognize Indigenous nations and provide the rights guaranteed to them through treaties and national laws; this affected approximately twelve thousand Indigenous peoples (Fixico 1986; Pinkins 2011).[1]

These policies and practices had devastating effects, but ironically, also sparked resurgence within Indigenous communities and alliances spanning both sides of the border. As termination efforts accelerated in the United States following World War II, these bonds continued to grow. It was through attendance at residential schools, termination and forced relocations, and service in the military that predecessors and early activists of the Red Power era began making wider connections with Indigenous peoples from other communities. This added to movements to reclaim traditional lifeways and regain tribal self-governance, or sovereignty; this activism was already gaining momentum in some communities in the earlier postwar period, but took on a radical new form (*Akwesasne Notes* 1976; Cobb 2008; Sanchez and Stuckey 2000). This movement evolved into Red Power activism, taking its cue from counterculture, civil rights, and global decolonization groups as well as longer traditions of alliance and diplomacy (Hauptman 1986).

Although coming from modest means, Indigenous activists of the late 1960s and early 1970s were resourceful, and some had received media production training through work at tribal newspapers or national institutions (George-Kanentiio 2011; Hauptman 1986). Others intuitively learned techniques for creating media events or orchestrating actions that would draw attention from the news media to shame the government (Sanchez and Stuckey 2000). They made do with little by tapping in to an intricate network of relationships with media makers and were media practitioners in their own right. They partnered with mainstream and underground media and created their own media outlets aimed at both majority audiences and their own communities.

Where Indigenous peoples had experienced both stereotyping and symbolic annihilation in the media (Merskin 1998; Raheja 2010), in the 1960s they began to mobilize the same institutions that had erased them for so long. With increasing national anxiety and distrust of the U.S. government during the Viet Nam era due to the large numbers of American casualties and anti-war dissent, these tactical appeals had a better chance of resonating with critical American audiences. Moreover, the public was becoming wary of corrupt officials as details of Richard Nixon's Watergate scandal began to emerge.

Scholars have examined the rhetorical strategies employed by groups such as the Indians of All Tribes and the American Indian Movement (Kelly 2009, 2014; Sanchez and Stuckey 2000; Chaat Smith and Warrior 1996) as well as rhetorical strategies and exclusion employed by government officials (Sanchez, Stuckey, and Morris 1999; Kelly 2007); others have examined press coverage of Indigenous activism (Anderson and Robertson 2011), and activists have also published their own accounts (e.g., *Akwesasne Notes* 1976; Boyer 1997; Banks 2004; Means 1995). However, it is important to think about how the early media activism of the late 1960s and early 1970s shaped subsequent tactics. As Leanne Simpson (2013) notes, while outsiders and mainstream news media tend to see Indigenous activism as isolated events, they are a continuation of the same struggles resulting from settler dispossession.

By highlighting some of the connections between early media activism in the Red Power movement and drawing comparisons, this chapter encourages an understanding of their impact and context beyond the singular event. Moreover, it encourages us to think about approaches that were more or less successful as historical conditions began to shift in the early 1970s. The scope of this chapter is far too brief to fully engage the rich history and dynamics of this era, and therefore I focus on a few key examples. As a non-Indigenous settler living on unceded, unsurrendered Algonquin territories, I am aware of my white privilege and the uncertainty I inhabit as an academic engaging in this topic (Mackey 2016; Tuck and Yang 2012). As an outsider, rather than offering a definitive work on Indigenous media activism, I offer this as an avenue of exploration that I hope will open up fruitful conversations.

From Community to Social Movement: *You Are on Indian Land*

As Indigenous leaders in the United States fought termination efforts in 1968, traditional Indigenous leaders in Akwesasne/St. Regis were imploring Parliament Hill to recognize the treaty rights of their community, which sits directly on the U.S./Canadian border. Activists asserted the rights of Kanien'kehá:ka (Mohawk) people established with the 1795 Jay Treaty to cross the border freely between the United States and Canada without paying a duty on goods purchased on either side; their community predates both nation-states, the provinces of Ontario and Quebec, and the state of New York, all of which community members must traverse as they move through their territories. In addition to imposing the national boundary that intersected Kanien'kehá:ka territories, Canadian officials built a bridge and customs house there without the consent of residents. Many Kanien'kehá:ka people cross the border regularly and even daily for work, school, or shopping and were subjected to tolls, duties, and harassment from customs officials for simply moving within their own community.

In 1968 a young Kanien'kehá:ka man from Akwesasne named Mike Kanentakeron Mitchell was instrumental in organizing a community protest, which was documented by the National Film Board of Canada (NFB). Mitchell had been working with a crew of Indigenous filmmakers trained through the NFB's Challenge for Change (CFC) program started in 1967 during the country's centennial celebration (Honarpisheh 2006). The program, which spanned ten years, was led by white executive director George Stoney, a filmmaker famous for his cinema verité–style documentaries that not only recorded events as they unfolded but acted as catalysts for community transformation. (e.g., *The Fogo Island Process* films, beginning 1967). This program reflected a shift to a national policy of Canadian multiculturalism following national French unrest in which film was enrolled to "promote citizen participation in the solution of social problems" (Barnouw 1993, 258). As Ginsburg states of Stoney, "few in documentary were as clear (and as legendary) as Stoney was about the importance of people being in control of the media being made about them" (Ginsburg 1999, 62). Importantly, a central tenet of the Challenge for Change program was to put the camera in the hands of traditionally marginalized people and provide training so that they could tell their own stories (Ginsburg 1999).

Ironically, the creation of this state-sponsored program meant opening up funding for scathing critiques of the government, which not surprisingly happened with the formation of the "Indian Film Crew," who directly challenged settler-colonial society in the process of promoting traditional cultures. Originally consisting of six male and one female Indigenous trainees from different communities, the group reached an international audience through the co-production of several films, including *These Are My People* (1969), directed by Willie Dunn, Mitchell, and Roy Daniels, *The Ballad of Crowfoot* (1968), directed by Dunn, and *Who Were the Ones?*, directed by Mitchell.

The most famous of these was the thirty-seven-minute documentary *You Are on Indian Land*. The film documents the December 1968 blockade of traffic along the U.S./Canadian Seaway International Bridge by Mike Mitchell and other community members to protest the imposition of the Canadian customs house and duties on Kanien'kehá:ka people travelling through their own territories. The film was co-created with Mitchell, non-Indigenous director Mort Ransen, Noel Starblanket, and the Akwesasne community, who are credited at the end of the film. In the film, protestors are confronted by a police force that clearly misunderstands the nature of their assertions, seeing the world through a law-and-order lens. Several unarmed members of the community are arrested as traditionalist Ernest Benedict tries to discourage violence and maintain a peaceful demonstration. The film begins and ends with a gathering in which Mitchell explains the protestors' position to officials and the press.

Initially, Mitchell and other community members organized a delegation to travel to Ottawa, the nation's capital, to lobby the government for their rights to cross the border freely, circumventing a Band Council that they saw as a government puppet. At the same time, Mitchell reached out to George Stoney, stating, "If we don't get satisfaction, which I doubt, we're coming back and we're going to block the international bridge. . . . If we block the bridge I want a film crew down there" (Ginsburg 1999, citing Stoney 1980, 64). Stoney sent the crew at Mitchell's behest. Not only did Stoney ensure that the event was recorded, he circulated the film in the community in keeping with his idea that it had great potential as a catalyst for social change. According to Ginsburg (1999), it was sent for processing soon after being shot so that it could be used as a tool for community building as protestors were arrested. Stoney also showed the footage to white officials with the Royal Canadian Mounted Police.

To understand the alliance with Stoney, we need to note that Mitchell and Benedict had come from a long line of Haudenosaunee (Iroquois

Confederacy) people who had strategically made alliances. Like all members of the Iroquois Confederacy, the Kanien'kehá:ka have a long history of diplomacy and interconnections with other Indigenous groups through trade, movement, and political engagement (Bonaparte 2006). Kanien'kehá:ka people have also had exposure to white settlers for hundreds of years, as evidenced by the Two Row Wampum, a fifteenth-century illustration of the agreement between the Haudenosaunee and Dutch settlers to live in peace alongside one another and to not interfere in the self-governance of the other (Rick Hill, in Maracle 2015). Haudenosaunee found themselves bound up with colonial allies in efforts to maintain trade relations and increasingly diminished territories through the Revolution, the French and Indian Wars, and the War of 1812.

Missing this important history of diplomacy, alliance, and activism, a white academic named Sol Worth criticized *You Are on Indian Land* by imposing a framework based on his own outsider experiences. Worth had collaborated with anthropologist John Adair to author the 1972 book *Through Navajo Eyes*, which documents his project with Adair in Pine Springs, Arizona, where they provided Navajo participants with equipment to make their own films. In his review of *You Are on Indian Land* in *American Anthropologist*, Worth accused the NFB film of being "a perfect example of the professional White liberal film made in 'consultation' with Indians" (74). This comment reflects the idea that the Indigenous youth trained through the NFB would not be savvy enough to create such a product. Worth seems unaware of the history of Akwesasne, its politics, and similar demonstrations like that of Standing Arrow in 1957, as well as the media savvy of leaders like Benedict, who had worked on tribal newspapers (George-Kanentiio 2011). In a flourish of ignorance, Worth asks, "How did these Indians to whom such behavior is quite alien get to learn about the use of mass media—film, TV, and newspapers—to mount a propaganda campaign of this magnitude?" (Worth 1972, 1031).

Yet other non-Indigenous academics helped to better contextualize this Indigenous/non-Indigenous alliance. Scholar Mary E. Fleming Mather (1973) noted that the community's "political sophistication" had developed over a long history of interactions with white settlers spanning hundreds of years. Similarly, she states, "these people would have to be incredibly naïve to be unfamiliar with mass media and civil rights techniques," a naïveté that Worth seems to assume is characteristic of all Indigenous peoples (75). She also describes the role of the traveling troupe of educators from the community, the White Roots of Peace, in communicating traditional messages more broadly to the public. It was clear that community members were aware of the multiple audiences to whom they were speaking, and how they might make appeals to them.

Despite critiques from misguided outsiders like Worth, *You Are on Indian Land* went on to be incredibly influential as a tool that demonstrated Indigenous political efficacy from eastern Canada to Alcatraz Island in the San Francisco Bay Area. When a group called the Indians of All Tribes took over Alcatraz in November of the following year, they held a screening of the film; they also painted the same mantra on a support wall so that approaching boats could read the words that summarized their movement so well: "YOU ARE ON INDIAN LAND" (National Film Board of Canada 2019; Strange and Loo 2001).

The Connections of Alcatraz Island

Although the two protests took place more than three thousand miles apart, there were many connections between the media activism displayed in Akwesasne/St. Regis through the aforementioned film and the Occupation of Alcatraz Island from 1969 to 1971. Most notably, they were both organized by young activists who understood the ways they could orchestrate media events around gathering together as Indigenous peoples to reclaim territories and reassert their presence. One of the key activists who helped to accomplish this was LaNada Boyer.

As a young woman in 1965, Shoshone/Bannock LaNada Boyer left her home in Blackfoot Idaho for San Francisco as part of a Bureau of Indian Affairs relocation program. It was there that she participated in the Alcatraz Island occupation with other Indigenous activists and students attending the University of California, Berkeley and San Francisco State University. This included Kanien'kehá:ka activist Richard Oakes, who was from Akwesasne/St. Regis and undoubtedly influenced by the media activism in that community. Both gained and managed press attention by building relationships with media practitioners and empathetic celebrities.

The Indians of All Tribes organized to call attention to a federal law and 1868 treaty stating that land deemed federal surplus, as with Alcatraz Island, would be returned to Indigenous peoples. Boyer assumed the assignment of public relations representative for the activists on the island, where international attention became key. She states,

> The international media focus embarrassed the federal government. The United States of America is always the first to point out human rights violations in other countries, without regard to its own treatment of Native Americans, blacks, Chicanos, Asians, and poor people. We hoped to expose the atrocities that the federal government had perpetrated and continues to perpetrate against our people. Every day, as news of the island takeover traveled throughout the country, our people kept arriving. We were in full view of the entire world, and the government made no move to take us off the island. (Boyer 1997, 92)

The group was known for making public declarations about its actions, and Boyer attempted to shape media messages with regular press briefings. For example, she notes that government agents were planting stories in the media to make the group appear to be armed and dangerous. In response, she held a press conference on the island to illustrate that there were no guns there, even disarming children of their toy guns in front of the media (Boyer 1997). Similarly, John Trudell, a Santee Dakota and Indigenous Mexican activist, brought attention to the island through "Radio Free Alcatraz," which was broadcast from the main cellblock and carried on the Pacifica radio network reaching Berkeley, Los Angeles, and New York (Pacifica Radio Archives 2017). Each evening broadcast began with Cree singer Buffy Sainte-Marie's "Now That the Buffalo's Gone" (ibid.).

While national and international press covered the events at Alcatraz, news of the occupation also spread throughout Indian country and across college campuses through *Akwesasne Notes*, a newsletter co-founded by Ernest Benedict, and at that time, distributed through numerous interpersonal networks and travelling troupes of educators (George-Kanentiio 2011; *Akwesasne Notes* 1969). Boyer also became the subject of media attention when the leftist magazine *Ramparts* wrote a feature centered on her story titled "The Red Man's Burden" (Collier

1970), and she graced the magazine's cover with the words "Better Red Than Dead." The magazine had paid a fine for Boyer resulting from the Third World Strike that she had helped to organize on the UC Berkeley campus and critiqued coverage from other media outlets, demonstrating its reciprocity as an ally (Collier 1970). This and other public relations efforts helped garner support from non-Indigenous celebrities like the musical group Credence Clearwater Revival. The band purchased a boat (dubbed the *Clearwater*) to transport fresh water to the island after the government confiscated the activists' barge (Boyer 1997, 93). White actress Jane Fonda also made an appearance on the island after reading the *Ramparts* article, and she used her connections to get Boyer a spot on the *Dick Cavett Show* in New York.

While each of these media events called more attention to the activists, Boyer notes that she felt ambivalent about working with celebrities and mainstream media. After being on the *Dick Cavett Show*, she states, "I had never been on a television show, and it made me feel extremely uncomfortable. . . . I felt awkward, wondering if I was supposed to be witty and funny about the injustices perpetrated against our people" (97). Her words point to the tensions that exist between the fleeting attention of mainstream audiences and ongoing Indigenous struggles.

While moments of celebrity orchestrated through the actions helped the group to gain attention, it was difficult to maintain public support. After many trying circumstances, the Indians of All Tribes eventually left the island; however, their actions were widely seen as a success in having made an impression through media and popular culture. Nearly fifty years later, during an alumni gathering at Alcatraz, occupiers described the event as the spark that inspired generations of Indigenous activism, noting that it continues to have symbolic importance. Navajo activist Lenny Foster makes the connection with more contemporary 2016 Indigenous actions in South Dakota: "It was a catalyst to what is happening at Standing Rock. The resistance goes from Alcatraz to Standing Rock" (Rickert 2017). But, while Alcatraz is noted as the initial catalyst for Indigenous activism, it is important to note the impact of the actions, players, and media coming out of Akwesasne.

Many other examples of Indigenous activism took their cue from these early years. But while Boyer stressed the importance of peaceful action, a new form of armed activism emerged shortly after, as exemplified by the 1973 seventy-three-day occupation of Wounded Knee by the American Indian Movement (AIM). The occupation was a highly symbolic media event where activists sought protection through press attention but was markedly different because of the militancy associated with AIM. As Sanchez and Stuckey note, "When it came to countering government and media-propagated images of activists, AIM's biggest hurdle was the portrayal of them as violent revolutionaries" (130). However, there were many similarities. As with the Indians of All Tribes, AIM found support with non-Indigenous celebrities like Marlon Brando, who famously refused his Academy Award in solidarity with the group. Millions of viewers saw the televised awards ceremony when Brando sent Sacheen Littlefeather in his place, and a national poll revealed that the majority of Americans sided with the Indigenous protestors, at least for a short time (Nelson 2010).[2] AIM activist Russell Means, who was also present in Alcatraz in 1969 and during an earlier demonstration in 1964, notes that AIM supporters were watching the awards ceremony broadcast from inside Wounded Knee; this gesture of support provided a significant boost when morale was low (Means in Diamond 2009; Lyons 1978). Although no lasting policy reforms resulted from this activism (Sanchez and Stuckey 2000), these moments nonetheless mark significant alliances between Indigenous and non-Indigenous media activists that became visible and meaningful through mediated narratives.

Arguably, we can still see some of the same media strategies used in more contemporary actions. These carefully consider audiences and staging, from the widely tweeted round dances in malls during the #IdleNoMore movement beginning in 2013, to the silk screen "Water Is Life" banners used in demonstrations, created by artists Isaac Murdoch (Ojibway) and Christi Belcourt (Métis) in collaboration with students during art workshops hosted on university campuses. While Indigenous media activist tactics transform according to contemporary needs, they are rooted in a long and rich history.

Conclusions

Because outsiders often view Indigenous activism in isolation without a broader historical context, it is important to note the connections between the media activism of the late 1960s and early 1970s and the profound impact it had on the media tactics that followed. The players involved developed sophisticated maneuvers to access mainstream resources through interpersonal relationships. Each media event raised awareness about Indigenous concerns while also serving to compete with the overwhelming resources at the disposal of authorities who sought to silence them. Although sometimes ambivalent or unsuccessful, the mobilization and clever tactics of Indigenous activists of that era reveal a creativity and energy that continue through Indigenous media activism today.

19

Black Gamers' Resistance

KISHONNA L. GRAY

platforms | video games | digital ethnography | live-streaming |
online spaces

Introduction: Live-Streaming and the Hegemonic Culture of Gaming

While we commonly think of video gamers as individuals who play
video games, in recent years another form of engaging with video games
has emerged—the use of live-streaming platforms that allow mass audiences to watch others play video games. Digital platforms like Mixer,
YouTube, and Twitch connect gamers around the world by allowing
them to broadcast, watch, and chat with one another from everywhere
they play. Twitch has been the most successful, attracting over 34 million
unique viewers a month (Edge 2013). Most live-streamers are afforded
the opportunity to make money from streaming and connecting to other
game fans, but their most valuable assets are the spectators. These are
the individuals who follow in-game, live-streaming experiences but are
not themselves currently immersed in game play. Because of this deep
engagement, video game live-streaming has the potential to promote
participatory engagement and alternative forms of community.

Yet this new form of community still falls prey to the racism that
plagues so many digital platforms and gaming cultures. This chapter
focuses on the way Black video gamers respond to racism, using live-
streaming platforms to disrupt and shift hegemonic video game narratives and cultural norms. By employing digital ethnography, critical
observations, and narrative interviewing, I aim to reveal the contentious
realities facing Black gamers and streamers. As one participant stated,

Of course nobody tunes in [to watch our live gaming streams]. We're
Black. And that's too Black for them [Twitch viewers]. No matter what
we talkin' about. But the few brothas that tune in? I try to do what I can.
To make sure they know. We got a community here. . . . I spend most my
time just talkin' 'bout us. (Interview with Black live-streamer)

The above statement expresses a common sentiment about live-
streaming by the many streamers who identify as Black. They have
understood and defined their realities in gaming culture as partially
hostile and perpetually isolating. But by using Twitch, Mixer, YouTube,
and other live-streaming technologies, these streamers, gamers, and
their tools, as social technologies, have the ability to transcend mediated
borders by creating a significant community that supports marginalized
identities and sustains their cultures. As this chapter will reveal, there
are particular dynamics that impede full participation and production
by these streamers, even as they continue to develop resistance practices
and activism that are specific to live-streaming platforms.

Digital Methods. Transmediated Realities. Black Lives

While traditional virtual ethnographies make sense of online environments and those who occupy those spaces, in this chapter I examine
how online spaces have been created by and for privileged bodies and
account for how Black users respond to marginalization. In particular, I
consider those who make no claims to these spaces, but instead continue
to exist on the margins to do the transformative work that is needed for
their communities. But the movement of these gamers in and out of
spaces, employing multiple modes of communication from textual to
oral to visual, is central to this digital ethnography. I move beyond seeing
these gamers as merely research participants who would have no control
over how their data were collected and analyzed—instead disrupting
and dismantling the traditional power hierarchy between researcher and
researched. I acknowledge these gamers as co-producers of knowledge,
as narrators who have access to making sense of how everyday Black
folk see themselves within these spaces created by hegemonic bodies,
but where they resist and transform communities, policies, and practices
within gaming culture. To work toward this goal, this chapter provides

a snapshot of my ten-year ethnography within digital gaming culture. I provide detailed narratives from a group of gamers referred to as a "clan" in gaming culture. The particular narratives outlined here stem from interactions after the deaths of unarmed Black men by police in the United States and surrounding the release of two video games featuring Black protagonists, Lincoln Clay (*Mafia III*) and Marcus Holloway (*Watch Dogs 2*). These experiences manifested digitally for this small group of Black gamers as they began incorporating their personal experiences and communal perspectives into their live-streaming content.

(Black) Games, Black Gamers, and Black Cultural Production

In allowing users the ability to create and produce content for an audience, platforms like YouTube, Twitch, and Mixer (among others) allow ordinary users to provide their own narratives and engage in digital cultural production (Strangelove 2010). This act of participation then extends the immersive value of games in particular for Black users who are often excluded and isolated from media production. Their contributions directly highlight resistance to traditional hegemonic stories and narratives, especially since gaming has long been criticized for its historical reproduction of othering and connections to the real-world ideologies of racism.

Mediated representations within games are often viewed through the dichotomy of positive or negative. Similar to other mediated imagery, Black narratives in games deploy the dangerous myth of assimilation for people of color without focusing on the racialized reality that people of color still reside within or the myths associated with meritocracy (Campbell 1995). Positive representations such as these are used to provide evidentiary claims that inequalities no longer exist (Bristor, Lee, and Hunt 1995; Villani 2001). Black characters are also often ghettoized with an emphasis on crime, drug abuse, and materialism; they are depicted as jobless, lazy, angry, often involved in conflicts, and possessing menial jobs, or painted as money-hungry criminals, hustlers, or gang members (Abraham 2003; Bristor, Lee, and Hunt 1995; Entman and Rojecki 2000; Harrell and Gallardo 2008; Ward 2004). When we do see narratives depicting Black characters in more progressive roles, they are still subject to White characters as heroes or saviors. Thus, the inscription of stereotypical media narratives into video games reveals the visible and invisible contours of collective and structural ideations that affirm long-standing cultural scripts about Black identity.

But the number of titles featuring Black protagonists in non-stereotypical positions has dramatically increased in recent years. As Samantha Blackmon (2016) states, the release of two Black heroes in popular culture who were "unapologetically . . . Black" reflects a recognition of inclusive stories within gaming culture—or the inability to continue ignoring the demands of gamers demanding more diversity. While she is referring to the Marvel superhero Luke Cage (which is not a video game) and Lincoln Clay from *Mafia III*, her analysis can extend to other video game titles such as *Watch Dogs 2*, *Battlefield 1*, and *Assassins Creed: Freedom Cry*. Examples such as these and others reveal to the gaming community that Blackness is increasingly unavoidable, and must be consumed holistically rather than through the singular lenses of the past.

Yet the Black gaming community has been divided in response to these Black in-game depictions, as many express that Blackness is still consumed through traditional tropes such as criminal narratives and the dangerous Black body. Others contend that the hypervisibility and hyperconsumption of Black death in *Battlefield 1* fit within the problematic framing deployed in mainstream media—the hyperconsumption of Black death and pain. As Catherine K. Steele and Jessica Lu (2018) explain, viral videos of Black men and women violently dying at the hands of the police have become a staple of digital media that stems from both cable news and lynching photography. This singular framing devalues their humanity by showing excessive images of Black pain, suffering, and death.

This kind of racism has been prevalent in streaming practices as well. For instance, the extremely popular YouTuber and gamer known as PewDiePie generated international attention for uttering a racial slur while live-streaming. While PewDiePie was no stranger to provocative acts on his videos, Black communities were particularly insulted when streaming services and gaming industry elites continued to support him even after these explicitly racist incidents. In doing so, they revealed the structural ways that gaming industries are implicated in productions of White supremacy and racial inequities—in excusing his behavior, such actions were affirmed as the norm within gaming. Racism has always been normalized through incidents like this that take place in public spaces, while even more go unchecked in private, anonymous spaces. Indeed, discussions about the rise of overt racism in relation to the "alt-right" and the election of Donald Trump elide the reality that these occurrences are far from new. The danger is not in individual instantiations of racist or sexist speech, but in the power of digital platforms that allow individuals to reach multitudes. In doing so, these platforms help to normalize racist behaviors and sustain the digital and physical violence associated with those behaviors.

The presence of Black gamers within live-streaming culture provides one way to counter these hegemonic norms, as they too bear the brunt of individual, structural, and institutional oppression. Their participation runs counter to the conformist cultural practices operating not only within live-streaming, but within the hegemonic Whiteness of gaming culture more broadly (K. Gray 2012a). There is a particular power through live-streaming that Black streamers are developing. The mostly unfettered and unregulated platforms provide an arena to disseminate Black knowledge for gamers who want to consume it—and in doing so, facilitate a form of Black resistance and activism within gaming.

Black Lives Don't Matter in Gaming

One of the key ways that Black participants have facilitated activism within digital game spaces has been to make connections between gaming and the #BlackLivesMatter movement. This makes sense, since activism surrounding #BlackLivesMatter and its struggle against anti-Blackness and police brutality has largely taken place online through social media (M. Hill 2018; Freelon, McIlwain, and Clark 2016a; S. Jackson 2016; Yang 2016; Flores 2015). As Jelani Ince, Fabio Rojas, and Clayton A. Davis (2017) explain, Twitter afforded activists the ability to promote the #BlackLivesMatter hashtag while also shaping the meaning of the movement through the use of related hashtags.

This movement then intersected with the gaming world through a campaign following the death of Eric Garner at the hands of the New York Police Department in 2014. Eric Garner succumbed to a state-sanctioned chokehold by officer Daniel Pantaleo for selling loose cigarettes. There were a plethora of responses to the unarmed Black man dying at the hands of the police—including from gaming communities. Kahlief Adams, co-creator of the video game podcast *Spawn on Me*, stated that he wanted to use his gaming and podcasting platforms to bring awareness to deaths of the unarmed by the police. His #Spawn4Good initiative was one of the first to use gaming technologies to discuss #BlackLivesMatter. As Kahlief Adams stated,

> I felt like both the gaming space and the real world had hit this level of toxicity that was unsustainable and for the first time in a long time I didn't know what or how to express how I felt about them. So I sat down, thought about what good could we do in the gaming space and how we could affect change in whatever small way we could as an entity. Then the Eric Garner incident happened and it was the proverbial back breaking straw. (K. Gray 2016, para. 8)

He used Twitch to stream messages about the racist treatment of Black people by law enforcement and generated funds to help the family of Eric Garner cover burial costs. During the two-day event, Adams also provided information on other victims of police abuse of power, such as Mike Brown and Ezell Ford. There was constant backlash and resistance by gamers who suggested that Twitch was not the platform to express support for #BlackLivesMatter. But Adams affirmed that he "streams for those who want to be the change they wish to see in the world." While this level of cultural production and activism may not generate a critical mass of followers, it is significant for those who are marginalized in gaming culture. It helps to make Blackness visible in gaming culture, and it is part of a growing trend to call attention to the changing demographics of gamers.

Black Gamers as Deviant Streamers

SILENTASSASSIN321: You're doing it wrong. That's what they tell me. That I'm doing it wrong. I'm like who gave you a twitch manual!

SHOTGUNKILLA: But what they saying is that you not doing it the white way.

SILENTASSASSIN321: Exactly. Like Chris Rock say, "it's all right if it's all White." . . .

SILENTASSASSIN321: And they lash out. No matter if we talking 'bout Black shit or not. Just being Black makes us outsiders. We can't win.

This interaction between two Black Twitch users highlights the reality that there is a universal standard they are unable to uphold because of their racial identity. Indeed, their mere presence in these gaming spaces as people of color deems them deviant because they are failing to uphold the norm of Whiteness (K. Gray 2012a). Deviant identities such as these are the result of being formally or informally sanctioned by social audiences. Because people of color are not recognized as legitimate participants in digital communities, these disparaging realities lead to their exclusion from full participation in these communities. No matter the content, the dominant culture of video gaming still gets to decide who is valid and who is not. This is what Pierre Bourdieu calls "symbolic exclusion," or the effort to impose a definition of "legitimate practice" and "universal essence" (Bourdieu 1993, 14). Any practice within cultural production then becomes the symbolic site of struggle over the power to enforce the dominant definition from a hegemonic standpoint, which delimits and restricts access to certain populations, delimiting who is entitled to take part in defining and shaping virtual spaces.

These kinds of delimiting practices extend into gaming as well, where Black players and characters are relegated to the margins. As many Black Twitch users expressed in interviews, they enjoy in-game representations and depictions of Black characters even as they struggle with them. One Mixer user stated,

> When I stream, I try to play games with Black characters. But that gets hard sometimes. Because they like real racist, like ColeTrain. I mean you got some good ones now like Mafia 3 and WatchDogs2, but its just a few.

As this user reveals, he chooses to center games that feature characters of color. But most Black characters are visually and narratively marked as other, as the previous discussion on Black characters illustrated.

Racializing Space and Place in Digital Gaming

The marginalization Black players face within gaming culture is also related to space and place. We often assume that space is a physical and permanent structure, but in reality, "space and place are not fixed or innate but rather created and re-created through the actions and meanings of people" (Gieseking et al. 2014, 3). Space and place are co-produced through many dimensions such as race and class, urban and suburban, gender and sexuality, public and private, bodies and buildings. While the era of public segregation may be gone, modern segregation mirrors the historical practice of culturally designating many spaces as "Whites only." These practices come in many forms, including lack of inclusion, toxic environments, as well as outright hostility, harassment, and violence. Black bodies have been severely censured by the threat and implementation of systematic forms of oppression, such as having the police called on them, being reported for violation of terms of service in online communities, and the threat of sexual violence for many Black women and transwomen. Being perpetually bound and conditioned to the legacies of racialized, sexualized, and gendered histories, Black bodies are subject to multiple forms of control and subordination that serve to remind them of "their place."

In spite of these limits, Black participants have employed a variety of responses to continue existing and residing in digital spaces. This includes strategies such as self-segregating and isolating themselves, as well as disrupting and invading the spaces anyway (K. Gray 2012a). Live-streaming is yet another way Black bodies strategically disrupt traditional gaming spaces. Black streamers act as agents of social change by their mere presence in these live-streaming spaces, their marginalized bodies serving to disrupt the norms of the space designated for privileged bodies. One example of this occurred in a forum that opened as a space for providing solace to women who were being attacked on Xbox Live as a result of the "Gamergate" controversy in 2014. As the conversation unfolds, we see the assumption that Black women are nothing but a disruption to gendered gaming spaces, as they are presumed to be restricted to serving the needs of White women.

SHEBANGS321: Everytime you come to this room, you start problems. We're not racist so stop saying that.

TASTYDIAMOND: The shit yall say make yall racist. Yall don't care what my color is? But yall want me to care about your pussy and the shit you go through? Fuk'd up logic.

SHEBANGS321: But this is an all girls space so of course we'd talk about girl shit.

TASTYDIAMOND: But I'm a girl too! Right! I'm just a black one!

SHEBANGS321: But we are addressing your needs too. We're talking about helping all women here.

TASTYDIAMOND: But you're not. When you fix the whole gender issue, I still have to deal with racism.

SHEBANGS321: racism isn't a problem tho! Gamergate's not racist. They're attacking women.

MZTEEVXV: Bitch that's fucked up! We been dealing with shit and yall just now got a problem in here. Where were yall when dem white boys was calling us black bitch and shit? Yall was playing with they cracka asses.

Throughout the conversation, Black women are reminded of their "place" and the fact that their racialized commentary is not welcome. In response, many Black women within the Xbox Live community began shifting the conversation toward raising awareness around the death of Mike Brown and the #BlackLivesMatter campaign. The discussion about toxic masculinity within the gaming community became an opportunity for Black women to discuss the invisibility they felt, and the issues that were important to them.

These conversations demonstrate the failure of White women to fully embrace the racialized nature of oppression, particularly in failing to recognize the privilege of Whiteness and their complicity in White supremacy. The policing of Black women's bodies in these digital spaces mirrors the way that police are weaponized to control Black movement in public spaces. From Starbucks to swimming pools to grilling in public parks, public spaces have become sites for power struggles as White women utilize the police to protect what they feel are their spaces. As Elijah Anderson (2015) explains, many White people have yet to accept the publicness of Black bodies in certain spaces, especially spaces once historically deemed White-only, such as parks and pools. When Black bodies are present in these once Whites-only spaces, there is a subconscious process to want to banish them to a place Anderson (2012) refers to as the "iconic ghetto," the stereotypical space in which they think all Black people belong. Live-streaming continues this practice of demarcating particular bodies as unwelcome, relegating them to the margins—but Black participants are not passive bystanders, and their actions as agents of change serve to disrupt the norms of these spaces designated for privileged bodies. They are engaging in a dynamic and ongoing process that serves to reshape discourses about what it means to be a true gamer.

Black Resistance in Digital Gaming Culture

While the Internet has aided in shaping marginalized communities by increasing their participation in civic society, manifestations of real-world inequalities in virtual spaces nonetheless continue to influence virtual realities. Even in a potentially liberatory space such as the Internet, racial and ethnic minorities are still marginalized and devalued. But Black resilience and resistance strategies must be explored, especially in these limiting conditions and terms. While there is extreme resistance to making Blackness legible and legitimate within digital culture, Black folk have utilized Internet technologies and digital communities to push back on these unequal power relations. Live-streaming and other forms of social media have offered new ways for marginalized users to articulate their identities and become visible. By critiquing racist norms and challenging oppressive practices, Black gamers use digital tools to defy the often simplistic and reductionist trends that have historically prevailed in media narratives. The continued barrage of stereotypical imagery of Blackness has led many Black gamers and users of gaming technologies to create their own empowering narratives that claim their autonomy by defining their own identities. The transmediated act of live-streaming offers an important component of countervisual resistance that not only allows Black users to reframe the racialized narratives of Blackness they encounter, but also allows them to do it in such a way that is readily accessible to other Black audiences consuming their gaming content.

While the current era of Black hypervisibility could simply be viewed within the narrative of consuming Black death, this limited vision of Black reality would render Blackness intelligible only under conditions imposed by White supremacy. In exploring other holistic instantiations of Black cultural practices in digital form, we can see the potential for Black digital practices in this transmediated era of engagement to disrupt traditional narratives. This includes inserting themselves into conversations and spaces that threaten to exclude them, as well as creating their own digital spaces for addressing the issues that are important to Black communities. In both cases, we see what gaming spaces can look like when Black folk are in charge of production and content creation. The innovative power on display in their live-streaming practices and engagements in digital communities illustrates the politics of viewing—a discursive struggle where these digital users are actively engaged in disrupting their historic marginalization.

20

Cosmopolitan Fan Activism

SUSAN NOH

fandom | cosmopolitanism | fan activism

On January 1, 2019, Netflix released a reality television show called *Tidying up with Marie Kondo*. The titular star of the show, Marie Kondo, is a lifestyle and self-help star from Japan who published the best-selling book *The Life-Changing Magic of Tidying Up* in 2011. Applying what has been called the *konmari* method, her central ideology of maintaining a respectful relationship with one's items and keeping only items that "spark joy" is faithfully replicated on-screen. Each episode shows Kondo going into the homes of disorganized Americans and advising them on modes of well-being through tidying their environment. Despite the rather benign premise of this reality show, Kondo proved to be a lightning rod figure for racial discourse, spurring heated online debates on Twitter and various news outlets between her fans and equally vocal anti-fans. Critiques leveled at Kondo ranged from her on-screen presence being a signal of America's waning hegemonic positionality on the global stage to accusations of anti-intellectualism within her practices and followers.

While mass critique of a racialized star persona is not a rare occurrence in today's media landscape, there is much to be gained from assessing the dialogue that emerged among Kondo's supporters. Indeed, both the fans and the anti-fans of Kondo use this opportunity to build and maintain their own identities in a similar fashion that serves to reinforce one another, hijacking one another's respective narratives in order to further secure their own agendas and identities. The debates around Kondo provide a generative site for racial discourse, as both fans and anti-fans alike structure their discourse around this Japanese woman and what her identities represent to them. In particular, it seems that fans of

Kondo use these critiques as a conduit for the enactment of cosmopolitan dispositions that reify the significance of the "Other" in contemporary culture. While race continues to be a specter in these discussions, it would be an oversimplification to frame the anti-fan's rhetoric as more racially charged than that of the fan. On the contrary, Kondo's perceived "Japaneseness" is simultaneously the primary means by which cosmopolitan fans justify her lifestyle, ideologies, and behaviors.

In this chapter, I analyze the ways in which the cosmopolitan fan identity is performed and how the moral framework that is encouraged by cosmopolitanism is sustained within Kondo fandom. The way anti-fan narrativity is formulated and subsequently hijacked by these cosmopolitan fans in order to destabilize the anti-fan identity remains one of the fundamental ways Kondo's fans use this discourse in order to engage in their critique of the broader issues of American race relations. We might assume that the affordances of digital platforms that allow for a more seamless flow of media from different nations and cultures would encourage a cosmopolitan desire that escapes parochial tendencies. Yet I argue that the cosmopolitan fans who support Kondo engage in a kind of ambivalent activism that sustains both essentialist and Orientalist formulations of race and culture.

Cosmopolitanism and Fandom

Philosopher Immanuel Kant first popularized the concept of "cosmopolitanism" in his essay *Perpetual Peace: A Philosophical Sketch*, where he calls for a "constitution conforming to the law of world citizenship, so far as men and states are considered citizens of a universal state of men, in their external mutual relationships (*ius cosmopoliticum*)" (Kant 2010, 1795). Cosmopolitanism is an ideology that is characterized by an openness to engage and empathize with different cultures as citizens of the global community, as opposed to limiting the self to a particular nation-state. Since Kant's forwarding of this idealized conceptualization, scholars have developed more nuanced frameworks for imagining the cosmopolitan disposition. In his interpretation of the political and cultural dimensions of "instrumental cosmopolitanism," Ulf Hannerz (2004) critiques cosmopolitan ideology for its often self-serving implications. This mode of cosmopolitanism is *instrumental* to the formation

of the self, by allowing individuals to define themselves by constructing binary differences in opposition to the foreign Other. Within this
paradigm, the "Other" is often framed as inferior or inhuman in relation to the self. Historically, cosmopolitan figures have existed among
the privileged classes, who are often endowed with the education to
de/re-contextualize foreign cultures and the means to travel and engage
with different facets of foreign communities (74). Often seen as symbolic
influencers and translators of foreign cultures for their local communities, these cosmopolitans wield significant influence in mediating the
way foreign cultures are perceived by locals. Because of the inherently
classed dimensions of cosmopolitanism, a Bourdieusian perspective
emerges that gestures toward the social capital involved in performing
cosmopolitanism, particularly against the face of "backwards" localism.[1]
Despite the inherent cultural openness that cosmopolitanism grounds
itself in, Hannerz cautiously notes that cosmopolitans do not necessarily encourage processes of "affirmative openness," but are more in the
position of curators who can actively reject foreignness that feels unac-
ceptable or alien. The political dimensions of cosmopolitanism are then
twofold: the first revolves around the construction of superiority that is
rooted in the performance of the cosmopolitan disposition, against the
lower-classed localists, who do not seem to have the capacity to imagine
a world broader than the boundaries of their own culture. The second
is the vapid displays of cultural cosmopolitanism, which revolve around
unchallenging engagements with the Other in cultural contact zones like
foreign cuisine, music, and art, but a refusal to engage meaningfully with
the global politics of the region and the power dynamics inherent in
one's own positionality as mediator of foreign cultures. In this manner,
instrumental cosmopolitanism remains deeply rooted in the structures
of a self-serving Orientalism, as defined by Edward Said (1978), where
the ever-present Other is framed, often in a reductive manner, to sub-
stantiate an Occidental identity.

In relation to instrumental cosmopolitanism, Henry Jenkins (2004c)
conceptualized "pop cosmopolitanism," which he defines as "the ways
that the transcultural flows of popular culture inspire new forms
of global consciousness and cultural competency" (117). Similar to
Hannerz, Jenkins is cautious in idealizing pop cosmopolitanism, which
"may not yet constitute a political consciousness of America's place in

the world . . . but it opens consumers to alternative cultural perspectives and the possibility of feeling . . . with others worldwide who share their tastes and interests" (117). In Jenkins's conception of the pop cosmopolitan media fan, he sees the potential for these globally minded fans to be able to accept foreign cultures wholesale, enabling the possibility for empathy for the Other in a way that avoids fetishization and reductive frameworks for understanding different cultures. However, there is always the risk that fans will default to an instrumental cosmopolitanism that is grounded in dilettantism, where the consumption of the foreign merely feeds into one's own ego (133). John Fiske (1992) outlines the ways alternative structures of capital exist within fandoms as a "shadow economy" that doesn't necessarily correspond to monetary gain, but nevertheless contribute to one's social standing. In particular, he states that fans can become "the experts—those who have accumulated the most knowledge—gain prestige within the group and act as opinion leaders. Knowledge, like money, is always a source of power" (43). Similarly, Mizuko Ito (2012) observes how "social belonging and reputation" are among the primary reasons why fans contribute their labor without economic compensation. Ito states that fans "enjoy knowledge exchange with respected peers, but they look down upon the mass of leechers and newbies who have yet to prove their self-worth" (194–95), demonstrating a direct correspondence between knowledge and social currency. In this manner, it seems only natural that the knowledge of the cosmopolitan fan would serve a similar function when dealing with media texts that have a global veneer, incentivizing fans to perform their knowledge in exchange for social capital.

Kondo's "unapologetically Japanese" (Romero 2019) disposition on the show has sparked a mode of fan engagement where the performance of cosmopolitan knowledge is weaponized in order to hierarchize fans and chastise those who reveal a parochial perspective. The instrumental performance of the cosmopolitan fan echoes uneasily with the narcissistic iteration of cosmopolitanism outlined above, where knowledge about the Other is utilized to reinforce the identity narrative of the cosmopolitan fan. However, this becomes further complicated when this cultural knowledge is deployed as an activist strategy to speak back against the racist remarks of the anti-fan, allowing for such cultural knowledge to do double duty.

Fan activism occurs when fans utilize their beloved texts as sites to engage in political action beyond the scope of the text or their respective fandom. This endeavor is often more complicated for fans of color, because they must negotiate their own racialized experiences and activist desires in a way that is legible to the broader public. Often, that demands a certain amount of essentialism and reduction in order to sustain a cohesive narrative that fans can effectively deploy in order to voice their discontent. This is exemplified in Lori Kido Lopez's (2012) scholarship on *Avatar: The Last Airbender* fans, who used their fandom to protest against Hollywood's whitewashing casting practices for the *Avatar* live-action film. According to Lopez, fan-activist endeavors rubbed uneasily against fan interpretations of what constitutes authentic "Asianness" and how Asian bodies should be portrayed on-screen. Such reductive and ossified interpretations of representation lack the "complexity or shading" that often characterize ethnic identities (435). Through the use of these double-edged methods, the strategies employed to protest against whitewashing "come uncomfortably close to replicating the very oppressive structures they aim to resist" (Pande 2018, 86). In the case of Marie Kondo, the cosmopolitan fan activist's attempts to legitimize her to the public by focusing on an essentialized view of her spiritual background imply a question about whether Kondo's ideologies and way of life can be given individual agency beyond these Orientalist assumptions of cultural and spiritual difference. Despite these complex negotiations between fandom, industry, and politics, the potential for effecting change and forming community through fan activist discourse should not be underestimated. We must also consider the ways performing a cosmopolitan identity and leveraging cultural knowledge, particularly for the fan of color, can be a rhetorical and discursive strategy to carve out space in a digital media landscape that persistently reverts back toward a hegemonic whiteness. In the next section, I will outline the Marie Kondo fandom and analyze the ways racialized discourse around her figure exemplifies the complexities of the cosmopolitan fan's positionality at the conjuncture of identity, self-narrative, and fan activism.

Defining Marie Kondo's Fandom

Unlike fandoms that have been more widely studied in the past, such as Trekkies or Harry Potter fans, practices of fan-fiction writing, fanart, and cosplay largely do not apply to Kondo's fandom. Similarly, unlike traditionally conceived star texts like actors or performers, Kondo does not have a large body of artistic work to draw upon. Instead, Kondo's fans engage with the fandom by following Kondo's methodology for tidying up one's surroundings. The subcultural currency of Konverts (the preferred name of Kondo's fans) revolves around before-and-after photos of their respective personal spaces, as they employ Kondo's neatening practices. Accompanying these images are often statements outlining the fans' respective struggles with cleaning and organizing, and their love for Kondo's methodologies. More intimate messages discuss how Kondo's practices have eased their mental afflictions and helped them regain control over their purchasing and living habits.

For the purposes of this study, I am looking at two moments of fan and anti-fan engagements on Twitter that gesture toward the way both communities construct their own identities in relation to Kondo's ideologies. The two moments of anti-fandom that exemplify the qualms of Kondo's dissenters are the following: tweets by sociologist Barbara Ehrenreich that reject Kondo by framing her presence as a signifier for America's waning positionality as a global hegemon, and tweets by author Anakana Schofield critiquing Kondo's supposed demand to throw away books. I will then look at the responses that these moments spurred from fan activists and observe the ways they disrupt, chastise, and hijack the anti-fan's narrative in order to perform a cosmopolitan disposition, while simultaneously using this rhetoric to critique the compromising mediations of Asian women on-screen. These moments are indicative of some of the major qualms that Kondo's anti-fans have gravitated toward, as is reflected by the surplus of media attention that these statements have received *beyond* Twitter. Further, the intensity of the reactions stirred by these moments across media platforms gesture toward how the convergent nature of digital platforms can amplify the fan and anti-fan's voice and encourage discourse within the fandom across many different outlets.

Kondo's Anti-Fans and Their Discontents

It is no surprise that Kondo's intimate presence inside American homes has caused discomfort for some viewers, as the questionable presence of

Japanese foreigners in the intimacy of one's personal space has inspired similar sentiments in the past. In the early 1990s, there was "an anxiety about exposure to, and penetration by, Japanese culture," particularly when Japan was experiencing an economic boom that enabled a rapid growth in global exports (Morley and Robins 2002, 150). The influx of Japanese pop culture and the increased banality of Japanese products in the United States have somewhat eased the foreignness of this presence in the contemporary moment. Yet the presence of a Japanese woman in the private space of the home who instructs American families on how to organize their lives strikes at these very same anxieties that arose two decades prior. The discomfort prompted by this perceived encroachment can be seen in Barbara Ehrenreich's (2019) attack on Kondo in a tweet that stated, "I will be convinced that America is not in decline only when our de-cluttering guru Marie Kondo learns to speak English." In this tweet, Ehrenreich returns to a kind of parochial localism that grates at the cosmopolitan sensibilities of Kondo's fans. This sentiment was only further exacerbated when Ehrenreich deleted that initial tweet, and responded with, "I hate Marie Kondo because, aesthetically speaking, I'm on the side of clutter. As for her language: it's OK with me that she doesn't speak English to her huge American audience but it does suggest that America is in decline as a superpower." This return to the safe realm of aesthetics, of benign "differences" of cultural taste, reduces the racial politics of Ehrenreich's statement to a flimsy, neoliberal pandering. Regardless, one can see that despite the deeply racist rhetoric employed by Ehrenreich, her anti-fan narrative primarily revolves around expressing the concerns of a nationalistic individual performing her duty as concerned citizen.

Similarly, one can see the ideological outline of the anti-fan's narrative in the backlash against Kondo and her statement on books. Anakana Schofield (2019) was among the first to weaponize this statement against Kondo with a tweet that read,

Do NOT listen to Marie Kondo or Konmari in relation to books. Fill your apartment & world with them. I don't give a shite if you throw out your knickers and Tupperware but the woman is very misguided about BOOKS. Every human needs a v extensive library not clean, boring shelves.

Other anti-fans were quick to jump onto this sentiment. In response to Schofield, Jennifer Wright (2019) created and circulated a meme of Kondo stating, "Ideally, keep less than thirty books" with the caption, "This woman is a monster." The fan backlash against these anti-fan sentiments rightfully addressed the willful misinterpretation of Kondo's words and the dangers of calling a person of color a monster. However, it is clear that the motivations behind this anti-fan sentiment were not necessarily rooted in racism, but in performing intellectualism. The ways the preservation of books within the home stands in for a symbol of intellectualism gesture toward the kind of cultural capital that performing this hate can yield. To perform disdain through the perceived attack on intellectualism and to have this sentiment be consumed and replicated across digital platforms is to once again reinforce one's own anti-fan identity and rearticulate communal borders.

Performing Fan Cosmopolitanism and Ambivalent Activism

In response to these two moments, fans exhibited strategies that weaponized their cosmopolitan knowledge, using their fan currency of before/after photos and collective narratives to effectively bolster the presence of fan-experts who have exhibited cosmopolitan identities. However, as mentioned before, the reinforcement of cosmopolitan dispositions as a mode of fan activism is often a double-edged tactic that simultaneously reinforces Orientalist interpretations. For example, Katha Pollitt's (2019) response to Ehrenreich's anti-fan comment was the following: "I think her speaking Japanese adds to her fairy-like delicacy and charm. It exaggerates the diff between herself and her lumpish, clueless American clients." While Pollitt raises Kondo above her "lumpish, clueless" counterparts, the use of terms like "fairy-like delicacy" betray the Orientalist fascination with the Other in a way that emphasizes attractive, yet inhuman difference over the self. This echoes the fantasy-ridden conceptual framework of nineteenth-century *Japonisme*, which also used the "rustic" and "innocent" Japanese as a convenient site of comparison to critique the indulgent and vapid nature of the civilized West (Napier 2007). While other fans of color were quick to respond to the Orientalizing nature of these comments, some of the most-cited Twitter users defending Kondo fell into similar trappings, as they used Kondo's spiritual background to simultaneously perform their own cultural expertise and police the parochial nature of the anti-fan. For example, Twitter user NoTotally (Lau 2019) emphasized the cultural background of Kondo's methodologies, stating,

> I think it's important to understand that a lot of the US-based negative reaction to Marie Kondo's philosophies parallels really basic cultural differences between Japan and the U.S. Japanese minimalism, as both a design aesthetic and normalized context for living, is hundreds of years old. It likely traces its roots to the arrival of what came to be known as Japanese Zen Buddhism.

While this observation may be entirely informed, the manner in which cultural and spiritual difference is the legitimating vehicle of Kondo causes tension between the cosmopolitan fan's activism against racism and the way this strategy figures Kondo as a kind of paradigmatic opposite. She is positioned as a figure inspired by Buddhism and Zen philosophies, in opposition to the somewhat spoilt United States whose culture is based in conspicuous consumption. NoTotally then continues his explanation by noting his own positionality as a fourth-generation Japanese American who was raised with much of the same ideologies, once again centering the self as a cosmopolitan figure and using this positionality to gain subcultural capital from the community. This, in turn, grants this activist legitimacy to be able to speak on this matter with a degree of authority. However, what is most interesting about his statement is that at the end of his lengthy explanation, validating Kondo's practices through her cultural difference, he states, "Fashioning Kondo herself as antithetical to the kind of consumption that a lot of people base their value on is cruel and ignorant. And she isn't, either, a tiny, magical Japanese fixer nymph. She's a Japanese woman who's found success communicating ways to implement what is, for her, standard cultural operating procedure."

This addendum reveals that NoTotally is fully aware of the Orientalist desires of fans and anti-fans alike when gazing upon Kondo, and he rightfully criticizes it. Yet he simultaneously falls into the same Orientalist trappings in his own analysis of Kondo through his emphasis on traditional Zen Buddhism and Kondo's different "standard cultural operating procedure." This friction between the need to perform the cosmopolitan self by emphasizing Kondo's difference and the desire to dispel Orientalist fixations reveals the multidirectional influences and negotiations that must be made by fans of color in order to engage in this mode of fan activism. Similar tensions can be found in the long response from Twitter user Jonah Ven (2019), who noted that the misunderstandings that arise from white people trying to make sense of Kondo's methodologies are based in a "misunderstanding [that] flows out of the fact that her process is informed by both Asian culture at large as well as Japanese culture. I'm not Japanese, but in many Asian cultures, it's not common to have the overindulgence and excess we have bc SPACE CONSTRAINTS." While Ven does not directly mention the spiritual dimensions of Kondo's ideology, he nevertheless positions himself as a cosmopolitan fan-expert, who leverages his knowledge of Asian lifestyles to heighten himself in comparison to the ignorance of perceived localists. He concludes by stating that the off-color comments and willful misinterpretations targeting Kondo are among the many ways that racially targeted hate continues to flourish within seemingly progressive communities. In order to use Marie Kondo as a site for activism, fans must negotiate between their own cosmopolitan identities and the Orientalist frameworks that often legitimize raced bodies in the American media landscape. Despite the fan's ambivalent positionality, it cannot be denied that these strategies are incredibly generative for fan discourse. These tweets foster conversation revolving around what features constitute Asian spirituality, and the double standards of raced and white individuals on reality television; they function as a site where one can police and discipline those who believe in damaging ideologies of nationalistic localism.

Similar trends can be observed in those who responded against what seemed to be deliberate misinterpretations of Kondo's advice pertaining to the number of books one should keep. While anti-fans used this quote to foster their own self-identity around values of intellectualism, fans hijacked this anti-fan narrative and framed it as one of deliberate misinterpretation. They targeted the misguided use of the term "monster" for people of color, who have already been, in many ways, dehumanized by mainstream media. For example, Patricia Theresa McCarthy (2019) tweeted, "Marie Kondo has proven irrefutably that no one is more annoying than people who think owning a lot of books is a personality"—implying the hypocrisy of such intellectualism that is fostered by the ignorance of tone-deaf asymmetrical racial dynamics. Another fan of color, Kat Cho (2019), used a more political approach to addressing this interpretation of calling Kondo a monster by stating, "Please don't call POC monsters. Please don't use language that dehumanize an already marginalized community. If you disagree that's fine but don't call someone something that paints them as subhuman. (Also not everyone has space to keep a lot of books)." It is critical to note that while these responses gained much attention from Twitter users, this does not necessarily mean that there was consensus in the response to the hijacking of these anti-fan statements. Other users expressed lack of familiarity with the idea that the term "monster" was racist, or affirmed that Japanese homes are very small—once again using cosmopolitan knowledge at the risk of Othering.

These discourses between fans and anti-fans are generative in the way that these tweets foster more coverage across different media platforms, amplifying both the exposure of anti-fan narratives and the responses from activist-minded fans. This reveals the resourceful ways that fans have used their numbers and sharp responses to gain attention from different news outlets to sustain and extend the presence of their activist narratives beyond the "immediacy of social media" (Click 2019, 19). The proliferation of different entry points into fan discourse within the digital environment allows for more opportunities to reexamine the star text of Marie Kondo. For example, articles from *Bustle*, *Paper*, *Vice*, MSN, Fox News, *Revelist*, and *Nylon*, among others, have directly quoted many of the tweets analyzed here, as well as from other users who have spoken about the issue of racism ignited through Kondo. Similarly, Barbara Ehrenreich was widely attributed throughout these articles. While the coverage of Ehrenreich was likely due to her preexisting fame as an author, other Twitter users utilized their cosmopolitan fan dispositions in order to inform and spread knowledge—occupying an "expert" positionality to gain additional coverage for their cause within the digital media landscape. This reiteration of cosmopolitan fan knowledge across multiple platforms aids in the process of sustaining the hegemonic signification of a "sign," like the meme of Kondo stating that people should keep fewer than thirty books. While anti-fans have taken this statement to signify a kind of anti-intellectualism, fan activists have co-opted the meme to demonstrate how people deliberately misunderstand Kondo's ideologies in order to paint her as less-than-human. They use this meme to reflect upon a hardship that people of color must often endure on a regular basis. Without the repetitive circulation of these interpretations, it would be all too easy to overwhelm the activist influence within fan discourse. Melissa Click states that "it is these attachments, repetitions, and accumulations of emotion that make individuals and collectives meaningful," and utilizing the reiterational dynamics of digital media to sustain favored interpretations is a strategy that fans prove to be incredibly capable at deploying (Click 2019, 13).

Conclusion

In this chapter, I examined the tensions that arise between cosmopolitan fan desires for the reinforcement of identity narratives and activism against racism. While these public displays of knowledge aid fans in earning subcultural capital and social standing within their respective communities, these demonstrations of cosmopolitanism often frame Kondo as a distinct "Other" through which the cosmopolitan fan can perform their expertise. This can be seen in the way Kondo is granted legitimacy through her personal history as a Shintoist shrine maiden, the cultural context of Zen Buddhism in Japan, as well as the focus on differences in Japanese living. While problematic, it is one strategy that cosmopolitans use to police the local and parochial perspectives of anti-fans. In regard to the way that both anti-fans and fans utilize their respective publics in order to perform certain parts of their identities and reinforce their own positionalities, the processes prove to be remarkably similar. However, despite the potentially "othering" mechanics utilized to secure fan cosmopolitan identities, I see the essentializing of Kondo as a strategic mode of branding that allows for fan activists to speak through her figure, exemplifying the treatment of Kondo as a broader cultural critique on the way race operates in Western society. The activist strategies of cosmopolitan fans and the friction caused by their own desire to reinforce their identity narratives are a negotiation with the broader context of power, race, class, and taste. While I remain critical of the fans' multidirectional desires, particularly in relation to how it potentially frames other cultures in difference as opposed to proximity, the case study of Kondo's cosmopolitan fandom proves that there is much to be gained from weaponizing these forms of knowledge.

ACKNOWLEDGMENTS

This book emerged from the Race and Media Conference, a small yearly gathering focusing on research at the intersection of critical race theory and media studies. When I started the conference in 2014 at the University of Wisconsin–Madison, I never imagined how it would blossom and expand, nourished by the strength of so many incredible scholars who were also hungry for a supportive scholarly community. Thanks to Jonathan Gray and all of my Communication Arts colleagues in Media and Cultural Studies who were my cheerleaders and support squad that first year, making it seem like running a conference was no big deal.

I dedicate this book to all of the amazing organizers who kept the Race and Media Conference alive by bringing it to their own campuses in subsequent years—to Myra Washington at the University of New Mexico, Isra Ali at New York University, LeiLani Nishime and Ralina L. Joseph at University of Washington, and Shilpa Davé and Camila Fojas at University of Virginia. Every year I am blown away by the intellect and kindness radiating from each of the participants, as well as the brilliance of the senior scholars who give keynotes and serve as mentors to us all. I also must give particular credit to Madhavi Mallapragada and Myra Washington for working with me for many years to assemble an edited journal issue on this subject; although that issue never found a home, it was your commitment to publishing scholarship from the conference that helped make this book possible.

Thanks to Eric Zinner and Dolma Ombadykow at New York University Press for your constant enthusiasm and support, to Aswin Punathambekar for being a generous advocate and advisor for this project, and to Angharad Valdivia and Shilpa Davé for reading each chapter and strengthening the collection with your incisive advice. Much gratitude also to my advisee Jacqueline Land for her labor and thoughtfulness in putting together the index. Finally, thanks to my personal support system who make all of this possible—my parents and siblings and in-laws, FBC, my fit fam, Boba, and Jason.

NOTES

CHAPTER 1. RACISM AND MAINSTREAM MEDIA

1 Large media corporations publish yearly data on the diversity of their workforce. Examples of this can be found in AT&T (2018), Walt Disney Company (2015), Comcast NBCUniversal (2018), and others. In addition, the FCC (2015) provides data on the ownership of commercial broadcast stations.

CHAPTER 3. VISUALIZING MIXED RACE AND GENETICS

1 Scholars use many terms to describe someone with a mixed-race background, including "multiracial," "multiethnic," and even "edgewalker" (Krebs 1999). Here, we are talking most specifically about first-generation mixed-race but want to note that there are also people who may be multigenerational mixed, meaning there is racial mixing in their heritage a few generations removed. DNA tests have been able to pick up on this multigenerational mixedness, which might have otherwise been lost in other genealogical methods. With technological advancements like the mapping of the human genome and thus new, direct-to-consumer genealogical methods and data, companies like 23andMe are complicating what "mixed" means. Scholars have focused on a spectrum of terms used to capture specific racial mixes such as Black-mixed (Dagbovie-Mullins 2013), Hapa (Fulbeck 2006), Cablanasian (Nishime 2012), and Mexipino (Guevarra 2012). Here, we focus on Black/White mixtures, which we simply call "mixed." As Michele Elam notes, "resisting the pressure common in mixed race studies to account for any and all racial combinations and variables," Black/White mixes "are a necessary precursor" to analyzing a wider comparison of racial dynamics (2011, xix). In the case of racialized genetic data, this is especially true.

2 23andMe notes in an educational video entitled *The Importance of Diversity in Research* that all humans are 99.5 percent genetically identical, meaning that in the case of race genetics, scientists are looking at just a sliver of that .5 percent difference between individuals (2018c).

3 Saperstein posits that census enumerators shaped racialization by determining who was mixed, most often visually (2012, 1485).

4 Within communication studies, there has been a shift away from using terms like "race" and "ethnicity" toward the use of the word "culture." Culture is "something different than, but categorically inclusive of, ethnicity and race," with race more increasingly seen as "noncultural and irrespective of ethnicity" but physiognomically located (Jackson and Garner 1998, 51).

5 Ralina L. Joseph (2018) defines "postracial" as the "far from neutral" "media-propagated notion that race and race-based discrimination are over, and that race and racism no longer affect the everyday lives of both Whites and people of color" (4).

6 Jayne Ifekwunigwe (2004), Miri Song (2017), and Cedric Essi (2017) note that this first generation of multiracial scholars lamented the question.

7 Alondra Nelson (2016) has explored the ways Black communities have utilized their genetic data for these purposes. She links AfricanAncestry with these efforts, noting the company's diversity of leadership and specific intent on serving the Black community.

8 As part of the daylong special live broadcast, Cari had her results revealed to her, with 86.9 percent sub-Saharan African and 10.4 percent European. On a live feed entitled *Cari Champion Discovers Her Ancestry* (23andMe 2018b), Cari moves from Black to a multigenerational multiracial. Although curious about the 10.4 percent, after hearing that the British/Irish component of her ancestry comes from four to seven generations out, with that relative having been born between 1770 and 1860, Cari calls that part of her DNA "a little far removed." Cari restates a desire to know more about the British/Irish in her DNA, and asks how to "delve further into that," but is just redirected back to the data.

9 For a comparative example, see: 23andMe, *Exploring the Pathways to His Past: Jordan's 23andMe Story* (2017b) and 23andMe, *Unexpected Discovery: Kristin's 23andMe Story* (2018e).

10 This type of testing is an add-on to the basic genetic test package and costs $50-$100, so class and issues of access are inevitably a part of this racialized trend as well.

11 For more on the debunking of racist theories such as biological determinism, see Stephen Jay Gould's *The Mismeasure of Man* (1996).

12 This amalgam of words destabilizes the results these tests render by blurring what differentiates populations. National borders, regions, and tribal delineations are constantly changing and negotiated. Complicated historical patterns of (forced) migration and colonization intersect with current national borders, regions, and nomenclatures.

13 The one-minute clip, filmed entirely in Veracruz, Mexico, has seen multiple iterations since its 2017 debut. One version plays a different soundtrack by Brigitte Bardot, which is entirely in French and entitled *Moi Je Joue*, which translates to *Me, I Play*, a lighthearted cat-and-mouse love song. Eating an insect with her dinner mates, making an impressive move in a game of chess, and the ending text, "Let your DNA be your guide" are some of the deviations that appear in the Brigitte Bardot version.

14 "Celebrate your DNA" resonates with what Ifekwunigwe calls the "Age of Celebration."

CHAPTER 4. LISTENING TO RACIAL INJUSTICE

1 Many scholars have turned our attention to the work of the ear and the historical practices of listening and use of sound within marginalized communities of color. These scholars include Aparicio 1998, Moten 2003, Weheliye 2005, Kun 2005, Brooks 2010, Stoever 2010, Casillas 2011, D. Vargas 2012, Quashie 2012, Bradley 2013, Davé 2013, E. Hill 2013, Lordi 2013, Redmond 2013, Obadike and Obadike 2014, Chude-Sokei 2016, Kheshti 2015, Mathes 2015, Sharpe 2016, Crawley 2016, Fiol-Matta 2017, Moriah 2017, Morrison 2017, Blue 2017, Dorr 2018, and Furlonge 2018, among others.

2 While this essay focuses on the sonic and linguistic profiling of Blackness, the term "vocal body" is embedded in a discussion of how Latinx people face related and similar—but not identical—issues regarding racialized sound in the United States. Gloria Anzaldúa (1987), for example, theorized about Chicanx "wild tongues" that defy being "tamed" by colonizing languages such as English and the refusal to accommodate to impositions of power by the dominant listeners of those languages. In one of the first ethnographic studies of listening, Frances Aparicio (1998) discusses how working-class Latinas in Chicago listen to salsa music with diverse intentions and for complex reasons often unexplored and misunderstood by both academia and mainstream American culture. Recently, Sara Hinojos (2019) uses the term "visual accent" to show how early popular magazines deliberately quoted Mexican film actors phonetically; Lupe Velez, for instance was famously quoted for saying "joo" rather than "you." reina alejandra prado's (2013) use of "sonic brownface" enables a conversation about how White American performers have exaggerated and distorted Latinx accents to create a stereotyped version of their voices used to demean and further racialize them. Deborah Vargas (2012) theorizes the term "dissonance" in order to help us understand how Chicana subjectivities are produced sonically at the intersections of race, class, gender, and sexuality (see also Vásquez 2013, Casillas 2014, Fiol-Matta 2017, Alarcón 2016, Anguiano 2018, McMahon and Herrera 2019).

3 While the term "earwitness" is usually attributed to R. Murray Schafer by sound studies scholars, James Parker (2015) notes that it evolved around the same time as "eyewitness" does in English legal contexts—the sixteenth century, according to the *Oxford English Dictionary*—although the term has had a quieter and far more complicated history.

4 This number comes from the *Hollywood Reporter* (O'Connell 2013). *Variety* also covered the upswing in cable viewers during the trial's final week, noting that it "rev[ved] up ratings" for Fox, MSNBC, CNN, and HLN (Kissell 2013).

5 The media footprint of a megaspectacle like this, however, can also be more diffuse and far-reaching. Joseph also argues that Shonda Rhimes diverged from her previous "white-woman-as-leading-lady formula" in developing her drama *Scandal*, which debuted in the spring of 2012, because of the very different media landscape that emerged in the wake of Martin's death (Joseph 2018, 96).

6 For more on the audiovisual "loudness" and performative "excess" associated with ratchetness, see Kristin J. Warner, "They Gon' Think You Loud Regardless: Ratchetness, Reality Television, and Black Womanhood" (2015).

CHAPTER 10. REMEDIATING TRANS VISUALITY

1 I prefer "trans*" when using a single term but use "trans" when modifying another term, such as "trans aesthetics."

2 I use "they/them/theirs" to refer to gender nonbinary and trans-identified performers.

CHAPTER 11. INTERSECTIONAL DISTRIBUTION

1 See the case study of "YouTube Black" in chapter 6 of *Open TV* (Christian 2018).

CHAPTER 12. PODCASTING BLACKNESS

1 This excludes many popular Black podcasts that are produced by media companies, such as Loud Speaker Network's *The Read*, Buzzfeed's *Another Round*, and the WNYC-produced *2 Dope Queens*. Of the podcasts included here, *The Black Guy Who Tips* is the only one to successfully monetize, though others generate some revenue that goes to offsetting their costs. However, they remain unaffiliated with any media company or entity.

CHAPTER 13. BLACK TWITTER AS SEMI-ENCLAVE

1 I follow scholars such as Racquel Gates (2018) to employ the term "Black" when referencing people (such as "Black users") and the lowercased "black" when indicating more abstract terms, such as "blackness" and "black cultures."

2 In consideration of the ethical guidelines of reproducing Twitter content, I have relied on public tweets in this paper and the names and Twitter handles have been de-identified. See Markham (2012) and Nissenbaum (2009) for further discussions on the ethical reproduction of Twitter data.

CHAPTER 15. DIASPORA AND DIGITAL MEDIA

1 This builds on John Durham Peters's (1999) coinage of "reconstitution-in-dispersion" (20).

2 For thoughtful discussions on the political possibilities and limitations of the term "South Asia," see Carsignol (2014) and Singh (2007). The term comes out of a U.S.-centric, Cold War-based vision of global "command and control," and is most frequently used by scholars and activists based in North America. Perhaps more than its clinical ring and associations with Western geopolitical hegemony, those who dislike the term within the communities it seeks to bring together see it as a euphemistic way to suggest solidarity while hiding the fact that most discussions about South Asia and South Asian America are dominated by Indian and Indian American concerns.

3 "Desi" is an identity term and adjective, derived from the Sanskrit-based word *desh* (country, homeland), which roughly translates as "someone or something of the homeland/country." It is most widely used as an inclusive term in the South Asian diaspora in North America, but some find it exclusionary as there are many South Asian languages that are not Sanskrit-based. When used in South Asia it carries more of a "country bumpkin" connotation.

CHAPTER 17. LATINX AUDIENCES AS MOSAIC

1 "Latinx" refers to communities of Latin American descent living in the United States. "Latinx" is sometimes preferred over the more widely used term "Latina/o" because it is gender-neutral and inclusive of nonconforming gender and transgender individuals. However, currently Latina/o studies is debating the widespread applicability of this term, especially because the term is less common among Spanish speakers and may reproduce language hierarchies that privilege English syntax. Given that "Latinx" is a highly contested label—though I find it more gender-inclusive than "Latina/o"—I oscillate between using the terms "Latinx" and "Latina/o" in this essay. It should be noted that the terms "Latinx" and "Latina/o" are rooted in experiences in the United States and are not synonymous with Latin American identities. See de Onis (2017) and R. Rodríguez (2017) for more extensive discussions on the term "Latinx."

2 See Cepeda (2016), Del Rio (2006), and Valdivia (2010, 2018) for overviews of the field.

3 The emphasis on Mexicans and Puerto Ricans is because these are the two largest Latinx groups in the United States.

CHAPTER 18. MEDIA ACTIVISM IN THE RED POWER MOVEMENT

1 Canadian prime minister Pierre Trudeau's White Papers in 1969 proposed a similar plan of termination.

2 Sacheen Littlefeather was a model and actress of White Mountain Apache and Yaqui descent.

CHAPTER 20. COSMOPOLITAN FAN ACTIVISM

1 Pierre Bourdieu explains that beyond economic capital, there is "cultural capital," which is rooted in the performance of certain sociocultural competencies. The accumulation of cultural capital provides power, distinction, and social status to the individual.

BIBLIOGRAPHY

23andMe. 2017a. *Breaking Down Stereotype Barriers: Angelina's 23andMe Story.* YouTube video, posted by "23andMe," June 19, 2017. www.youtube.com /watch?v=PLazxh2pBdQ.

———. 2017b. *Exploring the Pathways to His Past: Jordan's 23andMe Story.* YouTube video, posted by "23andMe," June 9, 2017. www.youtube.com /watch?v=akc6tbW8aOg.

———. 2018a. *100% Nicole.* YouTube video, posted by "23andMe," June 12, 2018. www .youtube.com/watch?v=jIhabIzB_Xs.

———. 2018b. *Cari Champion Discovers Her Ancestry.* YouTube video, posted by "23andMe," 2018. www.youtube.com/watch?v=GUoo4-bKN74.

———. 2018c. *The Importance of Diversity in Research.* YouTube video, posted by "23andMe," September 14, 2018. www.youtube.com/watch?time_continue=38&v =cgMqnNTEbh8.

———. 2018d. "A New Survey on Attitudes about Race and Genetics." *23andMeBlog,* August 15, 2018. https://blog.23andme.com/23andme-research/a-new-survey-on -attitudes-about-race-and-genetics/.

———. 2018e. *Unexpected Discovery: Kristin's 23andMe Story.* YouTube video, posted by "23andMe," January 2, 2018. www.youtube.com/watch?v=Mg101pbkozk.

———. 2018f. *We Are All Connected: Celebrate Your DNA.* YouTube video, posted by "23andMe," 2018. www.youtube.com/watch?v=ou3GOqU-YX8.

———. 2019a. "23andMe's Diversity Snapshot." https://mediacenter.23andme.com /company/diversity-snapshot/. Accessed February 9, 2019.

———. 2019b. "Diversity Matters in Research." *23andMeBlog,* February 1, 2019. https:// blog.23andme.com/23andme-research/diversity-matters-in-research/.

Abraham, Linus. 2003 "Media Stereotypes of African Americans." In *Images That Injure: Pictorial Stereotypes in the Media,* 2d ed., edited by Paul Martin Lester, 87–92. Santa Barbara: Praeger.

Abramowitsch, Simon. 2018. "The Black Communications Movement." *African American Review* 51 (4): 305–27. doi: 10.1353/afa.2018.0055.

Abu-Lughod, Lila. 2004. *Dreams of Nationhood: The Politics of Television in Egypt.* Chicago: University of Chicago Press.

Acham, Christine. 2004. *Revolution Televised: Prime Time and the Struggle for Black Power.* Minneapolis: University of Minnesota Press.

Acuña, Rudolfo. *Occupied America: A History of Chicanos.* 8th ed. London: Pearson, 2014.

Adalian, Josef. 2018. "Why Did Amazon, Netflix, and Hulu Kill a Bunch of Alternative Comedies?" *Vulture*, January 18, 2018. www.vulture.com/2018/01/amazon-cancels -i-love-dick-one-mississippi-heres-why.html.

Adande, J. A. 2014. "Purpose of 'I Can't Breathe' T-Shirts." ESPN.com, December 10, 2014. www.espn.com/nba/story/_/id/12010612/nba-stars-making-statement -wearing-breathe-shirts.

"Afrofuturism." 2017. In *obo* in Literary and Critical Theory. Oxford Bibliographies. www.oxfordbibliographies.com/view/document/obo-9780190221911/obo- 9780190221911-0004.xml. Accessed June 8, 2019.

Ahmed, Tanzila. 2012. "Taz's Top Ten and Thanks." *Sepia Mutiny*, April 1, 2012. http:// sepiamutiny.com/blog/2012/04/01/tazs-top-ten-and-thanks/.

Akwesasne Notes. 1969. "'Silent Too Damn Long' Alcatraz: Taken Back." 1 (10): 1. www .aidhp.com/items/show/2. Accessed March 18, 2019.

———. 1976. *Voices from Wounded Knee: 1973, in the Words of the Participants*. Roos- eveltown, NY: Akwesasne Notes.

Alarcón, Wanda. 2016. "Sounding Aztlán: Music, Literature, and the Chicana/o Sonic Imaginary." PhD diss., University of California, Berkeley.

Alim, H. Samy, and Geneva Smitherman. 2012. *Articulate While Black: Barack Obama, Language, and Race in the US*. Oxford: Oxford University Press.

Alsultany, Evelyn. 2012. *Arabs and Muslims in the Media: Race and Representation after 9/11*. New York: New York University Press.

American Civil Liberties Union. 2018. "Racial Profiling: A Definition." www.aclu.org /other/racial-profiling-definition.

Anderson, Elijah. 2012. "The Iconic Ghetto." *Annals of the American Academy of Politi- cal and Social Science* 642 (1): 8–24.

———. 2015. "The White Space." *Sociology of Race and Ethnicity* 1 (1): 10–21.

Anderson, Mark Cronlund, and Carmen L. Robertson. 2011. *Seeing Red: A History of Natives in Canadian Newspapers*. Winnipeg: University of Manitoba Press.

Andrejevic, Marc. 2007 *iSpy: Surveillance and Power in the Interactive Era*. Lawrence: University Press of Kansas.

Andrews, David, Ronald L. Mower, and Michael L. Silk. 2011. "Ghettocentrism and the Essentialized Black Male Athlete." In *Commodified and Criminalized: New Racism and African Americans in Contemporary Sports*, edited by David J. Leonard and C. Richard King, 69–94. Lanham, MD: Rowman and Littlefield.

Anguiano, Claudia, and Mari Castañeda. 2014. "Forging a Path: Past and Present Scope of Critical Race Theory and Latina/o Critical Race Theory in Communication Stud- ies." *Review of Communication* 14 (2): 107–24.

Anguiano, José. 2018. "Soundscapes of Labor and Belonging: Mexican Custodians' Radio Listening Practices at a Southern California University." *Journal of Popular Music Studies* 30 (1–2): 127–54.

Anzaldúa, Gloria. 1987. *Borderlands/La Frontera*. San Francisco: Aunt Lute.

Aparicio, Frances. 1998. *Listening to Salsa: Gender, Latin Popular Music, and Puerto Rican Cultures*. Lebanon, NH: University Press of New England.

Asen, Robert. 2000. "Seeking the 'Counter' in Counterpublics." *Communication Theory* 10 (4): 424–46.

AT&T. 2018. "2018 AT&T Diversity & Inclusion Annual Report." https://about.att.com /ecms/dam/pages/Diversity/Annual_Report/ATT_DI_Report_DIGITAL_5.pdf.

Ávila, Eric. 2006. *Popular Culture in the Age of White Flight: Fear and Fantasy in Suburban Los Angeles*. New ed. Berkeley: University of California Press.

Avilés-Santiago, Manuel G. 2018. "Digital Pulse: Looking at the Collective/Cultural Memorialization of the Puerto Rican Victims of the Terrorist Attack in Orlando." *Journal of Latin American Communication Research* 6 (1–2): 205–19.

Avilés-Santiago, Manuel G., and Jillian M. Báez. 2020. "Targeting the Billenials: Linguistic Flexibility and New Language Politics of Univision." *Communication Culture Critique*.

Bacle, Ariana. 2015. "'Fresh Off the Boat' Author Doesn't Watch the TV Series." *Entertainment*, April 8, 2015. ew.com/article/2015/04/08/eddie-huang-fresh -off-the-boat/.

Báez, Jillian M. 2015. "Television for All Women? Watching Lifetime's *Devious Maids*." In *Cupcakes, Pinterest, and Ladyporn: Feminized Popular Culture in the Early 21st Century*, edited by Elana Levine, 51–70. Urbana: University of Illinois Press.

———. 2016. "Voicing Citizenship: Undocumented Women and Social Media." *Chicana /Latina Studies Journal* 6 (1): 56–85.

———. 2017a. "Engaging in Consumer Citizenship: Latina Audiences and Advertising in Women's Ethnic Magazines." In *Feminists, Feminisms, and Advertising: Some Restrictions Apply*, edited by Kimberly Golombisky and Peggy J. Kreshel, 231–50. Lanham, MD: Lexington Books.

———. 2017b. "Spreadable Citizenship: Undocumented Youth Activists and Social Media." In *The Routledge Companion to Latina/o Media*, edited by María Elena Cepeda and Dolores Inés Casillas, 419–31. New York: Routledge.

———. 2017c. "Charting Latinx Fandoms." In *The Routledge Companion to Media Fandom*, edited by Melissa Click and Suzanne Scott, 271–79. New York: Routledge.

———. 2018a. *In Search of Belonging: Latinas, Media, and Citizenship*. Urbana: University of Illinois Press.

———. 2018b. "Media Literacy as Civic Engagement." In *Civic Engagement in Diverse Latina/o Communities: Learning from Social Justice Partnerships in Action*, edited by Mari Castañeda and Joseph Krupczynski, 201–14. New York: Peter Lang.

Baker, C. Edwin. 2006. *Media Concentration and Democracy: Why Ownership Matters*. Cambridge: Cambridge University Press.

Banet-Weiser, Sarah, Nancy K. Baym, Francesca Coppa, David Gauntlett, Jonathan Gray, Henry Jenkins, and Adrienne Shaw. 2014. "Participations: Dialogues on the Participatory Promise of Contemporary Culture and Politics—Part 1: Creativity." *International Journal of Communication* 8: 1069–88.

Banet-Weiser, Sarah, Roopali Mukherjee, and Herman Gray. 2019. "Introduction: Postrace Racial Projects." In *Racism Postrace*, by Sarah Banet-Weiser, Roopali Mukherjee, and Herman Gray, 1–22. Durham: Duke University Press.

Banks, Dennis, with Richard Erdoes. 2004. *Ojibwe Warrior: Dennis Banks and the Rise of the American Indian Movement.* Norman: University of Oklahoma Press.

Banks, Miranda. 2009. "Gender Below-the-Line: Defining Feminist Production Studies." In *Production Studies: Cultural Studies of Media Industries,* edited by Vicki Mayer, Miranda J. Banks, and John T. Caldwell, 87–98. New York: Routledge.

Barber, John T., and Alice Tait, eds. 2001. *The Information Society and the Black Community.* Westport, CT: Praeger.

Barnouw, Erik. 1993. *Documentary: A History of the Non-Fiction Film.* New York: Oxford University Press.

Barragan, Yesenia. 2016. "Afro-Colombian Strike in Choco: A Historical Reckoning." TeleSUR Online, August 27, 2016. www.telesurenglish.net/opinion/Afro-Colombian-Strike-in-Choco-A-Historical-Reckoning-20160827-0011.html.

Barthes, Roland. 1964. *Elements of Semiology.* New York: Hill and Wang.

———. 1972. *Mythologies.* New York: Hill and Wang.

BaselMeets. 2018. *Basel Meets Punny Pun Times [Comedy, How It All Started].* Video file, January 10, 2018. www.youtube.com/watch?v=bhj3M9NcBXQ.

Bashi, Vilna. 2004. "Globalized Anti-Blackness: Transnationalizing Western Immigration Law, Policy, and Practice." *Ethnic and Racial Studies* 27 (4): 584–606.

Baugh, John. 2003. "Linguistic Profiling." In *Black Linguistics: Language, Society, and Politics in Africa and the Americas,* edited by Sinfree Makoni, Geneva Smitherman, Arnetha Ball, and Arthur K. Spears, 155–68. London: Routledge.

Beltrán, Mary. 2016. "Latina/os on TV! A Proud (and Ongoing) Struggle over Representation and Authorship." In *The Routledge Companion to Latina/o Popular Culture,* edited by Frederick Aldama, 23–33. New York: Routledge.

———. 2018. "Representation." In *The Craft of Criticism: Critical Media Studies in Practice,* 97–108. New York: Routledge.

Berg, Charles Ramirez. 2002. *Latino Images in Film: Stereotypes, Subversion, Resistance.* Austin: University of Texas Press.

Berlant, Lauren. 2011. *Cruel Optimism.* Durham: Duke University Press.

Berry, Richard. 2006. "Will the iPod Kill the Radio Star? Profiling Podcasting as Radio." *Convergence* 12 (2): 143–62.

Billings, Andrew. 2008. *Olympic Media: Inside the Biggest Show on Television.* New York: Routledge.

Bird, Elizabeth S. 1999. "Gendered Construction of the American Indian in Popular Media." *Journal of Communication* 49 (3): 61–83.

The Black Guy Who Tips. 2014. "5 Star Reviews for Christmas 2014." *The Black Guy Who Tips.* Podcast audio, ep. 844. https://itunes.apple.com/us/podcast/the-black-guy-who-tips-podcast/id349830668?mt=2.

Blackmon, Samantha. 2016. "Be Real Black for Me: Luke Cage and Lincoln Clay as the Heroes We Need." *Not Your Mama's Gamer,* October 7, 2016. www.nymgamer.com/?p=15072.

Blue, Alex V. 2017. "'Hear What You Want': Sonic Politics, Blackness, and Racism-Canceling Headphones." *Current Musicology,* nos. 99–100, 95–114.

Bobo, Lawrence D. 2000. "Reclaiming a Du Boisian Perspective on Racial Attitudes." *Annals of the American Academy of Political and Social Science* 568: 186–202.

Bobo, Lawrence D., and Ryan A. Smith. 1998. "From Jim Crow Racism to Laissez-Faire Racism: The Transformation of Racial Attitudes." In *Beyond Pluralism: The Conception of Groups and Group Identity in America*, edited by Wendy F. Katkin, Ned Landsman, and Andrea Tyree, 182–220. Chicago: University of Illinois Press.

Bogle, Donald. 1973. *Toms, Coons, Mulattoes, Mammies and Bucks: An Interpretive History of Blacks in American Films*. New York: Bloomsbury.

Bolter, Jay David, and Richard Grusin. 2000. *Remediation: Understanding New Media*. Cambridge: MIT Press.

Bonaparte, Darren. 2006. *Creation and Confederation: The Living History of the Iroquois*. Akwesasne, NY: Wampum Chronicles.

Bonilla, Yarimar, and Jonathan Rosa. 2015. "#Ferguson: Digital Protest, Hashtag Ethnography, and the Racial Politics of Social Media in the United States." *American Ethnologist* 42 (1): 4–17.

Bonilla-Silva, Eduardo. 2003. *Racism without Racists: Color-Blind Racism and the Persistence of Racial Inequality in America*. Oxford: Rowman and Littlefield.

Bourdieu, Pierre. 1990. *In Other Words: Essays towards a Reflexive Sociology*. Stanford, CA: Stanford University Press.

———. 1993. *The Field of Cultural Production: Essays on Art and Literature*, edited by Randal Johnson. Cambridge, England: Polity.

Boyer, LaNada. 1997. "Reflections of Alcatraz." In *American Indian Activism: Alcatraz to the Longest Walk*, edited by Troy Johnson, Joane Nagel, and Duane Champagne, 88–103. Urbana: University of Illinois Press.

Bradley, Regina. 2013. "To Sir, with Ratchety Love: Listening to the (Dis)Respectability Politics of Rachel Jeantel." *Sounding Out!*, July 1, 2013. https://soundstudiesblog .com/2013/07/01/disrespectability-politics-of-rachel-jeantel/.

Brah, Avtar. 1996. *Cartographies of Diaspora: Contesting Identities*. New York: Routledge.

Braithwaite, A. 2016. "It's about Ethics in Games Journalism? Gamergaters and Geek Masculinity." *Social Media+ Society* 2 (4), 2056305116672484.

Bristor, Julia M., Renée Gravois Lee, and Michelle R. Hunt. 1995. "Race and Ideology: African-American Images in Television Advertising." *Journal of Public Policy & Marketing* 14 (1): 48–59.

Brock, André. 2011. "Beyond the Pale: The Blackbird Web Browser's Critical Reception." *New Media & Society* 13 (7): 1085–1103.

———. 2012. "From the Blackhand Side: Twitter as a Cultural Conversation." *Journal of Broadcasting & Electronic Media* 56 (4): 529–49.

———. 2016. "Critical Technocultural Discourse Analysis." *New Media & Society* 20 (3): 1–19. doi:10.1177/1461444816677532.

Brock, André, Lynette Kvasny, and Kayla Hales. 2010. "Cultural Appropriations of Technical Capital: Black Women, Weblogs, and the Digital Divide." *Information, Communication, and Society* 13 (7): 1040–59.

Brooks, Daphne. 2010. "'Sister, Can You Line It Out?': Zora Neale Hurston and the Sound of Angular Black Womanhood." *Amerikastudien/American Studies* 55 (4): 617–27.

Brown, Kennaria. 2010. "*West Side Story* Read from Below: Puerto Rican Women's Cultural Readings." *Communication Review* 13 (3): 193–215.

Bull, Michael. 2014. "iPod Use, Mediation, and Privatization in the Age of Mechanical Reproduction." In *The Oxford Handbook of Mobile Music Studies*, vol. 1, edited by Sumanth Gopinath and Jason Stanyek, 103–17. New York: Oxford University Press.

Burgos, Adrian. 2009. "Left Out: Afro-Latinos, Black Baseball, and the Revision of Baseball's Racial History." *Social Text* 27 (1): 37–58.

Burn. 2015. "Steam Community :: Burn :: Games." June 23, 2015. https://steamcommunity.com/id/Burn86/recommended/.

Burroughs, B., and P. Rama. 2015. "The eSports Trojan Horse: Twitch and Streaming Futures." *Journal for Virtual Worlds Research* 8 (2).

Butsch, Richard. 2000. *The Making of American Audiences: From Stage to Television, 1750–1990*. New York: Cambridge University Press.

Byrd, Jodi A. 2016. "'Do They Not Have Rational Souls?': Consolidation and Sovereignty in Digital New Worlds." *Settler Colonial Studies* 6 (4): 423–37.

———. 2018. "Beast of America: Sovereignty and the Wildness of Objects." *South Atlantic Quarterly* 117 (3): 599–615.

Cajayon, Gene, dir. 2001. *The Debut*. Film.

Campbell, Christopher P. 1995. *Race, Myth and the News*. Thousand Oaks, CA: Sage.

Campt, Tina. 2017. *Listening to Images*. Durham: Duke University Press.

Candelaria, Nash. 1988. *The Day the Cisco Kid Shot John Wayne*. Tempe, AZ: Bilingual Press.

Candelario, Ginetta E. B. 2008. *Black behind the Ears: Dominican Racial Identity from Museums to Beauty Shops*. Durham: Duke University Press.

Carr, P. R., and D. E. Lund. 2009. *The Great White North: Exploring Whiteness, Privilege, and Identity in Education*. Rotterdam: Sense Publishers.

Carsignol, Anouck. 2014. "The Construction, Mobilization and Limits of South Asianism in North America." *South Asia Multidisciplinary Academic Journal*, no. 10 (December). https://doi.org/10.4000/samaj.3766.

Casillas, Dolores Inés. 2011. "Sounds of Surveillance: U.S. Spanish-Language Radio Patrols La Migra." *American Quarterly* 63, no. 3 (September): 807–29.

———. 2014. *Sounds of Belonging: U.S. Spanish-Language Radio and Public Advocacy*. New York: New York University Press.

Casillas, Dolores Inés, Juan Sebastian Ferrada, and Sara Hinojos. 2018. "The 'Accent' on *Modern Family*: Listening to Vocal Representations of the Latina Body." *Aztlán: A Journal of Chicano Studies* 43, no. 1 (Spring): 61–88.

Castañeda, Mari. 2011. "¡Adelante! Advancing Social Justice through Latina/o Community Media." In *Media and Democracy: Critical Media Scholarship and Social Justice*, edited by Jeff Pooley, Sure Curry Jansen, and Lora Taub, 115–30. New York: Palgrave Macmillan.

———. 2014a. "The Role of Media Policy in Shaping the U.S. Latino Radio Industry." In *Contemporary Latina/o Media: Production, Circulation, Politics*, edited by Arlene Dávila and Yeidy Rivero, 267–84. New York: New York University Press.

———. 2014b. "La Lucha Sigue: Latina and Latino Labor in the U.S. Media Industries." *Kalfou: Journal of the UCSB Center for Black Studies Research* 1 (2): 203–20.

———. 2016. "Altering the U.S. Soundscape through Latina/o Community Radio." In *The Routledge Companion to Latina/o Media*, edited by María Elena Cepeda and Dolores Inés Casillas. New York: Routledge.

CBC Radio. 2017. "Thunderbird Strike: Controversial Video Game Takes Aim at Oil Industry." November 3, 2017. www.cbc.ca/radio/unreserved/from-video-games-to-ya-novels-how-indigenous-art-is-evolving-1.4384041/thunderbird-strike-controversial-video-game-takes-aim-at-oil-industry-1.4384559.

Cepeda, María Elena. 2008. "Survival Aesthetics: U.S. Latinas and the Negotiation of Popular Media." In *Latina/o Communication Studies Today*, edited by Angharad N. Valdivia, 237–56. New York: Peter Lang.

———. 2016. "Beyond 'Filling in the Gap': The State and Status of Latina/o Feminist Media Studies." *Feminist Media Studies* 16 (2): 344–60.

Cepeda, María Elena, and Alejandra Rosales. 2017. "An Indecent Proposal: Latino Masculinity and the Audience in Latina/o Music Video." In *The Routledge Companion to Latina/o Media*, edited by María Elena Cepeda and Dolores Inés Casillas, 385–401. New York: Routledge.

Chaat Smith, Paul, and Robert Allen Warrior. 1996. *Like a Hurricane: The Indian Movement from Alcatraz to Wounded Knee*. New York: New Press.

Chávez, Christopher. 2015. *Reinventing the Latino Television Viewer: Language, Ideology, and Practice*. Lanham, MD: Lexington Books.

Chess, Shira, and Adrienne Shaw. 2015. "A Conspiracy of Fishes, or, How We Learned to Stop Worrying about #Gamergate and Embrace Hegemonic Masculinity." *Journal of Broadcasting & Electronic Media* 59 (1): 208–20.

Chidester, P. 2008. "May the Circle Stay Unbroken: *Friends*, the Presence of Absence, and the Rhetorical Reinforcement of Whiteness." *Critical Studies in Media Communication* 25 (2): 157–74.

Chimezie, Amuzie. 1976. "The Dozens: An African-Heritage Theory." *Journal of Black Studies* 6 (4): 401–20.

Chin, Daryl. 1988. "After Ten Years: Some Notes on the Asian American International Film Festival." In *Asian CineVision Presents the Tenth Asian American International Film Festival* (film festival program), 11–17.

Chin, Frank, and Jeffery Paul Chan. 1972. "Racist Love." In *Seeing through Shuck*, edited by Richard Kostelanetz, 65–79. New York: Ballantine Books.

Cho, Kat. 2019. Twitter post, January 14, 2019. https://twitter.com/KatCho.

Choueiti, Marc, Stacy L. Smith, and Katherine Pieper. 2018. *Critic's Choice? Gender and Race/Ethnicity of Film Reviewers Across 100 Top Films of 2017*. Los Angeles: USC Annenberg Inclusion Initiative.

Christian, Aymar Jean. 2018. *Open TV: Innovation beyond Hollywood and the Rise of Web Television*. New York: New York University Press.

Chude-Sokei, Louis. 2016. *The Sound of Culture: Diaspora and Black Technopoetics*. Middletown, CT: Wesleyan University Press.

Chung, Wonho. 2010. *Wonho Chung Performs at Friday Night Live (part 1/2)*. Video file, May 14, 2010. www.youtube.com/watch?v=-BbJoJFu1Vc.

The Cisco Kid. 1950. "Boomerang." Ziv Television.

Clark, Kevito. 2016. "'Brown Girls' Producer Sam Bailey Talks Post-#OscarsSoWhite Vibes + Budding Show Hype." *Okayplayer*, November 16, 2016. www.okayplayer.com/news/brown-girls-series-sam-q-bailey-interview.html.

Clark, Lynn Schofield. 2003. *From Angels to Aliens: Teenagers, the Media, and the Supernatural*. New York: Oxford University Press.

Click, Melissa. 2019. *Anti-Fandom: Dislike and Hate in the Digital Age*. New York: New York University Press.

Clinard, B., and F. Meier. 1995. *Sociology of Deviant Behavior*. New York: Harcourt, Brace, Jovanovich College Publishers.

Cobb, Daniel. 2008. *Native Activism in Cold War America: The Struggle for Sovereignty*. Lawrence: University Press of Kansas.

Cohn, D'Vera. 2010. "Census History: Counting Hispanics." Pew Research Center, March 3, 2010. www.pewsocialtrends.org/2010/03/03/census-history-counting-hispanics-2/.

Collier, Peter. 1970. "The Red Man's Burden." *Ramparts*, February 1970, 26–38.

Collins, Patricia Hill. 2000. *Black Feminist Thought: Knowledge, Consciousness, and the Politics of Empowerment*. New York: Routledge.

Comcast NBCUniversal. 2018. "Diversity and Inclusion: Our People." https://corporate.comcast.com/values/diversityreport/2018/our-workforce/our-people.

Conwell, Jordan A. 2016. "Josephs without Pharaohs: The Du Boisian Framework for the Sociology of Education." *Journal of Negro Education*, no. 85, 28–45. doi:10.7709/jnegroeducation.85.1.0028.

Coombs, Danielle, and David Cassilo. 2017. "Athletes and/or Activists: LeBron James and Black Lives Matter." *Journal of Sport and Social Issues* 41 (5): 425–44.

Cooper, Brittney C. 2017. *Beyond Respectability: The Intellectual Thought of Race Women*. Chicago: University of Illinois Press.

———. 2018. *Eloquent Rage: A Black Feminist Discovers Her Superpower*. New York: St. Martin's.

Cornellier, Bruno. 2016. "Extracting Inuit: The *of the North* Controversy and the White Possessive." *American Indian Culture and Research Journal* 40 (4): 23–48.

Crawley, Ashon. 2016. *Black Pentecostal Breath: The Aesthetics of Possibility*. New York: Fordham University Press.

Crenshaw, Kimberlé. 1990. "Mapping the Margins: Intersectionality, Identity Politics, and Violence against Women of Color." *Stanford Law Review* 43 (6): 1241–1300.

Crey, Karrmen. 2016. "Indigeneity, Institutions of Media Culture, and the Canadian State since 1990." UCLA. http://oatd.org/oatd/record?record=california%5C%3Aqt 8j06t25o.

Cunningham, Philip Lamarr. 2009. "Please Don't Fine Me Again!!!!!": Black Athletic Defiance in the NBA and NFL." *Journal of Sport and Social Issues* 33 (1): 39–58.

Cunningham, Stuart. 2013. *Hidden Innovation: Policy, Industry and the Creative Sector.* Brisbane: University of Queensland Press.

Dagbovie-Mullins, Sika. 2013. *Crossing B(L)Ack: Mixed-Race Identity in Modern American Fiction and Culture.* Knoxville: University of Tennessee Press.

Daniels, Jesse. 2013. "Race and Racism in Internet Studies: A Review and Critique." *New Media & Society* 15 (5): 695–719.

Davé, Shilpa. 2013. *Indian Accents: Brown Voice and Racial Performance in American Television and Film.* Chicago: University of Illinois Press.

Dávila, Arlene. 2012. *Latinos, Inc.: The Marketing and Making of a People.* 2nd ed. Berkeley: University of California Press.

Dawnbug. 2018. "Steam Community :: Dawnbug :: Games." April 22, 2018. https:// steamcommunity.com/id/thehugthief/recommended/.

de B'béri, Boulou Ebanda, and Peter Hogarth. 2009. "White America's Construction of Black Bodies: The Case of Ron Artest as a Model of Covert Racial Ideology in the NBA's Discourse." *Journal of International and Intercultural Communication* 2 (2): 89–106.

de Certeau, Michel. 1984. *The Practice of Everyday Life.* Trans. Steven F. Rendall. Berkeley: University of California Press.

Del Rio, Esteban. 2006. "The Latina/o Problematic: Categories and Questions in Media Communication Research." *Communication Yearbook* 30 (1): 387–429.

de Onis, Catalina (Kathleen) M. 2017. "What's in an 'X'? An Exchange about the Politics of 'Latinx.'" *Chiricú Journal: Latina/o Literatures, Arts, and Cultures* 1 (2): 78–91.

Desai, Manan. 2014. "What B. R. Ambedkar Wrote to W. E. B. Du Bois." *TIDES*, April 22, 2014. www.saada.org/tides/article/ambedkar-du-bois.

de Saussure, Ferdinand. 1959. *Course in General Linguistics*, edited by Charles Bally and Albert Sechehaye, with Albert Reidlinger, translated by Wade Baskin. New York: Philosophical Library.

DeSipio, Louis. 1998. "Talking Back to Television: Latinos Discuss How Television Portrays Them and the Quality of Programming Options." Claremont: Tomás Rivera Policy Institute.

Diamond, Neil, dir. 2009. *Reel Injun.* Documentary film. Montreal: National Film Board of Canada.

Dixon, Travis L. 2006. "Psychological Reactions to Crime News Portrayals of Black Criminals: Understanding the Moderating Roles of Prior News Viewing and Stereotype Endorsement." *Communication Monographs* 73 (2): 162–87. https://doi .org/10.1080/03637750600690643.

———. 2008. "Network News and Racial Beliefs: Exploring the Connection between National Television News Exposure and Stereotypical Perceptions of African Americans." *Journal of Communication* 58: 321–37.

Dixon, Travis, and Daniel Linz. 2000. "Overrepresentation and Underrepresentation of Blacks and Latinos as Lawbreakers on Television News." *Journal of Communication* 50, no. 2 (Spring): 131–54.

Dorr, Kirstie. 2018. *In Site, in Sound: Performance Geographies in América Latina*. Durham: Duke University Press.

Douglas, Susan. 2004. *Listening In: Radio and the American Imagination*. Minneapolis: University of Minnesota Press.

Dovidio, John F., and Samuel L. Gaertner. 2000. "Aversive Racism and Selection Decisions: 1989 and 1999." *Psychological Science* 11 (4): 315–19.

Dovidio, John F., Brenda Major, and Jennifer Crocker. 2000. "Stigma: Introduction and Overview." In *The Social Psychology of Stigma*, edited by T. Heatherton, R. Kleck, M. Hebl, and J. Hull, 1–28. New York: Guilford.

Draper, Kevin, and Ken Belson. 2019. "Colin Kaepernick and the N.F.L. Settle Collusion Case." *New York Times*, February 15, 2019. www.nytimes.com/2019/02/15 /sports/nfl-colin-kaepernick.html.

Dubé, Jacob. 2017. "Destroy Oil Pipelines as a Thunderbird in This New Video Game." *Vice*, October 19, 2017. www.vice.com/en_us/article/59ymk5/thunderbird-strike -elizabeth-lapensee-video-game-imaginenative.

Dyer-Witheford, Nick, and Greig de Peuter. 2009. *Games of Empire: Global Capitalism and Video Games*. Minneapolis: University of Minnesota Press.

Edge, Nathan. 2013. "Evolution of the Gaming Experience: Live Video Streaming and the Emergence of a New Web Community." *Elon Journal of Undergraduate Research in Communications* 4 (2).

Edison Research. 2012. "The Podcast Consumer 2012." May 29, 2012. www.edisonresearch .com/the-podcast-consumer-2012/.

Edison Research and Triton Digital. 2014. "The Infinite Dial 2014." www.edisonre search.com/wp-content/uploads/2014/03/The-Infinite-Dial-2014-from-Edison -Research-and-Triton-Digital.pdf.

Edwards, Harry. 1969. *The Revolt of the Black Athlete*. New York: Free Press.

Ehrenreich, Barbara. 2019. Twitter post, February 4, 2019. https://twitter .com/B_Ehrenreich.

Elam, Michele. 2011. *The Souls of Mixed Folk: Race, Politics, and Aesthetics in the New Millennium*. Stanford, CA: Stanford University Press.

E-Line Media. 2016. *Never Alone—Game*. http://neveralonegame.com/game/.

Elliott, David. 2007. "In Asian Film, Kim's the Edge of Our Pacific Rim." *San Diego Union Tribune*, October 7, 2007.

Elliott, Matthew. 2014. "*Never Alone* Review." Gamesradar, November 18, 2014. www .gamesradar.com/never-alone-review/.

Entman, Robert, and Andrew Rojecki. 2000. *The Black Image in the White Mind*. Chicago: University of Chicago Press.

Erigha, Maryann. 2019. *The Hollywood Jim Crow: The Racial Politics of the Movie Industry*. New York: New York University Press.

Essi, Cedric. 2017. "'Mama's Baby, Papa's, Too'—Toward Critical Mixed Race Studies." *Zeitschrift für Anglistik und Amerikanistik* 65 (2).

Fahrenthold, David A., and Frances Stead Sellers. 2016. "How Bannon Flattered and Coaxed Trump on Policies Key to the Alt-Right." *Washington Post*, November 15, 2016. www.washingtonpost.com/politics/how-bannon-flattered-and-coaxed-trump-on-policies-key-to-the-alt-right/2016/11/15/53c66362-ab69-11e6-a31b-4b6397e625d0_story.html.

FCC (Federal Communications Commission). 2015. *Third Report on Ownership of Commercial Broadcast Stations*. Washington, DC: Industry Analysis Division, Media Bureau.

Feng, Peter. 1996. "Being Chinese American, Becoming Asian American: 'Chan Is Missing.'" *Cinema Journal* 35 (4): 88–118.

Feuer, Jane. 1983. "The Concept of Live Television: Ontology as Ideology." In *Regarding Television: Critical Approaches*, edited by E. Ann Kaplan, 12–33. Lanham, MD: University Publications of America.

Fields, Barbara Jeanne, and Karen E. Fields. 2012. *Racecraft: The Soul of Inequality in American Life*. New York: Verso.

Fiol-Matta, Licia. 2017. *The Great Woman Singer: Gender and Voice in Puerto Rican Music*. New York: New York University Press.

Fiske, John. 1992. "The Cultural Economy of Fandom." In *The Adoring Audience: Fan Culture and Popular Media*, edited by Lisa A. Lewis, 30–49. New York: Routledge.

Fixico, Donald. 1986. *Termination and Relocation: Federal Indian Policy, 1945–1960*. Albuquerque: University of New Mexico Press.

Flores, Joseph L. 2015. "#blacklivesmatter: The Investigation of Twitter as a Site of Agency in Social Movements." PhD diss., University of Texas at El Paso.

Florini, Sarah. 2014. "Tweets, Tweeps, and Signifyin': Communication and Cultural Performance on 'Black Twitter.'" *Television & New Media* 15 (3): 223–37.

———. 2017. "This Week in Blackness, the George Zimmerman Acquittal, and the Production of a Networked Collective Identity." *New Media & Society* 19 (3): 439–54.

Foley, Douglas E. 1997. "Deficit Thinking Models Based on Culture: The Anthropological Protest." In *The Evolution of Deficit Thinking: Educational Thought and Practice*, edited by R. Valencia, 113–31. London: Falmer.

Foster, Zachary J. 2017. "The Invention of Palestine." PhD diss., Princeton University.

Foucault, Michel. 1978. *The History of Sexuality: An Introduction*. New York: Random House.

———. 1988. *Technologies of the Self: A Seminar with Michel Foucault*. Amherst: University of Massachusetts Press.

France, David, dir. 2017. *The Death and Life of Marsha P. Johnson*. Film.

Fraser, Nancy. 2007. "Creating Model Citizens for the Information Age: Canadian Internet as Civilizing Discourse Policy." *Canadian Journal of Communication* 32 (2): 201–18.

Freelon, Deen, Charlton McIlwain, and Meredith D. Clark. 2016a. "Quantifying the Power and Consequences of Social Media Protest." *New Media & Society* 20 (3): 990–1011.

———. 2016b. "Beyond the Hashtags: #Ferguson, #BlackLivesMatter, and the Online Struggle for Offline Justice." Center for Media & Social Impact, American University.

Fulbeck, Kip. 2006. *Part Asian, 100% Hapa*. San Francisco: Chronicle Books.

Fuller, Jennifer. 2010. "Branding Blackness on US Cable Television." *Media, Culture & Society* 32 (2): 285–305.

Furlonge, Nicole Brittingham. 2018. *Race Sounds: The Art of Listening in African American Literature*. Iowa City: University of Iowa Press.

Galindo, René, and Jami Vigil. 2006. "Are Anti-Immigrant Statements Racist or Nativist? What Difference Does It Make?" *Latino Studies* 4 (4): 419–47.

Garza, Alicia. 2014. "A Herstory of the #BlackLivesMatter Movement by Alicia Garza." *Feminist Wire*, October 7, 2014. https://thefeministwire.com/2014/10/blacklivesmatter-2/.

Gates, Henry Louis, Jr. 1983. "The 'Blackness of Blackness': A Critique of the Sign and the Signifying Monkey." *Critical Inquiry* 9 (4): 685–723.

———. 1997. *Thirteen Ways of Looking at a Black Man*. New York: Random House.

Gates, Racquel J. 2018. *Double Negative: The Black Image and Popular Culture*. Durham: Duke University Press.

George-Kanentiio, Dan. 2011. "*Akwesasne Notes*: How the Mohawk Nation Created a Newspaper and Shaped Contemporary Native America." In *Insider Histories of the Vietnam Era Underground Press*, pt. 1, edited by Ken Wachsberger, 109–38. East Lansing: Michigan State University Press.

Gettell, Oliver. 2016. "Margaret Cho on Tilda Swinton Conversation: Emails Stand on Their Own." *Entertainment Weekly*, December 17, 2016. https://ew.com/article/2016/12/17/tilda-swinton-margaret-cho-emails-doctor-strange-whitewashing/.

Gibson, James. 2015. *The Ecological Approach to Visual Perception*. Classic ed. New York: Taylor and Francis.

Gieseking, Jen, William Mangold, Cindi Katz, Setha Low, and Susan Saegert, eds. 2014. *The People, Place, and Space Reader*. New York: Routledge.

Gillespie, Marie. 1995. *Television, Ethnicity, and Cultural Change*. London: Routledge.

Gillespie, Tarleton. 2011. "Can an Algorithm Be Wrong? Twitter Trends, the Specter of Censorship and Our Faith in the Algorithms around Us." *Culture Digitally*, October 19, 2011. http://culturedigitally.org/2011/10/can-an-algorithm-be-wrong/.

Gilliam, Franklin D., Jr., and Shanto Iyengar. 2000. "Prime Suspects: The Influence of Local Television News on the Viewing Public." *American Journal of Political Science* 44, no 3 (July): 560–73.

Gilliam, Franklin D., Jr., Nicholas A. Valentino, and Matthew N. Beckmann. 2002. "Where You Live and What You Watch: The Impact of Racial Proximity and Local

Television News on Attitudes about Race and Crime." *Political Research Quarterly* 55, no. 4 (July): 755–80.

Gilyard, Keith, and Adam Banks. 2018. *On African-American Rhetoric*. New York: Routledge.

Ginsburg, Faye D. 1999. "The After-Life of Documentary: The Impact of *You Are on Indian Land*." *Wide Angle* 21 (2): 60-67.

Ginwright, Shawn. 2008. "Collective Radical Imagination: Youth Participatory Action Research and the Art of Emancipatory Knowledge." In *Revolutionizing Education: Youth Participatory Action Research in Motion*, edited by Julio Cammarota and Michelle Fine, 22–31. New York: Routledge.

Giroux, Henry A. 1997. "White Squall: Resistance and the Pedagogy of Whiteness." *Cultural Studies* 11 (3): 376–89.

Goffman, Erving. 1963. *Stigma: Notes on the Management of Spoiled Identity*. New York: Simon and Schuster.

Goin, Keara K. 2017. "Zoe Saldana or Zoë Saldaña? Cinematic *dominicanidad* and the Hollywood Star." *Celebrity Studies* 8 (1): 1–19.

Goldberg, Leslie. 2015. "Eddie Huang Gives 'Fresh Off the Boat' a 'B'; Pushes for Domestic Violence Arc." *Hollywood Reporter*, February 4, 2015. www.hollywoodreporter.com/live-feed/fresh-boat-eddie-huang-interview-769874.

Gomez, Alan. 2016. "Another Election Surprise: Many Hispanics Backed Trump." *USA Today*, November 9, 2016. www.usatoday.com/story/news/politics/elections/2016/2016/11/09/hispanic-vote-election-2016-donald-trump-hillary-clinton/93540772/.

Gong, Stephen. 1991. "A History in Progress: Asian American Media Arts Centers, 1970–1990." In *Moving the Image: Independent Asian Pacific American Media Arts*, edited by Russell Leong, 1–9. Los Angeles: UCLA Asian American Studies Center and Visual Communications.

Goodridge, Tyler Patrice. 2016. "Black Lives Matter Timeline." Georgetown University Repository. https://repository.library.georgetown.edu/bitstream/handle/10822/1040691/Black%20Lives%20Matter%20Timeline%20.pdf?sequence=1.

Gordon, Lewis R., George Ciccariello-Maher, and Nelson Maldonado-Torres. 2013. "Frantz Fanon, Fifty Years On." *Radical Philosophy Review* 16 (1): 307–24.

Gould, Stephen Jay. 1996. *The Mismeasure of Man*. Rev. ed. New York: Norton.

Graham, Bob. 2001. "PROFILE / Gene Cajayon / Filipino American Film 'Debut' Getting Noticed." *San Francisco Chronicle*, April 24, 2001. www.sfgate.com/entertainment/article/PROFILE-Gene-Cajayon-Filipino-American-film-2928548.php.

Grainger, Andrew, Joshua I. Newman, and David L. Andrews. 2006. "Sports, the Media, and the Construction of Race." In *Handbook of Sports and Media*, edited by Arthur A. Raney and Jennings Bryant, 447–67. New York: Routledge.

Gray, Herman. 1995. *Watching Race: Television and the Struggle for Blackness*. Minneapolis: University of Minnesota Press.

———. 2005. *Culture Moves: African Americans and the Politics of Representation*. Berkeley: University of California Press.

Gray, Kishonna L. 2011. "Deviant Bodies Resisting Online: Examining the Intersecting Realities of Women of Color in Xbox Live." PhD diss., Arizona State University.

———. 2012a. "Deviant Bodies, Stigmatized Identities, and Racist Acts: Examining the Experiences of African-American Gamers in Xbox Live." *New Review of Hypermedia and Multimedia* 18 (4): 261–76.

———. 2012b. "Intersecting Oppressions and Online Communities: Examining the Experiences of Women of Color in Xbox Live." *Information, Communication & Society* 15 (3): 411–28.

———. 2014. *Race, Gender, and Deviance in Xbox Live: Theoretical Perspectives from the Virtual Margins.* London: Routledge.

———. 2015. "Cultural Production and Digital Resilience: Examining Female Gamers' Use of Social Media to Participate in Video Game Culture." In *Fan Girls and the Media: Creating Characters, Consuming Culture,* edited by Adrienne Trier-Bieniek, 85–100. Lanham, MD: Rowman and Littlefield.

———. 2016. "On Games and Activism: An Interview with Kahlief Adams." *Not Your Mama's Gamer,* May 23, 2016. www.nymgamer.com/?p=13784.

Gray, Kishonna L., and David J. Leonard. 2018. *Woke Gaming: Digital Challenges to Oppression and Social Injustice.* Seattle: University of Washington Press.

Gray, Tim. 2018. "Ryan Coogler on How 'Black Panther' Broke Barriers Below-the-Line, Too." *Variety,* December 12, 2018. https://variety.com/2018/artisans/production/ryan-coogler-black-panther-production-crew-1203087347/.

Green, Rachel Harris. 2013. "Reality TV Show *The First 48* Thrives Off America's Racist Justice System." *Guardian,* December 21, 2013. www.theguardian.com/commentisfree/2013/dec/21/first-48-tv-show-police-racism-entertainment.

Griffin, Rachel Alicia. 2012. "The Disgrace of Commodification and Shameful Convenience: A Critical Race Critique of the NBA." *Journal of Black Studies* 43 (2): 161–85.

Gruenewald, Jeff, Steven M. Chermak, and Jesenia M. Pizarro. 2013. "Covering Victims in the News: What Makes Minority Homicides Newsworthy?" *Justice Quarterly* 30 (5): 755–83. doi: 10.1080/07418825.2011.628945.

GrumpyReviewer. 2014. "Never Alone." Metacritic, December 2, 2014. www.metacritic.com/game/playstation-4/never-alone.

Gualtieri, Sarah. 2009. *Between Arab and White: Race and Ethnicity in the Early Syrian American Diaspora.* Berkeley: University of California Press.

Guerrero, Lisa. 2011. "One Nation under a Hoop: Race, Meritocracy, and Messiahs in the NBA." In *Commodified and Criminalized: New Racism and African Americans in Contemporary Sports,* edited by David J. Leonard and C. Richard King, 121–46. Lanham, MD: Rowman and Littlefield.

Guevarra, Rudy P. 2012. *Becoming Mexipino: Multiethnic Identities and Communities in San Diego.* New Brunswick, NJ: Rutgers University Press.

Haggins, Bambi. 2007. *Laughing Mad: The Black Comic Persona in Post-Soul America.* New Brunswick, NJ: Rutgers University Press.

Hagood, Mack. 2011. "Quiet Comfort: Noise, Otherness, and the Mobile Production of Personal Space." *American Quarterly* 63 (3): 573–89.

Halberstam, Jack. 2018. *Trans*: A Quick and Quirky Account of Gender Variability.* Berkeley: University of California Press.

Hall, Stuart, ed. 1973/2007. "Encoding/Decoding Model of Communication." In *The Cultural Studies Reader.* 3rd ed., edited by Simon During, 477–87. London: Routledge.

———. 1980. "Encoding/Decoding." In *Culture, Media, Language: Working Papers in Cultural Studies, 1972–79,* edited by Stuart Hall, Dorothy Hobson, Andrew Lowe, and Paul Willis, 128–38. London: Hutchinson.

———. 1981. "The Whites of Their Eyes: Racist Ideologies and the Media." In *The Race and Media Reader,* edited by Gilbert B. Rodman, 37–54. New York: Routledge.

———. 1992. "Race, Culture, and Communications: Looking Backward and Forward at Cultural Studies." *Rethinking Marxism* 5 (1): 10–18.

———. 1997a. "The Work of Representation." In *Representation: Cultural Representations and Signifying Practices,* edited by Stuart Hall, 13–74. London: Sage.

———. 1997b. "The Spectacle of the 'Other.'" In *Representation: Cultural Representations and Signifying Practices,* edited by Stuart Hall, 223–90. London: Sage.

Hannerz, Ulf. 2004. "Cosmopolitanism." In *A Companion to the Anthropology of Politics,* edited by David Nugent and Joan Vincent, 69–85. Malden, MA: Blackwell.

Harb, Ali. 2018. "US Census Fails to Add MENA Category: Arabs to Remain 'White' in Count." *Middle East Eye,* January 27, 2018. www.middleeasteye.net/news/us-census-continue-count-arabs-white-1206288795.

Harrell, Shelly P., and Miguel E. Gallardo. 2008. "Sociopolitical and Community Dynamics in the Development of a Multicultural Worldview." In *The Sage Handbook of Child Development, Multiculturalism, and Media,* edited by Joy Keiko Asamen and Mesha L. Ellis, 113–28. Thousand Oaks: Sage.

Harris-Lacewell, Melissa. 2004. *Barbershops, Bibles, and BET: Everyday Talk and Black Political Thought.* Princeton: Princeton University Press.

Harrison, Louis, and Anthony L. Brown. 2017. "Will the Real Black Dad Please Show Up?" *UT News,* June 19, 2017. https://news.utexas.edu/2017/06/19/will-the-real-black-dad-please-show-up/.

Hartmann, Douglas. 2003. *Race, Culture, and the Revolt of the Black Athlete.* Chicago: University of Chicago Press.

Harvey, Alison, and Tamara Shepherd. 2017. "When Passion Isn't Enough: Gender, Affect and Credibility in Digital Games Design." *International Journal of Cultural Studies* 20 (5): 492–508.

Hashmi, Mobina. 2006. "Outsourcing the American Dream? Representing the Stakes of IT Globalisation." *Economic and Political Weekly* 41 (3): 242–49.

Hauptman, Laurence M. 1986. *The Iroquois Struggle for Survival: World War II to Red Power.* Syracuse, NY: Syracuse University Press.

Havens, Tim. 2017. "The Algorithmic Audience and African American Media Cultures." *FlowTV,* October 30, 2017. www.flowjournal.org/2017/10/the-algorithmic-audience/.

Havens, Tim, Amanda D. Lotz, and Serra Tinic. 2009. "Critical Media Industry Studies: A Research Approach." *Communication, Culture & Critique* 2 (2): 234–53.

Hearne, Joanna. 2012. *Native Recognition: Indigenous Cinema and the Western*. Albany: State University of New York Press.

Hearne, Joanna, and Elizabeth LaPensée. 2017. "'We All Stand Side by Side': An Interview with Elizabeth LaPensée." *Studies in American Indian Literatures* 29 (1): 27–37.

Hernández, Tanya Katerí. 2003. "'Too Black to Be Latina/o': Blackness and Blacks as Foreigners in Latino Studies." *Latino Studies* 1 (1): 152–59.

Higgin, Tanner. 2008. "Blackless Fantasy: The Disappearance of Race in Massively Multiplayer Online Role-Playing Games." *Games and Culture* 4 (1): 3–26.

Hilger, Michael. 2016. *Native Americans in the Movies: Portrayals from Silent Films to the Present*. Lanham, MD: Rowman and Littlefield.

Hill, Edwin. 2013. *Black Soundscapes White Stages: The Meaning of Francophone Sound in the Black Atlantic*. Baltimore: Johns Hopkins University Press.

Hill, Marc Lamont. 2018. "'Thank You, Black Twitter': State Violence, Digital Counterpublics, and Pedagogies of Resistance." *Urban Education* 53 (2): 286–302.

Hinojos, Sara. 2019. "Lupe Vélez and Her Spicy Visual 'Accent' in English-Language Print Media." *Latino Studies* 17 (3): 338–61.

Hoffman, Kelly M., et al. 2016. "Racial Bias in Pain Assessment and Treatment Recommendations, and False Beliefs about Biological Differences between Blacks and Whites." *Proceedings of the National Academy of Sciences of the United States of America* 113 (16): 4296–301. doi:10.1073/pnas.1516047113.

Holt, Lanier Frush. 2013. "Writing the Wrong: Can Counter-Stereotypes Offset Negative Media Messages about African Americans?" *Journalism & Mass Communication Quarterly* 90 (1): 108–25. doi: 10.1177/1077699012468699.

Honarpisheh, Farbod. 2006. "You Are on Indian Land." In *The Cinema of Canada*, edited by Jerry White, 81–91. London: Wallflower Press.

hooks, bell. 1992. *Black Looks: Race and Representation*. Boston: South End.

Hosokawa, Shuhei. 1984. "The Walkman Effect." *Popular Music* 4: 165–80.

Hu, Brian. 2018. Interview by Jun Okada. Personal interview. March 31, 2018.

Huang, Eddie. 2013. *Fresh Off the Boat: A Memoir*. New York: Random House, Spiegel & Grau.

———. 2015. "Bamboo-Ceiling TV." *New York*, January 12, 2015.

Huber, Lindsay Perez, Corina Benavides Lopez, Maria C. Malagon, Veronica Velez, and Daniel G. Solorzano. 2008. "Getting beyond the 'Symptom,' Acknowledging the 'Disease': Theorizing Racist Nativism." *Contemporary Justice Review* 11 (1): 39–51.

Hunt, Darnell. 2016. "Renaissance in Reverse?" 2016 Hollywood Writers Reports, Writers Guild of America, West. March 2016. www.wga.org/uploadedFiles/who_we_are/HWR16.pdf.

Hurston, Zora Neale. 1935. *Mules and Men: Negro Folktales and Voodoo Practices in the South*. New York: Lippincott.

Ibrahim, Habiba. 2012. *Troubling the Family: The Promise of Personhood and the Rise of Multiracialism*. Minneapolis: University of Minnesota Press.

Ifekwunigwe, Jayne O. 2004. *"Mixed Race" Studies: A Reader.* New York: Routledge.

Ince, Jelani, Fabio Rojas, and Clayton A. Davis. 2017. "The Social Media Response to Black Lives Matter: How Twitter Users Interact with Black Lives Matter through Hashtag Use." *Ethnic and Racial Studies* 40 (11): 1814–30.

Ito, Mizuko. 2012. "Contributors versus Leechers: Fansubbing Ethics and a Hybrid Public Culture." In *Fandom Unbound: Otaku Culture in a Connected World*, edited by Mizuko Ito, Daisuke Okabe, and Izumi Tsuji, 179–204. New Haven: Yale University Press.

Jackson, Ronald L. 2006. *Scripting the Black Masculine Body: Identity, Discourse, and Racial Politics in Popular Media.* Albany: State University of New York Press.

Jackson, Ronald L., and T. Garner. 1998. "Tracing the Evolution of 'Race,' 'Ethnicity,' and 'Culture' in Communication Studies." *Howard Journal of Communications* 9 (1): 41–55.

Jackson, Sarah J. 2016. "(Re)imagining Intersectional Democracy from Black Feminism to Hashtag Activism." *Women's Studies in Communication* 39 (4): 375–79.

Jenkins, Henry. 2004a. *Convergence Culture: Where Old and New Media Collide.* New York: New York University Press.

———. 2004b. "The Cultural Logic of Media Convergence." *International Journal of Cultural Studies* 7 (1): 33–43.

———. 2004c. "Pop Cosmopolitanism: Mapping Cultural Flows in an Age of Media Convergence in the New Millennium." In *Globalization: Culture and Education in the New Millennium*, edited by Marcelo Suarez-Orozco and Desiree B. Qin-Hilliard, 114–40. Berkeley: University of California Press.

———. 2005. *Textual Poachers: Television Fans and Participatory Culture.* New York: Routledge.

———. 2006. "Pop Cosmopolitanism: Mapping Cultural Flows in an Age of Media Convergence." In *Fans, Bloggers and Gamers: Exploring Participatory Culture*, 152–72. New York: New York University Press.

———. 2008. *Convergence Culture: Where Old and New Media Collide.* New York: New York University Press.

———. 2016. "Youth Voice, Media, and Political Engagement: Introducing the Core Concepts." In *By Any Media Necessary: The New Youth Activism*, edited by Henry Jenkins, Sangita Shresthova, Liana Gamber-Thompson, Neta Kliger-Vilenchik, and Arely M. Zimmerman, 1–60. New York: New York University Press.

Jenkins, Henry, and Nico Carpentier. 2013. "Theorizing Participatory Intensities: A Conversation about Participation and Politics." *Convergence* 19 (3): 265–86.

Jenkins, Henry, Sam Ford, and Joshua Green. 2018. *Spreadable Media: Creating Value and Meaning in a Networked Culture.* New York: New York University Press.

Jenkins, Henry, Ravi Purushotma, Margaret Weigel, Katie Clinton, and Alice J. Robison. 2009. *Confronting the Challenges of Participatory Culture: Media Education for the 21st Century.* Cambridge: MIT Press.

Johnson, Catherine. 2012. *Branding Television*. New York: Routledge.

Johnson, E. Patrick. 2003. *Appropriating Blackness: Performance and the Politics of Authenticity*. Durham: Duke University Press.

Johnson, Kevin R. 1996. "Fear of an Alien Nation: Race, Immigration, and Immigrants." *Stanford Law & Policy Review* 7 (2): 111–31.

Jones, Bomani. 2017. "Colin Kaepernick Is Called a Distraction, but from What?" TheUndefeated.com, March 27, 2017. https://theundefeated.com/features/colin-kaepernick-is-called-a-distraction-but-from-what/.

Jordenö, Sara, dir. 2016. *Kiki*. Film.

Joseph, Ralina L. 2013. *Transcending Blackness: From the New Millennium Mulatta to the Exceptional Multiracial*. Durham: Duke University Press.

———. 2018. *Postracial Resistance: Black Women, Media, and the Uses of Strategic Ambiguity*. New York: New York University Press.

Juul, Jesper. 2010. *A Casual Revolution: Reinventing Video Games and Their Players*. Cambridge: MIT Press.

Kant, Immanuel. 2010. "Idea for a Universal History with a Cosmopolitan Purpose." In *The Cosmopolitanism Reader*, edited by Garrett Wallace Brown and David Held, 15–26. Malden, MA: Polity.

Karenga, Maulana, and Tiamoyo Karenga. 2007. "The *Nguzo Saba* and the Black Family: Principles and Practices of Well-Being and Flourishing." In *Black Families*, 4th ed., edited by Harriette Pipes McAdoo, 7–29. Thousand Oaks: Sage.

Katz, Irwin, and R. Glen Hass. 1988. "Racial Ambivalence and American Value Conflict: Correlational and Priming Studies of Dual Cognitive Structures." *Journal of Personality and Social Psychology* 55 (6): 893–905.

Kellner, Douglas. 2002. *Media Spectacle*. London: Routledge.

Kelly, Casey Ryan. 2007. "Rhetorical Counterinsurgency: The FBI and the American Indian Movement." *Advances in the History of Rhetoric* 10 (1): 223–58.

———. 2009. "The Rhetoric of Red Power and the American Indian Occupation of Alcatraz Island (1969–1971)." PhD diss., University of Minnesota. https://conservancy.umn.edu/handle/11299/54605.

———. 2014. "Détournement, Decolonization, and the American Indian Occupation of Alcatraz Island (1969-1971)." *Rhetoric Society Quarterly* 44 (2): 168–90.

Kelty, Christopher M. 2013. "From Participation to Power." In *The Participatory Cultures Handbook*, edited by Aaron Delwiche and Jennifer Jacobs Henderson, 22–32. New York: Routledge. http://recursivepublic.net/wp-content/uploads/2010/11/Kelty-Hdbk-Participation-0.3.pdf.

The Kerner Report: The 1968 Report of the National Advisory Commission on Civil Disorders. 1968. New York: Pantheon.

Khanna, Nikki. 2004. "The Role of Reflected Appraisals in Racial Identity: The Case of Multiracial Asians." *Social Psychology Quarterly* 67 (2): 115–31.

———. 2010. "'IF YOU'RE HALF BLACK, YOU'RE JUST BLACK': Reflected Appraisals and the Persistence of the One-Drop Rule." *Sociological Quarterly* 51 (1): 96–121.

———. 2011. *Biracial in America: Forming and Performing Racial Identity*. Lanham, MD: Lexington Books.

Kheshti, Roshanak. 2015. *Modernity's Ear: Listening to Race and Gender in World Music*. New York: New York University Press.

Kilpatrick, Jacquelyn. 1999. *Celluloid Indians: Native Americans and Film*. Lincoln: University of Nebraska Press.

Kim, Claire Jean. 1999. "The Racial Triangulation of Asian Americans." *Politics & Society* 27 (1): 105–38.

Kinder, Donald R., and David O. Sears. 1981. "Prejudice and Politics: Symbolic Racism versus Racial Threats to the Good Life." *Journal of Personality and Social Psychology* 40 (3): 414–31.

Kissell, Rick. 2013. "Zimmerman Trial Revs Up Ratings for Cable News Networks." *Variety*, July 12, 2013. https://variety.com/2013/tv/news/zimmerman-trial-revs-up-ratings-for-cable-news-networks-1200561565/.

Kraker, Dan. 2017. "Video Game Prompts Charges of 'Eco-Terrorism' from Oil Pipeline Advocates." *MPR News*, October 26, 2017. www.mprnews.org/story/2017/10/26/video-game-enabling-fantasy-pipeline-attacks-draws-fire.

Krebs, Nina. 1999. *Edgewalkers: Defusing Cultural Boundaries on the New Frontier*. Liberty Corner, NJ: New Horizon Press.

Kress, Tricia M. 2009. "In the Shadow of Whiteness: (Re)exploring Connections between History, Enacted Culture, and Identity in a Digital Divide Initiative." *Cultural Studies of Science Education* 4 (1): 41–49.

Krogstad, Jorge Manuel, and Antonio Flores. 2016. "Unlike Other Latinos, about Half of Cuban Voters in Florida Backed Trump." Pew Research Center, November 15, 2016. www.pewresearch.org/fact-tank/2016/11/15/unlike-other-latinos-about-half-of-cuban-voters-in-florida-backed-trump/.

Kubo, Duane, and Robert A. Nakamura, dirs. 1980. *Hito Hata: Raise the Banner*. Film. Visual Communications.

Kun, Josh. 2005. *Audiotopia*. Berkeley: University of California Press.

Kuo, Rachel. 2018. "Racial Justice Activist Hashtags: Counterpublics and Discourse Circulation." *New Media & Society* 20 (2): 495–514.

Lal, Vinay. 2007. *The Other Indians: Politics and Culture of South Asians in America*. Los Angeles: Asian American Studies Center Press.

LaPensée, Elizabeth. 2014. "Survivance among Social Impact Games." *Loading: The Journal of the Canadian Game Studies Association* 8 (13). http://journals.sfu.ca/loading/index.php/loading/article/view/141.

———. 2018. "Self-Determination in Indigenous Games." In *The Routledge Companion to Media Studies and Digital Humanities*, edited by Jentery Sayers, 128–37. New York: Routledge.

Lau, Sean. 2019. Twitter post, January 14, 2019. https://twitter.com/nototally.

Lauletta, Tyler. 2017. "Colin Kaepernick May Have a Better Shot at Proving Collusion Than Initially Suspected." *Business Insider*, October 18, 2017. www.businessinsider.com/colin-kaepernick-collusion-grievance-case-2017-10.

Lee, Erika. 2015. "Legacies of the 1965 Immigration Act." *TIDES: Magazine of the South Asian American Digital Archive*, October 1, 2015. www.saada.org/tides /article/20151001-4458.

Leeman, Jennifer. 2012. "Illegal Accents: Qualifications, Discrimination and Distraction in Arizona's Monitoring of Teachers." In *Arizona Firestorm: Global Immigration Realities, National Media, and Provincial Politics*, edited by Otto Santa Ana and Celeste González de Bustamante, 145–66. Lanham, MD: Rowman and Littlefield.

Leonard, David J. 2006. "'The Real Color of Money: Controlling Black Bodies in the NBA." *Journal of Sport and Social Issues* 30 (2): 158–79.

———. 2014. "Antiblack Racism and Moral Panics." *Black Scholar*, September 20, 2014. www.theblackscholar.org/a-national-pastime-antiblack-racism-and-moral-panics/.

Levine, Lawrence W. 1977. *Black Culture and Black Consciousness: Afro-American Folk Thought from Slavery to Freedom*. Oxford: Oxford University Press.

Lewis, Jason Edwards. 2014. "A Better Dance and Better Prayers: Systems, Structures, and the Future Imaginary in Aboriginal New Media." In *Coded Territories: Tracing Indigenous Pathways in New Media*, edited by Steven Loft and Kerry Swanson, 48–77. Alberta: University of Calgary Press.

Lewis, Jason Edwards, and Beth Aileen LaPensée. 2011. "Skins: Designing Games with First Nations Youth." *Journal of Game Design & Development Education* 1 (1) : 54–63.

Lichter, S. Robert, and Daniel R. Amundson. 1997. "Distorted Reality: Hispanic Characters in TV Entertainment." In *Latin Looks: Images of Latinas and Latinos in the U.S. Media*, edited by Clara E. Rodríguez, 57–72. Boulder: Westview.

Lin, Justin, dir. 2002. *Better Luck Tomorrow*. Film.

Lipkin, Nadav D. 2013. "Examining Indie's Independence: The Meaning of 'Indie' Games, the Politics of Production, and Mainstream Cooptation." *Loading. . .* , 7 (11).

Lipsitz, George. 2007. *Footsteps in the Dark: Hidden Histories of Popular Music*. Minneapolis: University of Minnesota Press.

Littlefield, Marci B. 2008. "The Media as a System of Racialization: Exploring Images of African American Women and the New Racism." *American Behavioral Scientist* 51 (5): 675–85.

Livingston, Jenny, dir. 1992. *Paris Is Burning*. Film.

Lopez, Lori Kido. 2012. "Fan Activists and the Politics of Race in *The Last Airbender*." *International Journal of Cultural Studies* 15 (September): 431–45.

———. 2016a. *Asian American Media Activism: Fighting for Cultural Citizenship*. New York: New York University Press.

———. 2016b. "Mobile Phones as Participatory Radio: Developing Hmong Mass Communication in the Diaspora." *International Journal of Communication* 10: 2038–55.

Lorde, Audre. 1984. *Sister Outsider: Essays and Speeches*. Freedom, CA: Crossing Press.

Lordi, Emily. 2013. *Black Resonance: Iconic Women Singers and African American Literature*. New Brunswick, NJ: Rutgers University Press.

Love, Heather. 2010. "Truth and Consequences: On Paranoid Reading and Reparative Reading." *Criticism* 52, no. 2 (Spring 2010): 235–41.

"Love Punks." N.d. Yijala Yala Project. https://yijalayala.bighart.org/neomad/love-punks/. Accessed May 16, 2019.

Lowe, Lisa. 1996. *Immigrant Acts: On Asian American Cultural Politics*. Durham: Duke University Press.

Lury, Celia. 2004. *Brands: The Logos of the Global Economy*. New York: Routledge.

Lyons, Oren-Foagquisho. 1978. Preamble to *Basic Call to Consciousness*, edited by *Akwesasne Notes*, 13–25. Summertown: Book Publishing Company.

Mackey, Eva. 2016. *Unsettled Expectations: Uncertainty, Land and Settler Decolonization*. Halifax: Fernwood.

Madsen, Deborah L. 2017. "The Mechanics of Survivance in Indigenously-Directed Video-Games: Invaders and *Never Alone*." *Transmotion* 3 (2): 79–110.

Mancini, Christina, Daniel P. Mears, Eric A. Stewart, Kevin M. Beaver, and Justin T. Pickett. 2013. "Whites' Perceptions about Black Criminality: A Closer Look at the Contact Hypothesis." *Crime & Delinquency* 61 (7): 996–1022. doi: 10.1177/0011128712461900.

Maracle, Candace, dir. 2015. *Grandfather of All Treaties*. Documentary. Vtape: Toronto.

Maragh, Raven S. 2016. "'Our Struggles Are Unequal': Black Women's Affective Labor between Television and Twitter." *Journal of Communication Inquiry* 40 (4): 351–69.

Markham, Annette. 2012. "Fabrication as Ethical Practice." *Information, Communication & Society* 15 (3): 334–53.

Marubbio, Elise. 2006. *Killing the Indian Maiden: Images of Native American Women in Film*. Lexington: University of Kentucky Press.

Marx, Karl. 1978. "The Eighteenth Brumaire of Louis Bonaparte." In *The Marx-Engels Reader*, 2nd ed., edited by Robert C. Tucker, 594–616. New York: Norton.

Massanari, Adrienne. 2015. "#Gamergate and The Fappening: How Reddit's Algorithm, Governance, and Culture Support Toxic Technocultures." *New Media & Society* 19 (3): 329–46. doi/10.1177/1461444815608807.

Massey, Doreen. 1994. *Space, Place, and Gender*. Minneapolis: University of Minnesota Press.

Mastro, Dana E., Elizabeth Behm-Morawitz, and Michelle Ortiz. 2007. "The Cultivation of Social Perceptions of Latinos: A Mental Models Approach." *Media Psychology* 9 (2): 347–65.

Mastro, Dana, Maria Knight Lapinski, Maria A. Kopacz, and Elizabeth Behm-Morawitz. 2009. "The Influence of Exposure to Depictions of Race and Crime in TV News on Viewer's Social Judgments." *Journal of Broadcasting & Electronic Media* 53 (4): 615–35.

Mather, Mary E. Fleming. 1973. "Iroquois Talk, Mr. Worth: A Reply to Sol Worth's Review of *You Are on Indian Land*." *American Anthropologist* 75 (6): 2052–53.

Mathes, Carter. 2015. *Imagine the Sound: Experimental African American Literature after Civil Rights*. Minneapolis: University of Minnesota Press.

Mattingly, David. 2014. "Transcript of Interview with Rachel Jeantel." CNN, July 13, 2014. http://edition.cnn.com/TRANSCRIPTS/1407/13/cnr.03.html.

Mayer, Vicki. 2003. *Producing Dreams, Consuming Youth: Mexican Americans and Mass Media*. New Brunswick, NJ: Rutgers University Press.

———. 2004. "Please Pass the Pan: Retheorizing the Map of Panlatinidad in Communication Research." *Communication Review* 7 (2): 113–24.

McCarthy, Patricia Theresa. 2019. Twitter post, January 14, 2019. https://twitter.com/FruitOnBottom.

McMahon, Marci, and Patricia Herrera. 2019. "¡Oye, Oye!: A Manifesto for Listening to Latinx Theater." *Aztlán: A Journal of Chicana/o Studies* 44 (1): 239–48.

McManamon, Pat. 2017. "Joe Thomas: NFL Views Colin Kaepernick as Unworthy Distraction." ESPN.com, March 26, 2017. www.espn.com/nfl/story/_/id/19011238/colin-kaepernick-viewed-distraction-joe-thomas-cleveland-browns-says.

McWhorter, John. 2013. "Rachel Jeantel Explained Linguistically." *Time*, June 28, 2013. http://ideas.time.com/2013/06/28/rachel-jeantel-explained-linguistically/.

———. 2019. "Could Black English Mean a Prison Sentence?" *Atlantic*, January 31, 2019. www.theatlantic.com/ideas/archive/2019/01/stenographers-need-understand-black-english/581671/.

McWilliams, Carey. 2016. *North from Mexico: The Spanish-Speaking People of the United States*. 3rd ed. 2nd ed. updated by Matt S. Meier, 3rd ed. updated by Alma M. García. Santa Barbara: Praeger.

Means, Russell. 1995. *Where White Men Fear to Tread: The Autobiography of Russell Means*. Brooklyn: Antenna Books.

Mercer, Kobena. 1994. *Welcome to the Jungle: New Positions in Black Cultural Studies*. New York: Routledge.

Merskin, Debra. 1998. "Sending Up Signals: A Survey of Native American Media Use and Representation in Mass Media." *Howard Journal of Communication* 9: 333–45.

Meyer, John C. 2000. "Humor as a Double-Edged Sword: Four Functions of Humor in Communication." *Communication Theory* 10 (3): 310–31.

Miller, Daniel, and Don Slater. 2000. *The Internet: An Ethnographic Approach*. New York: Berg.

Miller, Toby, and Richard Maxwell. 2011. "For a Better Deal, Harass Your Governor!: Neoliberalism and Hollywood." In *Neoliberalism and Global Cinema: Capital, Culture, and Marxist Critique*, edited by Jyotsna Kapur and Keith B. Wagner. New York: Routledge.

Milloy, Jonathan. 1999. *A National Crime: The Canadian Government and the Residential School System, 1879–1986*. Winnipeg: University of Manitoba Press.

Minnesota Senate Republican Caucus. 2017. "Sen. David Osmek: MN Taxpayers Should Not Be Funding *Angry Birds* for Eco-Terrorists." October 26, 2017. www.mnsenaterepublicans.com/sen-david-osmek-mn-taxpayers-not-funding-angry-birds-eco-terrorists/

Mishra, Debasish. 2001. "American Backlash: Terrorists Bring War Home in More Ways Than One." SAALT: South Asian Americans Leading Together, 2001. http://saalt.org/wp-content/uploads/2012/09/American-Backlash-Terrorist-Bring-War-Home-in-More-Ways-Than-One.pdf.

Mittell, Jason. 2003. "The Great Saturday Morning Exile: Scheduling Cartoons on Television's Periphery in the 1960s." In *Prime Time Animation: Television Animation and American Culture*, edited by Carol Stabile and Mark Harrison, 33–54. New York: Routledge.

Molina-Guzmán, Isabel. 2016. "#OscarsSoWhite: How Stuart Hall Explains Why Nothing Changes in Hollywood and Everything Is Changing." *Critical Studies in Media Communication* 33 (5): 438–54.

Mora, Adolfo R., and Viviana Rojas. 2017. "Latina/os' Facebook Usage: An Inter-Ethnic and Inter-Generational Exploration of Their Engagement with a Social Networking Site." In *The Routledge Companion to Latina/o Media*, edited by María Elena Cepeda and Dolores Inés Casillas, 365–84. New York: Routledge.

Mora, Cristina G. 2014. *Making Hispanics: How Activists, Bureaucrats, and Media Constructed a New American*. Chicago: University of Chicago Press.

Morales, Orquidea. 2016. "Direct to DVD: The Possibilities and Limitations of New Distribution Platforms." In *The Routledge Companion to Latina/o Media*, edited by María Elena Cepeda and Dolores Inés Casillas, 143–55. New York: Routledge.

Moran, Kristin C. 2011. *Listening to Latina/o Youth: Television Consumption within Families*. New York: Peter Lang.

———. 2016. "Beyond the Market: Lessons Learned from Latina/o Families." In *The Routledge Companion to Latina/o Media*, edited by María Elena Cepeda and Dolores Inés Casillas, 88–101. New York: Routledge.

Moriah, Kristin. 2017. "Dark Stars of the Evening: Performing African American Citizenship and Identity in Germany, 1890–1920." PhD diss., CUNY Graduate Center.

Morley, David, and Kevin Robins. 2002. *Spaces of Identity: Global Media, Electronic Landscapes and Cultural Boundaries*. New York: Routledge.

Morrison, Matthew D. 2017. "The Sound(s) of Subjection: Constructing American Popular Music and Racial Identity through Blacksound." *Women & Performance* 27 (1): 13–24.

Mosby, Ian. 2013. "Administering Colonial Science: Nutrition Research and Human Biomedical Experimentation in Aboriginal Communities and Residential Schools, 1942–1952." *Social History* 46 (91): 145–72.

Moten, Fred. 2003. *In the Break*. Minneapolis: University of Minnesota Press.

Muhawi, Ibrahim. 1994. "The Metalinguistic Joke: Sociolinguistic Dimensions of an Arabic Folk Genre." In *Arabic Sociolinguistics: Issues and Perspectives*, edited by Yasir Suleiman, 155–76. New York: Routledge.

Mukherjee, Roopali. 2006. *The Racial Order of Things: Cultural Imaginaries of the Post-Soul Era*. Minneapolis: University of Minnesota Press.

Munshi, Sherally. 2018. "Beyond the Muslim Ban." *TIDES*, October 10, 2018. www.saada.org/tides/article/beyond-the-muslim-ban.

Naber, Nadine C. 2012. *Arab America: Gender, Cultural Politics, and Activism*. New York: New York University Press.

Nagy, Peter, and Gina Neff. 2015. "Imagined Affordances: Reconstructing a Keyword for Communication Theory." *Social Media + Society* 1 (2).

Nakamura, Lisa. 2002. *Cybertypes: Race, Ethnicity, and Identity on the Internet.* New York: Routledge.

———. 2017. "Afterword: Racism, Sexism, and Gaming's Cruel Optimism." In *Gaming Representation: Race, Gender, and Sexuality in Video Games,* edited by Jennifer Malkowski and Treaandrea M. Russworm. Bloomington: Indiana University Press.

Nakamura, Robert A., dir. 1976. *Manzanar.* Film.

Namakkal, Jessica L. 2017. "Peanut Butter Dosas: Becoming Desi in the Midwest." *TIDES,* April 18, 2017. www.saada.org/tides/article/peanut-butter-dosas.

Napier, Susan Jolliffe. 2007. *From Impressionism to Anime: Japan as Fantasy and Fan Cult in the Mind of the West.* New York: Palgrave Macmillan.

National Film Board of Canada. 2019. "*You Are on Indian Land*: Synopsis." www.nfb .ca/film/you_are_on_indian_land/.

Navarrette, Ruben, Jr. 2017. "Latino Americans Love This Country—But Does It Love Them Back?" *East Bay Times,* July 4, 2017. www.eastbaytimes.com/2017/07/04 /navarrette-latino-americans-love-this-country-but-does-it-love-them-back/.

NBA. 2019a. NBA Cares. https://cares.nba.com.

———. 2019b. NBA Voices. https://voices.nba.com.

Neal, Shane Paul. 2013. "Black Podcasts Bring the Barbershop to the Internet." *Huffington Post,* March 13, 2013.

Negrón-Muntaner, Frances, and Chelsea Abbas. 2016. "The Latino Disconnect: Latinos in the Age of Media Mergers." New York: Columbia Center for the Study of Ethnicity and Race.

Negrón-Muntaner, Frances, with Chelsea Abbas, Luis Figueroa, and Samuel Robson. 2014. "The Latino Media Gap: A Report on the State of Latinos in U.S. Media." New York: Columbia Center for the Study of Ethnicity and Race.

Nelson, Alondra. 2016. *The Social Life of DNA: Race, Reparations, and Reconciliation after the Genome.* Boston: Beacon.

Nelson, Stanley, dir. 2010. *We Shall Remain: America through Native Eyes.* Pt. 5, *Wounded Knee.* Documentary. American Experience. Arlington, VA: PBS.

Netflix. 2019. Twitter post, March 14, 2019. https://twitter.com/netflix/ status/1106246147771764736.

"Never Alone." 2015. *Edge,* January 9, 2015. www.metacritic.com/game/playstation-4 /never-alone.

Newman, Alyssa M. 2019. "Desiring the Standard Light Skin: Black Multiracial Boys, Masculinity and Exotification." *Identities* 26 (1): 107–25.

"New Web Series 'Brown Girls' Stars Two Women of Color." 2016. *NowThis Her,* December 7, 2016.

NFL. 2019. *Let's Listen Together.* www.nfl.com/letslistentogether.

Nielsen. 2013. "Latina Power Shift." Nielsen Consumer Report, August 1, 2013. www .nielsen.com/us/en/insights/reports/2013/latina-power-shift.html.

———. 2017. "Latina 2.0." Nielsen Consumer Report, September 12, 2017. www.nielsen .com/content/dam/corporate/us/en/reports-downloads/2017-reports/Latina%20 2.0.pdf.

Nightengale, Virginia. 1996. *Studying Audiences: The Shock of the Real*. London: Routledge.

Nishime, LeiLani. 2012. "The Case for Cablinasian: Multiracial Naming from Plessy to Tiger Woods." *Communication Theory* 22 (1): 92–111.

———. 2014. *Undercover Asian: Multiracial Asian Americans in Visual Culture*. Urbana: University of Illinois Press.

Nissenbaum, Helen. 2009. *Privacy in Context: Technology, Policy, and the Integrity of Social Life*. Stanford, CA: Stanford University Press.

Noble, Saifya Umoja. 2018. *Algorithms of Oppression: How Search Engines Reinforce Racism*. New York: New York University Press.

Noriega, Chon A. 2000. *Shot in America: Television, the State, and the Rise of Chicano Cinema*. Minneapolis: University of Minnesota Press.

Norman, Don. 2013. *The Design of Everyday Things*. Rev. ed. New York: Basic Books.

Nunely, Vorris. 2011. *Keepin' It Hushed: The Barbershop and African American Hush Harbor Rhetoric*. Detroit: Wayne State University Press.

Obadike, Mendi, and Keith Obadike. 2014. *Big House/Disclosure*. New York: 1913 Press.

O'Connell, Michael. 2013. "TV Ratings: Cable Viewership Swells Past 10 Million with George Zimmerman Verdict." *Variety*, July 15, 2013. www.hollywoodreporter.com /live-feed/tv-ratings-cable-viewership-swells-585498.

OED Online. 2018. "ear-witness, n." Oxford University Press. www.oed.com/view /Entry/59071.

Omi, Michael, and Howard Winant. 1986. *Racial Formation in the United States: From the 1960s to the 1990s*. New York: Routledge.

O'Neal, Lonnae. 2015. "Laughing While Black: Not on the Wine Train." *Washington Post*, August 27, 2015. www.washingtonpost.com/lifestyle/style/lonnae-oneal-laughing-while-Black-not-on-the-wine-train/2015/08/26/93dd9718-4bf2-11e5-902f-39e9219e574b_story.html?utm_term=.3361592b0ceb.

Ong, Aihwa. 1999. *Flexible Citizenship: The Cultural Logics of Transnationality*. Durham: Duke University Press.

Ono, Kent, and Vincent Pham. 2009. *Asian Americans and the Media*. New York: Polity.

Oriard, Michael. 2003. *Brand NFL: Making and Selling America's Favorite Sport*. Chapel Hill: University of North Carolina Press.

Osajima, Keith. 1988. "Asian Americans as the Model Minority: An Analysis of the Popular Press Image in the 1960s and 1980s." In *Reflections on Shattered Windows: Promises and Prospects for Asian American Studies*, edited by Gary Okihiro et al., 165–74. Pullman: Washington State University Press.

Otterson, Joe. 2018. "487 Scripted Series Aired in 2017, FX Chief John Landgraf Says." *Variety*, January 5, 2018. https://variety.com/2018/tv/news/2017-scripted-tv-series -fx-john-landgraf-1202653856.

Pacifica Radio Archives. 2017. "Radio Free Alcatraz: Series Record." https://pacificara dioarchives.org/recording/bb545701-bb545740.

Palumbo-Liu, David. 1999. *Asian/American: Historical Crossings of a Racial Frontier.* Palo Alto: Stanford University Press.

Pande, Rukmini. 2018. *Squee from the Margins: Fandom and Race.* Iowa City: University of Iowa Press.

Paredez, Deborah. 2009. *Selenidad: Selena, Latinos, and the Performance of Memory.* Durham: Duke University Press.

Parker, James. 2015. *Acoustic Jurisprudence: Listening to the Trial of Simon Bikindi.* Oxford: Oxford University Press.

Passel, Jeffrey S., and D'Vera Cohn. 2016. "Overall Number of US Unauthorized Immigrants Holds Steady since 2009." Pew Research Center's Hispanic Trends Project, September 20, 2016. www.pewhispanic.org/2016/09/20/overall-number-of -u-s-unauthorized-immigrants-holds-steady-since-2009/.

Penney, Joel, and Caroline Dadas. 2014. "(Re)Tweeting in the Service of Protest: Digital Composition and Circulation in the Occupy Wall Street Movement." *New Media & Society* 16 (1): 74–90. doi: 10.1177/1461444813479593.

Perks, Lisa G. 2012. "The Ancient Roots of Humor Theory." *Humor* 25 (2): 119–32.

Peters, John Durham. 1999. "Exile, Nomadism, and Diaspora: The Stakes of Mobility in the Western Canon." In *Home, Exile, Homeland: Film, Media, and the Politics of Place*, edited by Hamid Naficy, 17–44. New York: Routledge.

Petersen, William. 1966. "Success Story, Japanese-American Style." *New York Times Magazine*, January 9, 1966.

Pew Research Center. 2016. "Digital Divide Narrows for Latinos as More Spanish Speakers and Immigrants Go Online." July 20, 2016. www.pewhispanic.org/2016/07 /20/1-internet-use-among-hispanics/.

———. 2017. "Social Media Use by Race." January 11, 2017. www.pewinternet.org/chart /social-media-use-by-race/.

———. 2018. "Demographics of Social Media Users and Adoption in the United States." www.pewinternet.org/fact-sheet/social-media/.

Phoenix, Nikia. 2017. Nikia Phoenix Instagram page. www.instagram.com/nikiaphoenix /?hl=en.

Phu, Thy N. 2008. "Shooting the Movement: Black Panther Party Photography and African American Protest Traditions." *Canadian Review of American Studies* 26: 165–89.

Pinkins, Carlyn N. 2011. "One Nation, Separate Spheres: An Examination of Red Power Activism between Two Mohawk Communities." M.A. thesis, Georgia Southern University. https://digitalcommons.georgiasouthern.edu/etd/601.

Pixley, Tara L. 2017. "Why We Need More Visual Journalists and Editors of Color." *Nieman Reports*, May 15, 2017. https://niemanreports.org/articles/a-new-focus/.

Pollitt, Katha. 2019. Twitter post, February 4, 2019. https://twitter.com/kathapollitt.

prado, reina alejandra. 2013. "Sonic Brownface: Representations of Mexicanness in an Era of Discontent." *Sounding Out!*, June 10, 2013. https://soundstudiesblog .com/2013/06/10/sonic-brownface-representations-of-mexicanness-in-an-era-of -discontent/.

Prashad, Vijay. 1999. "From Multiculture to Polyculture in South Asian American Studies." *Diaspora: A Journal of Transnational Studies* 8 (2): 185–204. https://doi.org/10.1353/dsp.1999.0006.

Price, John, Neil Farrington, and Lee Hall. 2013. "Changing the Game? The Impact of Twitter on Relationships between Football Clubs, Supporters and the Sports Media." *Soccer and Society* 14 (4): 446–61.

Priyadarshini, Meha. 2014. "The 'Mughal Princess' of Mexico." *TIDES: Magazine of the South Asian American Digital Archive*, May 5, 2014. www.saada.org/tides/article/mughal-princess-of-mexico.

Prothero, G. W. 1888. "Gneist on the English Constitution." *English Historical Review* 3 (9): 1–33.

Punny Pun Times. N.d. About Page, *Facebook*. www.facebook.com/pg/punnypuntimes/about/?ref=page_internal.

———. 2016. *Punny Pun Times*, episode 1, "Random Word Play," December 28, 2016. Video file. www.youtube.com/watch?v=kP-Nk_6IXuo.

———. 2017a. *Punny Pun Times*, episode 3, January 4, 2017. Video file. www.youtube.com/watch?v=KyVFDb4QMKk.

———. 2017b. *Punny Pun Times*, episode 5, January 4, 2017. Video file. www.youtube.com/watch?v=Wlemd7MXqlY.

Quashie, Kevin. 2012. *The Sovereignty of Quiet: Beyond Resistance in Black Culture.* New Brunswick, NJ: Rutgers University Press.

The Quick Draw McGraw Show. 1959a. "Bad Guy Disguise." October 5, 1959. Written by Michael Maltese. Produced by Hannah-Barbera Productions, syndicated by Screen Gems.

———. 1959b. "Masking for Trouble." October 17, 1959. Written by Michael Maltese. Produced by Hannah-Barbera Productions, syndicated by Screen Gems.

———. 1959c. "Slick City Slicker." Written by Michael Maltese. Produced by Hannah-Barbera Productions, syndicated by Screen Gems.

Radtke, Dina. 2017. "Three Ways Hispanic Media Has Changed in the Trump Era." *Media Matters*, October 15, 2017. www.mediamatters.org/donald-trump/three-ways-hispanic-media-has-changed-trump-era.

Raheja, Michelle. 2010. *Reservation Reelism: Redfacing, Visual Sovereignty, and Representations of Native Americans in Film*. Lincoln: University of Nebraska Press.

Rainie, Lee, and Barry Wellman. 2012. *Networked: The New Social Operating System.* Cambridge, MA: MIT Press.

Rait, Robert S. 1915. "Parliamentary Representation in Scotland." *Scottish Historical Review* 12 (36): 115–34.

Redmond, Shana L. 2013. *Anthem: Social Movements and the Sound of Solidarity in the African Diaspora*. New York: New York University Press.

Reign, April. 2018. "#OscarsSoWhite Is Still Relevant This Year." *Vanity Fair*, March 2, 2018. www.vanityfair.com/hollywood/2018/03/oscarssowhite-is-still-relevant-this-year.

Reynolds, Tracey. 2009. "Exploring the Absent/Present Dilemma: Black Fathers, Family Relationships, and Social Capital in Britain." *Annals of the American Academy of Political & Social Science* 624 (1): 12–28. doi:10.1177/0002716209334440.

Rhoden, William C. 2006. *$40 Million Slaves: The Rise, Fall, and Redemption of the Black Athlete.* New York: Crown.

Rickert, Levi. 2017. "Alcatraz Occupation Alumni Gather on Island to Remember 1969 Takeover." *Native News*, January 29, 2017. https://nativenewsonline.net/currents /alcatraz-occupation-alumni-gather-island-remember-1969-takeover/.

Rickford, John R., and Sharese King. 2016. "Language and Linguistics on Trial: Hearing Vernacular Speakers." *Language* 92 (4): 948–88.

Riggs, Marlon, dir. 1989. *Tongues Untied*. Film.

Ríos, Diana I. 2000. "Chicana/o and Latina/o Gazing: Audiences of the Mass Media." In *Chicano Renaissance: Contemporary Cultural Trends*, edited by David R. Maciel, Isidro D. Ortiz, and María Herrera-Sobek, 169–90. Tucson: University of Arizona Press.

———. 2003. "U.S. Latino Audiences of Telenovelas." *Journal of Latinos in Education* 2 (1): 59–65.

Ríos, Diana E., and Stanley Gaines Jr. 1998. "Latino Media Use for Cultural Maintenance." *Journalism and Mass Communication Quarterly* 75 (4): 746–61.

Rivadeneyra, Rocio. 2006. "Do You See What I See? Latino Adolescents' Perceptions of the Images on Television." *Journal of Adolescent Research* 21: 393–414.

Rivadeneyra, Rocio, and L. Monique Ward. 2005. "From Ally McBeal to Sábado Gigante: Contributions of Television Viewing to the Gender Role Attitudes of Latino Adolescents." *Journal of Adolescent Research* 20: 453–75.

Rivadeneyra, Rocio, L. Monique Ward, and Maya Gordon. 2007. "Distorted Reflections: Media Exposure and Latino Adolescents' Conceptions of Self." *Media Psychology* 9: 261–90.

Rivera, Michelle M. 2019. "Just Sexual Games and Twenty-Four Hour Parties? Anti-Fans Contest the Global Crossover of Reggaetón Music Online." In *Anti-Fandom: Dislike and Hate in the Digital Age*, edited by Melissa A. Click, 84–204. New York: New York University Press.

Rivero, Yeidy M. 2003. "The Performance and Reception of Televisual 'Ugliness' in *Yo soy Betty la fea*." *Feminist Media Studies* 3 (1): 65–81.

———. 2014. "*Grey's Anatomy*, Colombia's *A corazón abierto*, and the Politicization of a Format." In *Contemporary Latina/o Media*, edited by Arlene Dávila and Yeidy M. Rivero. New York: New York University Press.

Rodríguez, Clara. 2007. "Film Viewing in Latino Communities, 1896–1934: Puerto Rico as Microcosm." In *From Bananas to Buttocks: The Latina Body in Popular Film and Culture*, edited by Myra Mendible, 31–50. Austin: University of Texas Press.

Rodríguez, Richard T. 2017. "X Marks the Spot." *Cultural Dynamics* 29 (3): 202–13.

Rojas, Viviana. 2004. "The Gender of Latinidad: Latinas Speak about Hispanic Television." *Communication Review* 7 (2): 125–53.

Rojas, Viviana, and Juan Piñón. 2017. "Voices from the Borderlands: Young Latina/os Discuss the Impact That Culture and Identity Have on Their Media Consumption."

In *The Routledge Companion to Latina/o Media*, edited by María Elena Cepeda and Dolores Inés Casillas, 347–66. New York: Routledge.

Román, Miriam J., and Juan Flores. 2010. *The Afro-Latin@ Reader: History and Culture in the United States*. Durham: Duke University Press.

Romero, Eliza. 2019. "The Backlash against Marie Kondo Is So Stupid (and Racist)." *Medium*, January 21, 2019. medium.com/@AestheticDistance/the-backlash-against -marie-kondo-is-so-stupid-and-racist-6def7fbd78b2.

Root, Maria P. P. 1996. *The Multiracial Experience: Racial Borders as the New Frontier*. Thousand Oaks, CA: Sage.

———. 2001. *Love's Revolution: Interracial Marriage*. Philadelphia: Temple University Press.

Roth, Lorna. 2009. "The Fade-Out Shirley, a Once-Ultimate Norm: Colour Balance, Image Technologies, and Cognitive Equity." *Canadian Journal of Communication* 34: 111–36.

Ruberg, Bonnie. 2018. "Queer Indie Video Games as an Alternative Digital Humanities: Counterstrategies for Cultural Critique through Interactive Media." *American Quarterly* 70 (3): 417–38.

Ruiz, Vicki L. 2008. *From Out of the Shadows: Mexican American Women in Twentieth Century America*. 10th ed. New York: Oxford University Press.

Said, Edward W. 1978. *Orientalism*. New York: Vintage.

Sami Game Jam. N.d. https://samigamejam.com/. Accessed May 16, 2019.

Sanchez, George J. 1997. "Face the Nation: Race, Immigration, and the Rise of Nativism in Late Twentieth Century America." *International Migration Review* 31 (4): 1009–1131.

Sanchez, John, and Mary Stuckey. 2000. "The Rhetoric of American Indian Activism in the 1960s and 1970s." *Communication Quarterly* 48 (2): 120–36.

Sanchez, John, Mary Stuckey, and Richard Morris. 1999. "Rhetorical Exclusion: The Government's Case against American Indian Activists, AIM, and Leonard Peltier." *American Indian Culture and Research Journal* 23 (2): 27–52.

Saperstein, Aliya. 2012. "Capturing Complexity in the United States: Which Aspects of Race Matter and When?" *Ethnic and Racial Studies* 35 (8): 1484–1502.

———. 2013. "Race in the Eye of the Beholder." *Made in America: Notes on American Life from American History* (blog), May 21, 2013. https://madeinamericathebook .wordpress.com/2013/05/21/race-in-the-eye-of-the-beholder/.

Schafer, R. Murray. 1978. *The Soundscape: Our Sonic Environment and the Tuning of the World*. Rochester, NY: Destiny Books.

Schmittel, Annelie, and Jimmy Sanderson. 2015. "Talking about Trayvon in 140 Characters: Exploring NFL Players' Tweets about the George Zimmerman Verdict." *Journal of Sport and Social Issues* 39 (4): 332–45.

Schofield, Anakana. 2019. Twitter post, January 4, 2019. https://twitter.com /AnakanaSchofiel.

Sedgwick, Eve Kosofsky. 2003. "Paranoid Reading and Reparative Reading, or, You're So Paranoid You Probably Think This Essay Is about You." In *Touching Feeling: Affect, Pedagogy, Performativity*. Durham: Duke University Press.

Semple, Kirk. 2014. "Immigrants Who Speak Indigenous Languages Encounter Isolation." *New York Times*, July 10, 2014. www.nytimes.com/2014/07/11/nyregion /immigrants-who-speak-indigenous-mexican-languages-encounter-isolation.html.

Sewell, Christopher Scott. 2016. *The Cherokee Paradox: Unexpected Ancestry at the Crossroads of Identity and Genetics.* Crofton, KY: Backintyme.

Sharam, C. 2011. "Native Americans in Video Games: Racism, Stereotypes, and The Digitized Indian." Project COE, April 5, 2011. www.projectcoe.com/2011/04/04 /native-americans-in-video-games-racism-stereotypes-and-progress/.

Sharma, Sanjay. 2013. "Black Twitter? Racial Hashtags, Networks and Contagion." *New Formations*, no. 78, 46–64.

Sharpe, Christina. 2016. *In the Wake: On Blackness and Being.* Durham: Duke University Press.

Shifman, Limor. 2012. "An Anatomy of a YouTube Meme." *New Media and Society* 14 (2): 187–203.

Shohat, Ella, and Robert Stam. 1994. *Unthinking Eurocentrism: Multiculturalism and the Media.* London: Routledge.

Simon, Frank, dir. 1968. *The Queen.* Film.

Simón, Yara. 2016. "#BlackLatinxHistory Highlights Afro-Latinos Who Changed History." *Remezcla.* February 15, 2016. https://remezcla.com/lists/culture/10-afro -latinos-who-changed-the-world-as-told-by-blacklatinxhistory/.

Simpson, Leanne Betasamosake. 2013. "Elsipogtog Everywhere." www.leannesimpson .ca/writings/2013/10/20/elsipogtog-everywhere.

Sims, Jennifer Patrice. 2016. "Reevaluation of the Influence of Appearance and Reflected Appraisals for Mixed-Race Identity: The Role of Consistent Inconsistent Racial Perception." *Sociology of Race and Ethnicity* 2 (4): 569–83.

Singh, Amardeep. 2007. "'Names Can Wait': The Misnaming of the South Asian Diaspora in Theory and Practice." *South Asian Review* 28 (1): 13–27.

Smith, John Matthew. 2009. "'It's Not Really My Country': Lew Alcindor and the Revolt of the Black Athlete." *Journal of Sport History* 36 (2): 223–44.

Smith, Stacy L., Marc Choueiti, Angel Choi, and Katherine Pieper. 2019. *Inclusion in the Director's Chair: Gender, Race, and Age of Directors across 1,200 Top Films from 2007 to 2018.* Los Angeles: USC Annenberg Inclusion Initiative.

Smith, Stacy L., Marc Choueiti, and Katherine Pieper. 2016. "Inequality in 800 Popular Films: Examining Portrayals of Gender, Race/Ethnicity, LGBT, and Disability from 2007–2015." Los Angeles: USC Annenberg School for Communication and Journalism, University of Southern California. https://annenberg.usc.edu/sites/default /files/2017/04/10/MDSCI_Inequality_in_800_Films_FINAL.pdf.

Smith, Stacy L., Marc Choueiti, Katherine Pieper, Ariana Case, and Angel Choi. 2018. *Inequality in 1,100 Popular Films: Examining Portrayals of Gender, Race/Ethnicity, LGBT & Disability from 2007 to 2017.* Los Angeles: USC Annenberg Inclusion Initiative.

Song, Miri. 2017. "Generational Change and How We Conceptualize and Measure Multiracial People and 'Mixture.'" *Ethnic and Racial Studies* 40 (13): 2333–39.

Soruco, Gonzalo R. 1996. *Cubans and the Media in South Florida*. Gainesville: University Press of Florida.

Spivak, Gayatri Chakravorty. 1999. *A Critique of Postcolonial Reason: Toward a History of the Vanishing Present*. Cambridge, MA: Harvard University Press.

Squires, Catherine. 2002. "Rethinking the Black Public Sphere: An Alternative Vocabulary for Multiple Public Spheres." *Communication Theory* 12 (4): 446–68.

———. 2014. *The Post-Racial Mystique: Media and Race in the Twenty-First Century*. New York: New York University Press

Srinivasan, Ramesh. 2006. "Indigenous, Ethnic and Cultural Articulations of New Media." *International Journal of Cultural Studies* 9 (4): 497–518.

Steele, Catherine. 2016. "Signifyin', Bitching, and Blogging: Black Women and Resistance Discourse Online." In *The Intersectional Internet: Race, Class, Sex, and Culture Online*, edited by Safiya Umoja Noble and Brendesha M. Tynes, 73–93. New York: Peter Lang.

Steele, Catherine, and Jessica Lu. 2018. "Defying Death: Black Joy as Resistance Online." In *A Networked Self and Birth, Life, Death*, edited by Zizi Papacharissi, 143–59. New York: Routledge.

Steinbock, Eliza. 2019. *Shimmering Images: Trans Cinema, Embodiment, and the Aesthetics of Change*. Durham: Duke University Press.

Stewart, Katherine. "Eighty-One Percent of White Evangelicals Voted for Donald Trump. Why?" *Nation*, November 17, 2016. www.thenation.com/article/eighty-one -percent-of-white-evangelicals-voted-for-donald-trump-why/.

Stoever, Jennifer Lynn. 2010. "Splicing the Sonic Color-Line: Tony Schwartz Remixes Postwar Nueva York." *Social Text* 102 (Spring): 59–85.

———. 2016. *The Sonic Color Line: Race and the Cultural Politics of Listening*. New York: New York University Press.

Stoney, George. 1980. "You Are on Indian Land." In *The Documentary Conscience: A Casebook in Film Making*, by Alan Rosenthal. Berkeley: University of California Press.

Strange, Carolyn, and Tina Loo. 2001. "Holding the Rock: The 'Indianization' of Alcatraz Island, 1969–1999." *Public Historian* 23 (1): 55–74.

Strangelove, Michael. 2010. *Watching YouTube: Extraordinary Videos by Ordinary People*. Toronto: University of Toronto Press.

Strauss, Chris, and Nate Scott. 2014. "LeBron James Wears 'I Can't Breathe' Shirt before Cavs Game." *USA Today*, December 8, 2014. www.usatoday.com/story/sports /basketball/2014/12/08/lebron-james-cant-breathe-t-shirt/20119047/.

Suarez, Ray. 2013. *Latino Americans: The 500-Year Legacy That Shaped a Nation*. New York: Celebra.

Subervi-Vélez, Federico. 2008. *The Mass Media and Latino Politics: Studies of U.S. Media Content, Campaign Strategies and Survey Research: 1984–2004*. New York: Routledge.

Sudarkasa, Niara. 2007. "African American Female-Headed Households: Some Neglected Dimensions." In *Black Families*, edited by Harriette Pipes McAdoo, 172–83. Thousand Oaks: Sage.

Sullivan, Emily. 2018. "Laura Ingraham Told LeBron James to Shut Up and Dribble; He Went to the Hoop." NPR, February 19, 2018. www.npr.org/sections/thetwo-way /2018/02/19/587097707/laura-ingraham-told-lebron-james-to-shutup-and-dribble -he-went-to-the-hoop.

Sweeney, Miriam E. 2017. "The Ms. Dewey 'Experience': Technoculture, Gender, and Race." In Digital Sociologies, edited by Jessie Daniels, Karen Gregory, and Tressie McMillan Cottom, 401–20. Cambridge: Polity.

Szekely, Balazs. 2018. "Downtown LA's 90014 Heads the List of Fastest-Gentrifying ZIPS since the Turn of the Millennium." Rentcafe Blog, February 26, 2018. www .rentcafe.com/blog/rental-market/real-estate-news/top-20-gentrified-zip-codes/.

Tagg, John. 1988. The Burden of Representation: Essays on Photographies and Histories. Amherst: University of Massachusetts Press.

Tasker, Yvonne. 1993. Spectacular Bodies: Gender, Genre and the Action Cinema. London: Routledge.

Terranova, Tiziana. 2000. "Producing Culture for the Digital Economy." Social Text 63 (1): 33–58.

Thompson, Krissah, and Lonnae O'Neal Parker. 2014. "For Trayvon Martin's Friend Rachel Jeantel, a 'Village' of Mentors Trying to Keep Her on Track." Washington Post, June 4, 2014. www.washingtonpost.com/lifestyle/style/for-rachel-jeantel -travyon-martins-friend-the-journey-continues/2014/06/04/0135d5a2-ec11-11e3 -93d2-edd4be1f5d9e_story.html?noredirect=on&utm_term=.3cbcbef16c78.

Tiku, Nitasha. 2018. "Why Netflix Features Black Actors in Promos to Black Users." Wired, October 14, 2018. www.wired.com/story/why-netflix-features-black-actors -promos-to-black-users/.

Tilly, Charles. 1986. The Contentious French. Cambridge: Harvard University Press.
———. 1995. Popular Contention in Great Britain, 1758–1834. New York: Routledge.
———. 2008. Contentious Performances. London: Cambridge University Press.

Torres-Saillant, Silvio. 2008. "Problematic Paradigms: Racial Diversity and Corporate Identity in the Latino Community." Review of International American Studies 3 (1–2): 45–61.

Tourmaline and Wortzel, Sasha, dirs. 2018. Happy Birthday Marsha! Film.

Tristan. 2018. "'You Name It!'—The Gospel Origins of This Thanksgiving Meme." EpicPew, November 26, 2018. https://epicpew.com/you-name-it-the-gospel-origins -of-this-thanksgiving-meme/.

Truth and Reconciliation Commission of Canada. 2015. Honouring the Truth, Reconciling for the Future: Summary of the Final Report of the Truth and Reconciliation Commission. www.trc.ca/assets/pdf/Honouring_the_Truth_Reconciling_for_the _Future_July_23_2015.pdf.

Tuchman, Gaye. 1979. "Women's Depiction by the Mass Media." Signs: Journal of Women in Culture and Society 4 (3): 528–42.

Tuck, Eve, and K. Wayne Yang. 2012. "Decolonization Is Not a Metaphor." Decolonization: Indigeneity, Education & Society 1 (1): 1–40.

Tukachinsky, Riva, Dana Mastro, and Moran Yarchi. 2017. "The Effect of Prime-Time Television Ethnic/Racial Stereotypes on Latino and Black Americans: A Longitudinal National Level Study." *Journal of Broadcasting & Electronic Media* 61 (3): 538–56.

Tynes, Brendesha, Joshua Schuschke, and Safiya Noble. 2016. "Digital Intersectionality Theory and the #BlackLivesMatter Movement." In *The Intersectional Internet: Race, Class, Sex, and Culture Online*, edited by Safiya Umoja Noble and Brendesha M. Tynes, 21–40. New York: Peter Lang.

Univision. 2017. Press release, November 8, 2017. https://corporate.univision.com /corporate/press/2017/11/08/ilia-calderon-join-jorge-ramos-co-anchor-univisions -flagship-newscast-noticiero-univision/.

Upper One Games. 2013a. "Launch Release." Press kit, December 2013.

———. 2013b. "Upper One Games Overview." Press kit, December 2013.

U.S. Census Bureau. 2017. "Facts for Features: Hispanic Heritage Month." August 31, 2017. www.census.gov/newsroom/facts-for-features/2017/hispanic-heritage.html.

USC Annenberg. 2018. "Why an 'Inclusion Rider' Is the Answer We Need Now." March 5, 2018. https://annenberg.usc.edu/research/why-inclusion-rider-answer -we-need-now.

Valdivia, Angharad N. 2000. *A Latina in the Land of Hollywood: And Other Essays on Media Culture*. Tucson: University of Arizona Press.

———. 2003. "Radical Hybridity: Latinas/os as the Paradigmatic Transnational Post-Subculture." In *The Post-Subcultures Reader*, edited by David Muggleton and Rupert Weinzierl, 151–65. New York: Berg.

———. 2010. *Latina/os and the Media*. Malden, MA: Polity.

———. 2018. "Latina Media Studies." *Feminist Media Histories* 4 (2): 101–6.

Vanderhoef, John. 2013. "Casual Threats: The Feminization of Casual Video Games." *Ada: A Journal of Gender, New Media, and Technology*, no. 2. doi:10.7264/ N3V40S4D.

van Dijk, Teun A. 1992. "Discourse and the Denial of Racism." *Discourse & Society* 3 (1): 87–118.

Vargas, Deborah. 2012. *Dissonant Divas: The Limits of La Onda*. Minneapolis: University of Minnesota Press.

Vargas, Lucila. 2009. *Latina Teens, Migration, and Popular Culture*. New York: Peter Lang.

Vásquez, Alejandra T. 2013. *Listening in Detail: Performances of Cuban Music*. Durham: Duke University Press.

Ven, Jonah. 2019. Twitter post, January 13, 2019. https://twitter.com/jonah_ven.

Villani, Susan. 2001. "Impact of Media on Children and Adolescents: A 10-Year Review of the Research." *Journal of the American Academy of Child & Adolescent Psychiatry* 40 (4): 392–401.

Visweswaran, Kamala. 1997. "Diaspora by Design: Flexible Citizenship and South Asians in US Racial Formations." *Diaspora: A Journal of Transnational Studies* 6 (1): 5–29.

Walt Disney Company. 2015. "Disney Citizenship Data Table." www.thewaltdisneycom
pany.com/wp-content/uploads/FY15-Data-Table-Final.pdf.

Wang, Wayne, dir. 1982. *Chan Is Missing*. Film.

Ward, L. Monique. 2004. "Wading through the Stereotypes: Positive and Negative
Associations between Media Use and Black Adolescents' Conceptions of Self."
Developmental Psychology 40 (2): 284–94.

Warner, Kristen J. 2015. "'They Gon' Think You Loud Regardless: Ratchetness, Reality Television, and Black Womanhood." *Camera Obscura: Feminism, Culture, and
Media Studies* 30 (1): 129–53.

———. 2017. "In the Time of Plastic Representation." *Film Quarterly* 71 (2). https://film-
quarterly.org/2017/12/04/in-the-time-of-plastic-representation/.

Watkins, Mel. 1999. *On the Real Side: A History of African American Comedy*. Chicago:
Lawrence Hill.

Weaver, Hilary N. 2009. "The Colonial Context of Violence: Reflections on Violence
in the Lives of Native American Women." *Journal of Interpersonal Violence* 24 (9):
1552–63.

Weheliye, Alexander G. 2005. *Phonographies: Grooves in Sonic Afro-Modernity*. Durham: Duke University Press.

———. 2014. *Habeas Viscus: Racializing Assemblages, Biopolitics, and Black Feminist
Theories of the Human*. Durham: Duke University Press.

West, Cornel. 1982. *Prophesy Deliverance! An Afro-American Revolutionary Christian-
ity*. Philadelphia: Westminster.

Westgate, Christopher Joseph. 2014. "One Language, One Nation, and One Vision:
NBC Latino, Fusion, and Fox News Latino." In *Contemporary Latina/o Media: Pro-
duction, Circulation, Politics*, edited by Arlene Dávila and Yeidy M. Rivero, 82–102.
New York: New York University Press.

Weststar, Johanna, Victoria O'Meara, and Marie-Josée Legault. 2018. "Developer Satisfaction Survey 2017 Summary Report." *International Game Developers Association*,
January 8, 2018. https://s3-us-east-2.amazonaws.com/igda-website/wp-content
/uploads/2019/04/11143720/IGDA_DSS_2017_SummaryReport.pdf.

Williams, Kim M. 2006. *Mark One or More: Civil Rights in Multiracial America*. Ann
Arbor: University of Michigan Press.

Williams-León, Teresa, and Cynthia L. Nakashima. 2001. *The Sum of Our Parts: Mixed-
Heritage Asian Americans*. Philadelphia: Temple University Press.

Wilson, Pamela, and Michelle Stewart. 2008. "Introduction: Indigeneity and Indigenous
Media on the Global Stage." In *Global Indigenous Media: Cultures, Poetics, and Politics*,
edited by Pamela Wilson and Michelle Stewart, 1–38. Durham: Duke University Press.

Winters, Loretta I., and Herman L. DeBose. 2003. *New Faces in a Changing America:
Multiracial Identity in the 21st Century*. Thousand Oaks: Sage.

Wong, Eddie, dir. 1971. *Wong Sinsaang*. Film.

Woo, Michelle. 2014. "20 Years Later, Margaret Cho Looks Back on 'All-American
Girl.'" *KoreAm*, August–September 2014. https://charactermedia.com/20-years
-later-margaret-cho-looks-back-on-all-american-girl/.

Worth, Sol. 1972. "Audiovisuals Reviews: You Are on Indian Land." *American Anthropologist* 74 (4): 1029–31.

Worth, Sol, and John Adair. 1972. *Through Navajo Eyes: An Exploration in Film Communication and Anthropology.* Albuquerque: University of New Mexico Press.

Wright, Jennifer. 2019. Twitter post, January 13, 2019. https://twitter.com /JenAshleyWright.

Yang, Guobin. 2016. "Narrative Agency in Hashtag Activism: The Case of #Black LivesMatter." *Media and Communication* 4 (4): 13–17.

Yosso, Tara J. 2005. "Whose Culture Has Capital? A Critical Race Theory Discussion of Community Cultural Wealth." *Race Ethnicity and Education* 8 (1): 69–91.

Yuen, Nancy Wang. 2016. *Reel Inequality: Hollywood Actors and Racism.* New Brunswick, NJ: Rutgers University Press.

Zinoman, Jason. 2018. "The Netflix Executives Who Bent Comedy to Their Will." *New York Times*, September 9, 2018. www.nytimes.com/2018/09/09/arts/television /netflix-comedy-strategy-exclusive.html.

Zogby, James J. 2019. "A Historic Day in Congress." January 5, 2019. Arab American Institute. www.aaiusa.org/a_historic_day_in_congress.

Zwahlen, Christie. 2015. "Listening to and through 'Need': Sound Studies and Civic Engagement," *Sounding Out!*, April 6, 2015. https://soundstudiesblog .com/2015/04/06/14961/.

Lori Kido Lopez is an Associate Professor of Media and Cultural Studies in the Communication Arts Department at the University of Wisconsin–Madison. She is also Affiliate Faculty in the Asian American Studies Program, the Chican@ and Latin@ Studies Program, and the Department of Gender and Women's Studies. She is the author of *Asian American Media Activism: Fighting for Cultural Citizenship* and co-editor of *The Routledge Companion to Asian American Media*. She is a Co-Editor for the *International Journal of Cultural Studies*.

Jillian M. Báez is an Associate Professor of Africana and Puerto Rican/Latino Studies at Hunter College. She is also an Affiliated Faculty member at the CUNY Mexican Studies Institute and the Center for the Study of Women and Society at the CUNY Graduate Center. Dr. Báez is the author of *In Search of Belonging: Latinas, Media, and Citizenship*, which won the 2019 National Communication Association's Bonnie Ritter Award for Outstanding Feminist Book. She is a former Co-General Editor of *WSQ: Women's Studies Quarterly*.

Mary Beltrán is an Associate Professor in the Department of Radio-Television-Film, an affiliate of Mexican American and Latina/o Studies and Women's and Gender Studies, and Director of the Latino Media Arts & Studies Program at the University of Texas at Austin. She is the author of *Latina/o Stars in U.S. Eyes*, co-editor with Camilla Fojas of *Mixed Race Hollywood*, and author of the forthcoming *Latino, Latina, and Latinx Television: Navigations of U.S. Storytelling*.

Miranda J. Brady is an Associate Professor in the School of Journalism and Communication at Carleton University. She is a settler who lives on unceded Algonquin territory. In addition to her community-based and scholarly work in Indigenous media, she currently writes about the social constructions of Autism Spectrum Disorder and mothers.

Dolores Inés Casillas is an Associate Professor in the Department of Chicana and Chicano Studies at the University of California, Santa Barbara (UCSB). She is the author of *Sounds of Belonging: U.S. Spanish-Language Radio and Public Advocacy*, which received two book prizes; co-editor with María Elena Cepeda of *The Routledge Companion to Latina/o Media*; and co-editor with Mary Bucholtz and Jin Sook Lee of *Feeling It: Language, Race and Affect in Latinx Youth Learning*.

Mari Castañeda is a Professor in the Department of Communication and Associate Dean for Equity and Inclusion in the College of Social and Behavioral Sciences at the University of Massachusetts Amherst. She is also affiliated with the Center for Latin American, Caribbean and Latina/o Studies, and Women, Gender, Sexuality Studies. Dr. Castañeda's fields of study include Latinx/Chicana communication studies, academic labor, digital media, and communications policy. Her engaged scholarship has appeared in multiple journals/monographs and she has published three co-edited books: *Telenovelas and Soap Operas in the Digital Age: Global Industries and New Audiences*; *Mothers in Academia*; and *Civic Engagement in Latinx Communities: Learning from Social Justice Partnerships in Action*.

Aymar Jean Christian is an Associate Professor of Communication Studies at Northwestern University. His book *Open TV: Innovation beyond Hollywood and the Rise of Web Television* argues that the web brought innovation to television by opening development to independent producers. His work has been published in numerous academic journals, including the *International Journal of Communication, Television & New Media, Cinema Journal, Continuum*, and *Transformative Works and Cultures*.

Meredith D. Clark is an Assistant Professor in the Department of Media Studies at the University of Virginia.

Peter X Feng is an Associate Professor of English and Women and Gender Studies at the University of Delaware. He is the author of *Identities in Motion: Asian American Film and Video*, the editor of *Screening Asian Americans*, and a co-editor of *Chinese Connections: Critical Perspectives on Film, Identity, and Diaspora*. He has published essays on Asian American cinema in *Schirmer Encyclopedia of Film*, *Cineaste*, *Amerasia Journal*, *Jump Cut*, *Quarterly Review of Film and Video*, *Camera Obscura*, and *Cinema Journal*.

Sarah Florini is an Assistant Professor of Film and Media Studies in the Department of English at Arizona State University. Her research explores the intersection of race, technology, and Black culture. Her monograph, *Beyond Hashtags: Racial Politics and Black Digital Networks*, explores how Black Americans used digital technologies to navigate U.S. racial dynamics from 2010 to 2016.

Kishonna L. Gray (@kishonnagray) is an Assistant Professor in the Department of Communication and Gender and Women's Studies at the University of Illinois–Chicago. She is also a Faculty Associate at the Berkman Klein Center for Internet and Society at Harvard University. Dr. Gray is an interdisciplinary, intersectional, digital media scholar and "digital herstorian" whose areas of research include identity, performance and online environments, embodied deviance, cultural production, video games, and Black Cyberfeminism. Dr. Gray is the author of *Race, Gender, and Deviance in Xbox Live*, and is completing a manuscript tentatively titled *Intersectional Tech*.

Ralina L. Joseph is a scholar, teacher, and facilitator of race and communication. She is a Professor of Communication and the founding director of the Center for Communication, Difference, and Equity at the University of Washington. Her book *Postracial Resistance: Black Women, Media, and the Uses of Strategic Ambiguity* is the 2019 winner of the International Communication Association's Outstanding Book of the Year. She is also author of *Transcending Blackness: From the New Millennium Mulatta to the Exceptional Multiracial* and is currently writing *Generation Mixed Goes to School* (with Allison Briscoe-Smith) and *Interrupting Privilege*.

Jacqueline Land is a Doctoral Candidate of Media and Cultural Studies in the Communication Arts Department at the University of

Wisconsin–Madison. Her research focuses on contemporary Indigenous media activism and digital cultures. She is on the editorial board for the *Playback* blog and is a co-editor of the Center for Critical Race and Digital Studies public syllabus.

Jason Kido Lopez is an Assistant Professor of Media and Cultural Studies in the Communication Arts Department at the University of Wisconsin–Madison. He is the author of *Self-Deception's Puzzles and Processes: A Return to a Sartrean View*. His current research focuses on the intersection of sports, race, athlete activism, and labor. He is also working on a manuscript on games around games like sports betting, fantasy sports, and March Madness brackets.

Raven Maragh-Lloyd is an Assistant Professor at Gonzaga University. Her research looks at the ways that marginalized communities reflect, resist, and uniquely deploy digital media culture, exploring how racialized and gendered identities influence digital structures in their pursuit of community goals. Dr. Maragh-Lloyd's work has appeared in *Communication, Culture & Critique; Television and New Media; Journal of Communication Inquiry*; and *The Handbook of Diasporas, Media, and Culture*.

Susan Noh is a Doctoral Candidate in the Media and Cultural Studies Program at the University of Wisconsin–Madison. Her academic interests revolve around global media flows, the effects of the platformization of the web, and trends in fan-driven activism as it relates to the digital media landscape. She has written on the practical applications and potentials of metadata activism.

Jun Okada is an Associate Professor of Visual and Media Arts at Emerson College, where she teaches courses in Media Studies. She published her book *Making Asian American Film and Video: History, Institutions, Movements* in 2015. She has also published in *Film Quarterly, Velvet Light Trap, Journal of Cinema and Media Studies*, and the *Routledge Companion to Asian American Media*.

Jennifer Lynn Stoever is the Editor in Chief of *Sounding Out!* and an Associate Professor of English at the State University of New York at

Binghamton. She is the author of *The Sonic Color Line: Race and the Cultural Politics of Listening* and numerous essays on the relationship between race and sound published in *American Quarterly*, the *Radical History Review, Social Text*, and *The Oxford Handbook of Hip Hop Studies*.

Meshell Sturgis is a Doctoral Candidate in the Department of Communication at the University of Washington, where she critically looks at visual culture and the politics of self-representation and how queer Black women communicate identity and difference using alternative media. She has a BA in English from the University of North Carolina at Chapel Hill and an MA in Cultural Studies from the University of Washington, Bothell. She is a GO-MAP Presidential Dissertation Fellow.

Amy Villarejo is the Frederic J. Whiton Professor of Humanities at Cornell University, where she teaches cinema and media studies in the Department of Performing and Media Arts and Department of Comparative Literature. She is author of *Lesbian Rule: Cultural Criticism and the Value of Desire* and *Ethereal Queer: Television, Historicity, Desire*, and she is co-editor with Ron Gregg of the forthcoming *Oxford Handbook to Queer Cinema*. Her articles have appeared in *Film Quarterly, Journal of Cinema and Media Studies, Social Text*, and other journals and edited collections.

Lia Wolock is an Assistant Professor of Media Studies at the University of Wisconsin–Milwaukee. Her research examines the media production and curation cultures of diasporic and minority communities. Her research has been published in journals like *Television and New Media* and she is currently working on a book project tentatively titled *Producing South Asian America: Diasporic Community and Digital Activism*.

Sulafa Zidani is a Doctoral Candidate in Communication at the University of Southern California's Annenberg School for Communication and Journalism. Her research is concentrated in participatory culture, culture mixing and hybridity, and global power dynamics in digital media.

Ms. Zidani's educational background includes a dual-major BA and MA in Asia Studies and Communication and Journalism from the Hebrew University of Jerusalem, as well as an MA in Communication from USC Annenberg. Her work has been published in *Social Media + Society* and *Asian Communication Research*.

INDEX